ApPETiTeS

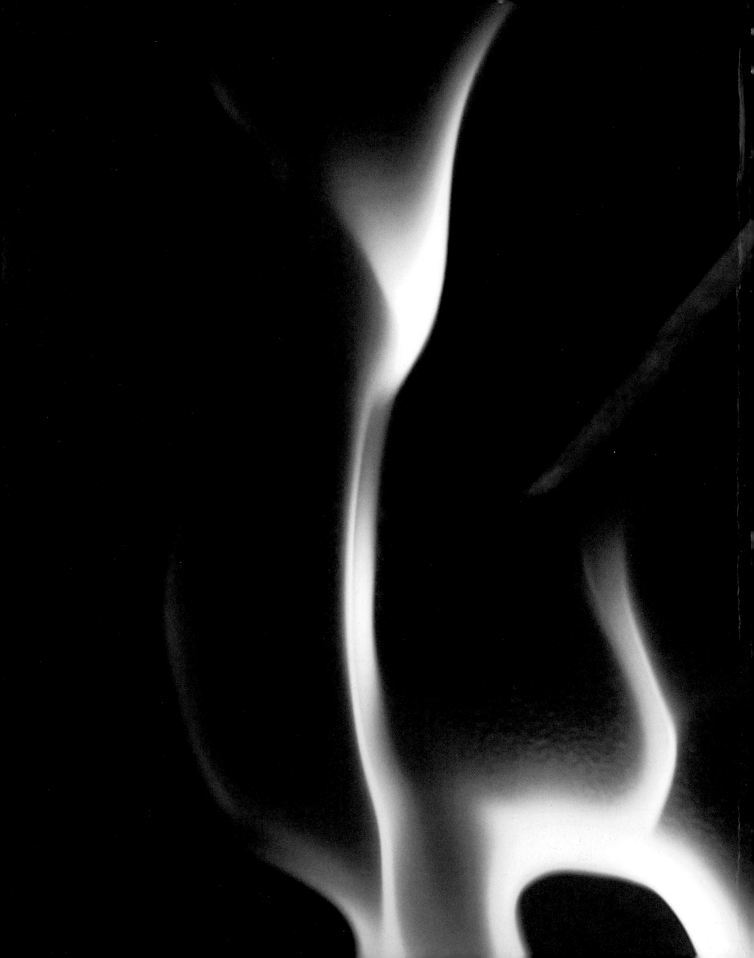

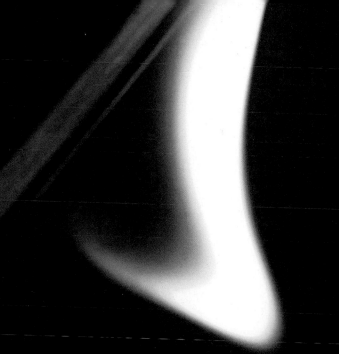

ALSO BY ANTHONY BOURDAIN

nonfiction

KITCHEN CONFIDENTIAL

A COOK'S TOUR: IN SEARCH OF THE PERFECT MEAL

TYPHOID MARY: AN URBAN HISTORICAL

ANTHONY BOURDAIN'S LES HALLES COOKBOOK

THE NASTY BITS

NO RESERVATIONS: AROUND THE WORLD ON AN EMPTY STOMACH

MEDIUM RAW: A BLOODY VALENTINE TO THE WORLD
OF FOOD AND THE PEOPLE WHO COOK

fiction

BONE IN THE THROAT

GONE BAMBOO

THE BOBBY GOLD STORIES

GET JIRO!

GET JIRO: BLOOD AND SUSHI

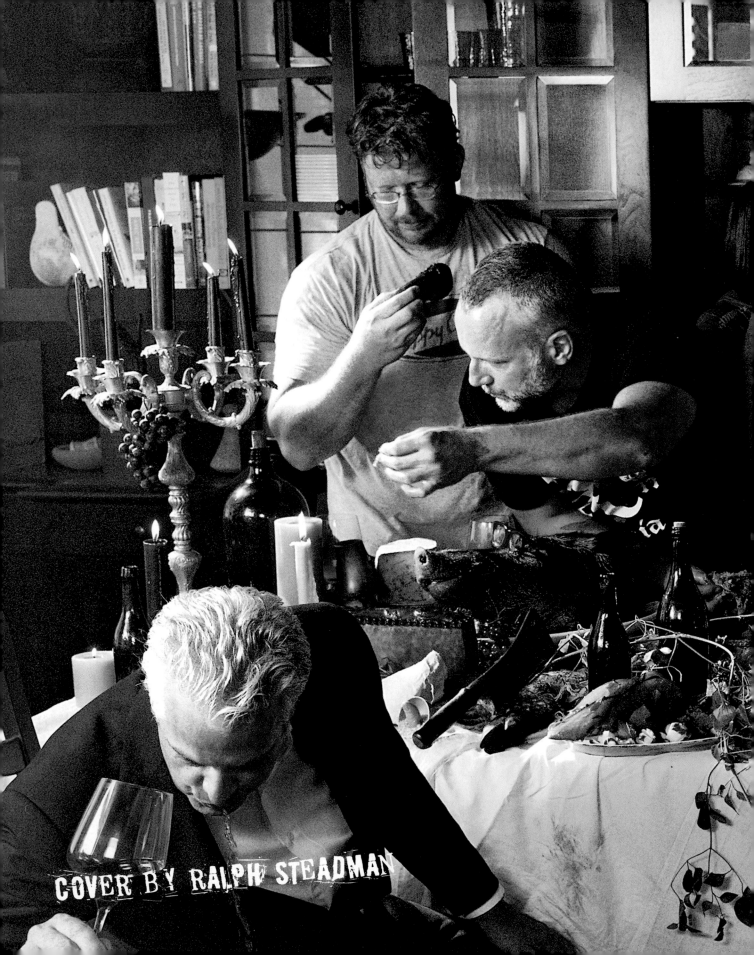

COVER BY RALPH STEADMAN

APPETITES

ANTHONY BOURDAIN

with LAURIE WOOLEVER

PHOTOGRAPHS BY BOBBY FISHER

ecco

An Imprint of HarperCollinsPublishers

HarperCollins books may be purchased for educational, business, or sales promotional use. For information please e-mail the Special Markets Department at SPsales@harper collins.com.

FIRST EDITION

Interior design by Suet Yee Chong
Cover design by Ralph Steadman
"Bourdain Perfect Burger" text courtesy of Nathan Myhrvold/The Cooking Lab. © The Cooking Lab, LLC
"Bourdain Perfect Burger" illustration © Theo van den Boogard

Library of Congress Cataloging-in-Publication Data has been applied for.

ISBN 978-0-06-240995-9 (hardcover)
ISBN 978-0-06-266278-1 (jacketed edition)

18 19 20 LSCW 10 9 8 7

To Ariane and Jacques

CONTENTS

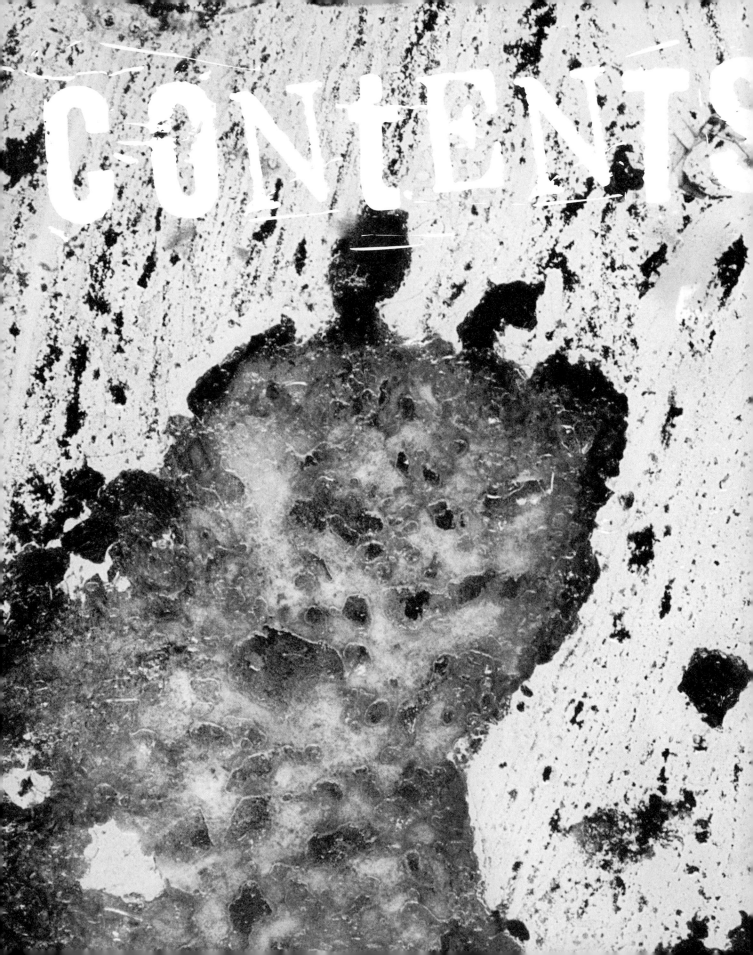

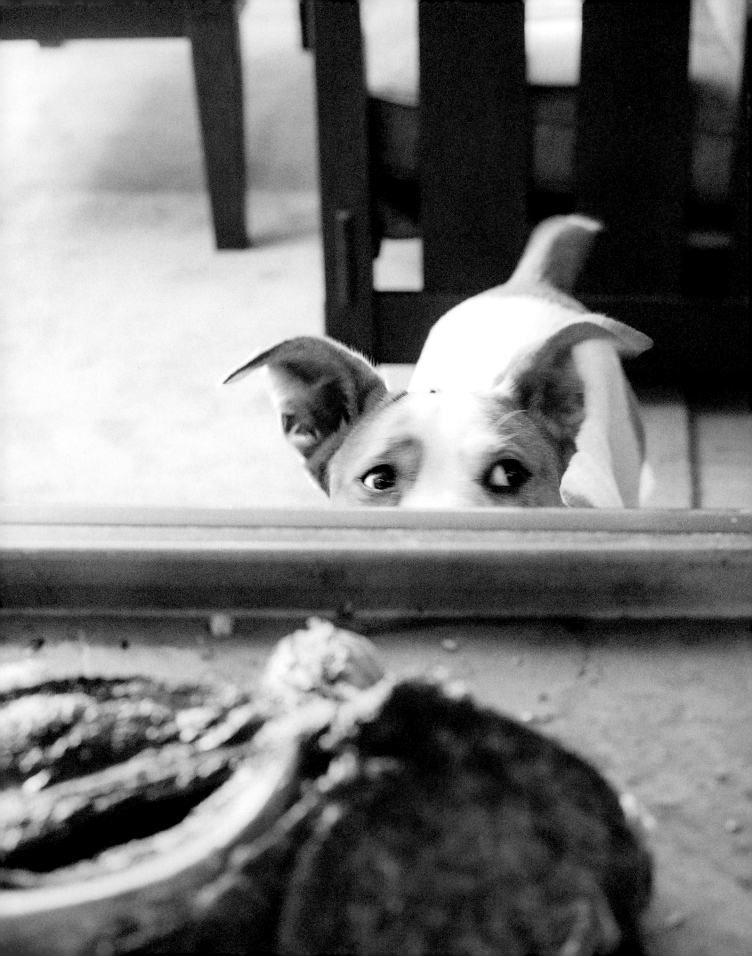

ACKNOWLEDGMENTS

For their large and small contributions to the making of this book, we'd like to thank:

Paul Ackerina

Olivia Mack Anderson

Beth Aretsky

Eddie Barrera

Ruby Basdeo

Anna Billingskog

Danny Bowien

Andreana Busia

Angelo Busia

Ariane Busia-Bourdain

Ottavia Busia-Bourdain

Sonya Cheuse

Helen Cho

Suet Yee Chong

John Cogan

Chris Collins

Milo Collins

Neko Collins

Ariane Daguin

Lizzie Roller Dilworth

Angela Dimayuga

Lolis Elie

Chris Faulkner

Josh Ferrell

Bobby Fisher

Dahlia Galler

Giacomo Gambineri

Ashley Garland

Theo Granof

Victoria Granof

Daniel Halpern

Jon Heindemause

Anya Hoffman

Ruby Hoffman-Werle

Tema Hoffman-Werle

Nicholas Krasznai

Alison Tozzi Liu

Caleb Liu

Micah Liu

Tony Liu

Dave Luebker

Melissa Lukach

Peter Meehan

Rachel Meyers

Emily Miller

Flavio Moledda

Joshua Monesson

Max Monesson

Nathan Myhrvold

Patty Nusser

Nick Olivieri

Sophia Pappas

Miriam Parker

Jason Perez

Buster Quint

Doug Quint

Jacques Quizon

Marcus Quizon

Myra Quizon

Rommel "Giant" Quizon

Bridget Read

Eric Ripert

Matt Roady

Mark Rosati

Allison Saltzman

Cathy Sheary

Ralph Steadman

Lydia Tenaglia

Ashley Tucker

Theo van den Boogaard

Kaitlyn DuRoss Walker

Jonathan Werle

Maisie Wilhelm

Kimberly Witherspoon

Monika Woods

John Woolever

Patricia Woolever

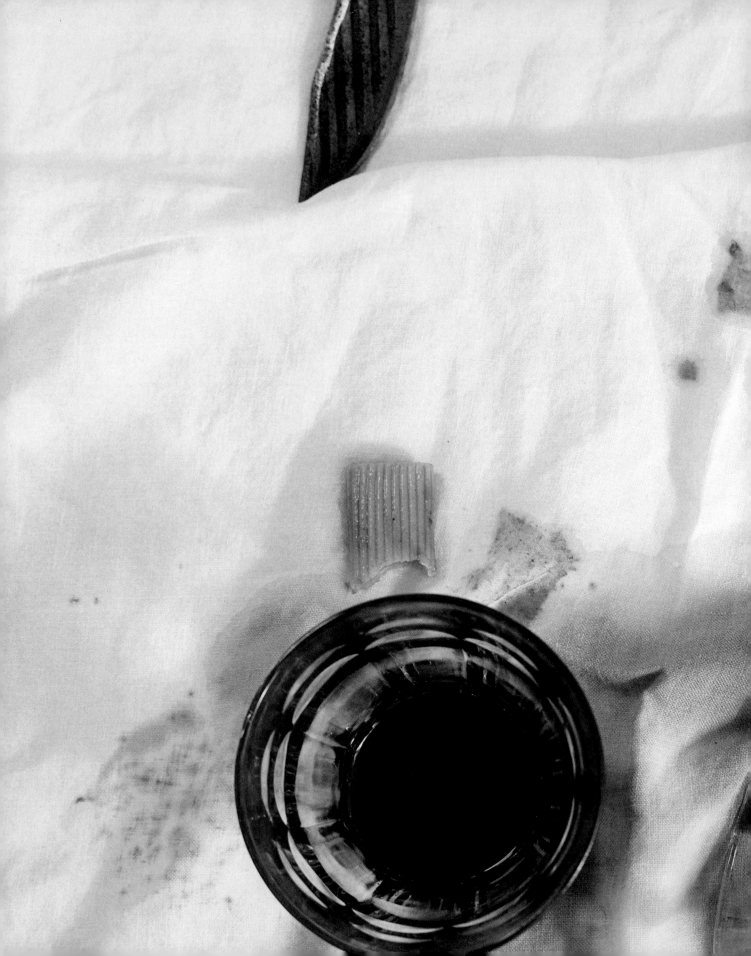

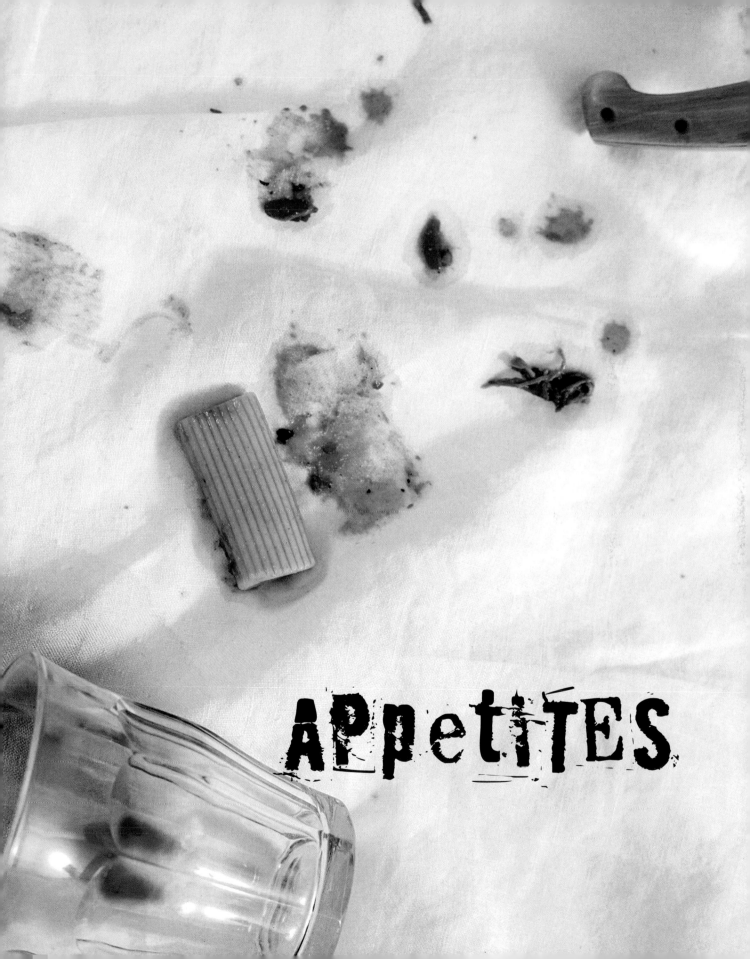

APPetiTES

INTRODUCTION

All happy families are alike . . .

—Leo Tolstoy, *Anna Karenina*

Tolstoy clearly never spent any time with my happy family.

My eight-year-old daughter, Ariane, does a terrific imitation of my wife threatening to choke a taxi driver. It's something she's seen often enough to get dead right—my wife's Italian accent, her anger, her exasperation as the driver takes yet another wrong turn on the way to my daughter's school, and finally the kicker: "I'm going to *keel* you with my bare-a hands!"

It has been many months, maybe years, since anyone has seen my wife out of her regular attire of rash guard and spats. She's a martial artist, a purple belt in Brazilian jiujitsu, and she trains full-time, seven days a week. Most of her efforts are spent practicing horrifying new ways to quickly, forcibly manipulate opponents' feet, ankles, and knees in such ways as to permanently damage their tendons and ligaments.

I travel the world for a living. On any given day, I'm as likely to be found in a longhouse in Sarawak, Borneo; in a cafe in Marseille; or in an airport transit lounge in Doha as I am to be found at home. My daughter is used to seeing her father's face on TV and on the sides of city buses, accustomed to seeing him approached by strangers—and is decidedly unimpressed.

Her best friend, Jacques (pronounced "Jax"), from whom she has been inseparable most of her life, is Filipino, part of an extended family who easily spends as much time in our home as anywhere else. English, Italian, and Tagalog are heard interchangeably. My daughter is increasingly fluent in Italian. I am not.

What is it that "normal" people do?

What makes a "normal" happy family?

How do they behave? What do they eat at home? How do they live their lives?

I had little clue how to answer these questions for most of my working life, as I'd been living it on the margins. I didn't know any normal people. From age seventeen on, normal people had been my customers. They were abstractions, literally shadowy silhouettes in the dining rooms of wherever it was I was working at the time. I looked at them through the perspective of the lifelong professional cook and chef—which is to say, as someone who did not have a family life, who knew and associated only with fellow restaurant professionals, who worked while normal people played, and who played while normal people slept.

To the extent that I knew or understood normal people's behaviors, it was to anticipate their immediate desires: Would they be ordering the chicken or the salmon?

I usually saw them only at their worst: hungry, drunk, horny, ill tempered, celebrating good fortune or taking out the bad on their servers.

What they did at home, what it might be like to wake up late on a Sunday morning, make pancakes for a child, watch cartoons, throw a ball around a backyard—these were things I only knew from movies.

The human heart was—and remains—a mystery to me. But I'm learning. I have to.

I became a father at fifty years of age. That's late, I know. But for me, it was just right. At no point previously had I been old enough, settled enough, or mature enough for this, the biggest and most important of jobs: the love and care of another human being.

From the second I saw my daughter's head corkscrewing out of the womb, I began making some major changes in my life. I was no longer the star of my own movie—or any movie. From that point on, it was all about the girl. Like most people who write books or appear on television, who think that anyone would or should care about their story, I am a monster of self-regard. Fatherhood has been an enormous relief, as I am now genetically, instinctually compelled to care more about someone other than myself. I like being a father. No, I love being a father. Everything about it.

I'm sure my wife has a different view on this, but if I could go back to the diaper-changing, wake-up-in-the-middle-of-the-night-to-soothe-crying-baby phase of fatherhood? I'd be overjoyed.

I recognize that I am, in some ways, overenthusiastic about this late-in-life move into responsible parenting. And that I have a tendency to try to make up for lost time. Since so many of my happiest memories of childhood—summer vacations at the Jersey shore, off-season Montauk, trips to France—are associated with the tastes and smells of the things I ate, I feel uncontrollable urges to smother the people I love with food. I've become the sort of passive-aggressive yenta or Italian grandmother stereotype from films who's always urging people, "Eat! Eat!" and sulking inconsolably when they don't.

This pathology is further complicated by my time as a professional. I have developed work habits that, over three decades, imprinted on me the need to be organized, to have a plan, to rotate stock, to label prepared foodstuffs, and to keep a clean work area.

So on top of my desire to make up for lost time, and my psycho–Ina Garten–like need to feed the people around me, I am obsessive-compulsive in my work habits and anally retentive in ways that you'd find ideal in a professional brunch cook, but probably disturbing in a husband or parent.

That's our family. And this is our family cookbook

These are the dishes I like to eat and that I like to feed my family and friends. They are the recipes that "work," meaning they've been developed over time and have been informed by repetition and long—and often painful—experience.

As happens in the restaurant business, I will, from time to time, make small incremental sacrifices in "quality" for the often more important matter of serviceability. While it is a laudable ambition to prepare the best risotto in the world, that doesn't mean shit if your guests are sitting around with their stomachs growling, getting progressively drunker, while you dick around in the kitchen, interminably stirring rice.

Fish served on the bone is admittedly "better." You, uncertain of your knife skills, struggling to lift a fillet from a cooked Dover sole, tableside, in front of eight guests, might not be.

There is nothing remotely innovative about the recipes in this book. If you are looking for a culinary genius to take you to the Promised Land of next-level creativity, look elsewhere. That ain't me.

Mostly, these recipes are direct lifts from imperfect memories of childhood favorites: things my mom fed me, things I liked or loved to eat during the happier moments of my life—the kind of food memories I like to share with my daughter—along with a few greatest hits from my travels, and some boiled-down wisdom on subjects like breakfasts and Thanksgiving dinner, presented in an organized and tactically efficient, stress-free way.

One of the first things I discovered as I transitioned into my new "Daddy" phase was that I was usually more frantic preparing a dinner party for five friends at home than I was cranking out five hundred à la carte dinners in a restaurant. The remedy for this anxiety, I've found, is to treat my friends or family just like another five-top in a sea of customers—until the food is served. Then I can sit down with them, relax, and enjoy their company. Just like a "normal" dad.

A Note About My Daughter

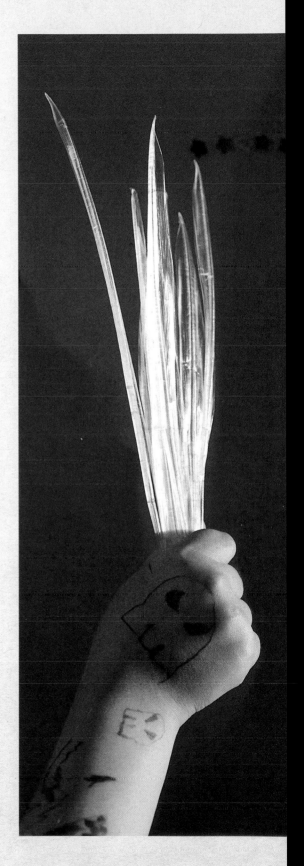

My daughter, Ariane, is eight years old at the time of this writing. She is mostly obscured in the photos in this book. Being recognized by strangers is as weird and unnatural a thing as I have ever known, but I'm a big boy. I made my bed, and I won't complain when I have to lie in it. If I'm running through an airport, frantically looking for a bathroom, and a fan stops me for a photograph, this is a small price to pay for all the freedoms and the good things that being the sort of person who gets recognized in airports has brought me. It sure as shit beats working a busy brunch shift. I made an informed decision by writing book after book, by choosing to appear on television. At eighteen, my daughter will be old enough to make those kinds of decisions for herself. It would be wrong for me, or anyone else, to make those decisions for her.

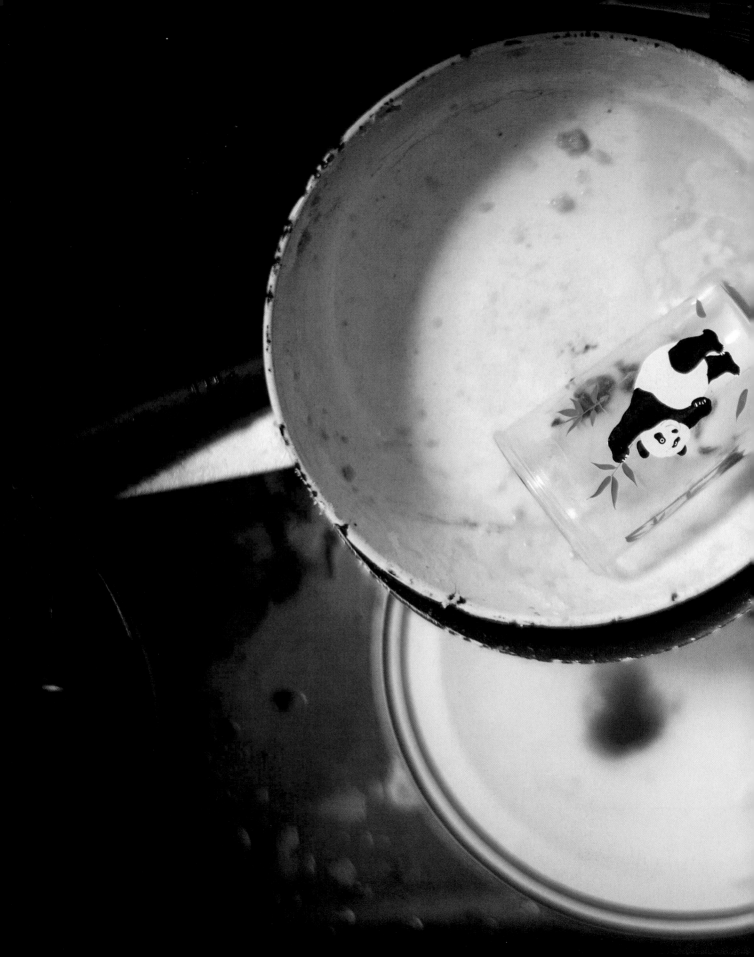

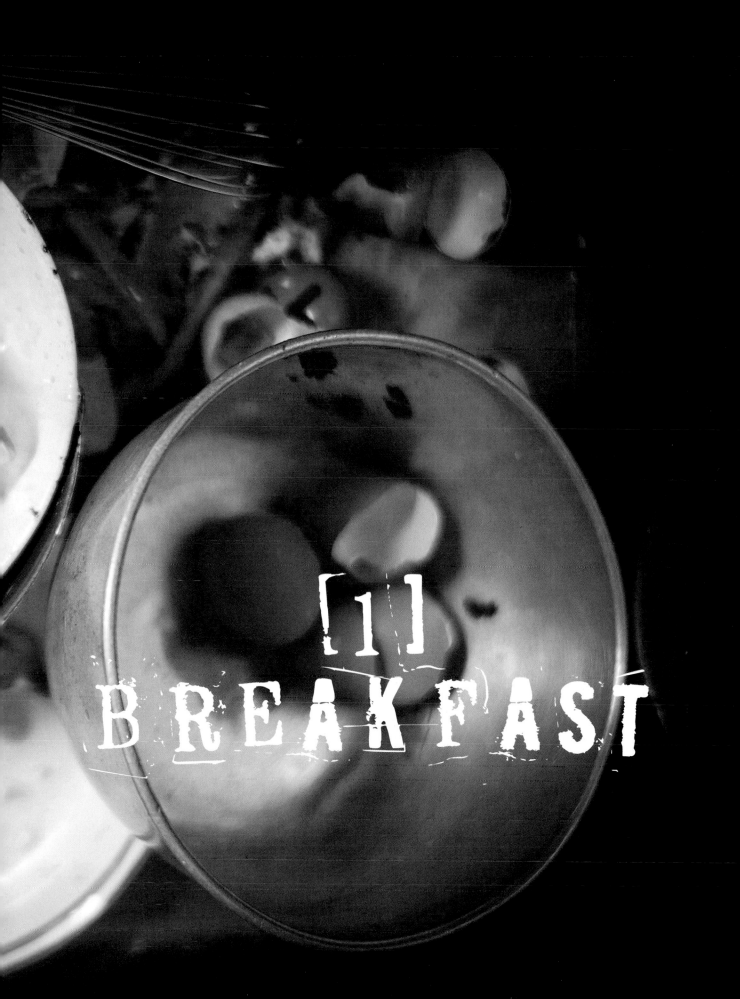

[1]
BREAKFAST

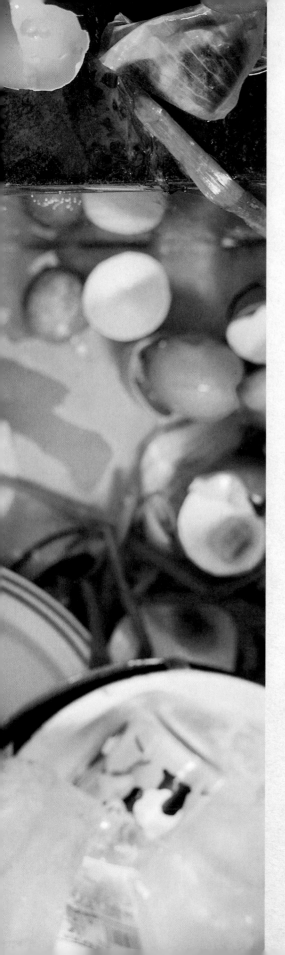

I am a very good breakfast and brunch cook. This was, during the darker periods of my employment history, both a blessing and a curse.

No matter how bad things were, how messed up I might have been, however disgraced, however unemployable by polite society, I could always get a job as a brunch cook.

And while it's nice to know that I can, in a pinch, fall back on a reliable income stream, the smell of breakfast to me will always be the smell of defeat and remind me of the low points of my life when I'd wake up early on Saturdays and Sundays to cook off the bacon, put up the home fries, beat up a shitload of hollandaise, and then sling eggs by the hundreds.

It is because of all those bad associations that, for a long time, I avoided cooking breakfast—at all.

I've lately had to draw frequently on those experiences, because I'm the father of an eight-year-old, who, like most eight-year-olds, digs pancakes, and breakfast in general. So now that I'm cooking for an eight-year-old and her friends, I've acquired more joyous associations with that meal.

For instance, I'm frequently called upon these days to provide efficient pancake service to sleepover parties involving numerous children. And on vacation, I'm more inclined than not to have breakfast ready for houseguests.

So, after all those years of cooking what was essentially—and often literally—short order breakfasts, here is what I've learned.

SCRAMBLED EGGS

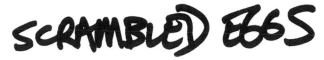

Escoffier was said to beat his eggs for scrambling with a fork, a secret clove of garlic affixed to the tines. I don't do that. I believe in eggs, salt, black pepper, and the whole butter that the eggs are cooked in. No milk or cream—or added water—will make a properly cooked order of scrambled eggs any better. I do, however, use a fork.

On a foodie message board a while back, some insufferable food nerd was commenting on an episode of one of Jacques Pépin's PBS cooking shows, in which Jacques had cooked scrambled eggs in a nonstick pan and stirred them with a fork. The offended poster worried out loud that the metal fork would be destructive to the nonstick pan's surface.

You know what? If Jacques Pépin tells you this is how you make a fucking egg? The matter is settled, fuck nuts. Now go back to arguing about Bundt cake recipes.

Here's how to scramble an egg: Break a fresh egg against a flat surface, like a cutting board, and empty it from its shell into a bowl so that you can inspect it for bits of shell, which you should of course remove and discard. Beat it lightly with a fork, dragging the yellow and white through each other. Heat whole butter in a pan. Pour in the egg and work your fork through. Not too vigorously; you want to gently pile the layers as they cook. When the egg is fluffy yet still moist, plate it quickly and serve it immediately. Remember, the eggs will continue to cook out of the pan.

OMELETS

Use fresh eggs, and as with scrambled eggs, break them on a flat surface and into a small bowl. Season with salt and freshly cracked pepper. I do not add milk or water. Just before cooking, and not a moment before, beat the eggs vigorously with a fork, but don't overdo it. Texturally, you want a rippling effect between yolk and albumen—not strips of visible egg white running through your omelet (which you want in scrambled eggs), but not a homogenous, totally smooth consistency either. Beat just until uniformly yellow. No more.

In a nonstick pan, heat a little whole butter. Do *not* brown.

When butter is bubbling, add the eggs and immediately move them around. I use a (relatively) heat-resistant rubber spatula. Jacques Pépin uses a fork. Whatever utensil you use, move it in a figure-eight pattern, drawing the wet eggs to the center and north (twelve o'clock) of the pan, letting the empty spaces that you've created become filled in with wet egg. Incorporate any egg splatter from the edges, not allowing anything to get crisp or more cooked than any other part. Do *not* flip an omelet.

The center of the omelet should still be moist and a tiny bit wet when you remove it from the heat—what the French call *baveuse*.

Plating your omelet is a very important step, and while it looks tricky, it's actually not.

Using a towel to protect your hand from heat, grasp the pan's handle from *underneath* in a V grip with one hand. Lift it up. Holding your plate in the other hand, tilt the pan onto the plate like a closing door, flopping the omelet onto the plate so it folds shut on itself.

If it looks like a pile of crap, not to worry. Lay a clean paper towel over the omelet like a blanket—like you're putting a child to bed. With hands together almost like praying, shape the omelet into a neat crescent: fat in the center, narrower at both ends. This will also sop up any excess butter or oozing egg.

If you're using fillings in your omelet, cook "dry" ingredients like onions, peppers, or ham in the butter in the pan before adding the egg, incorporating them into the actual omelet. Cheese, or anything else soft and likely to ooze, should be gently laid into the center of the cooking eggs just before removing from the fire and plating.

You should be able to make two omelets at once. Probably no more. Unless you're like me.

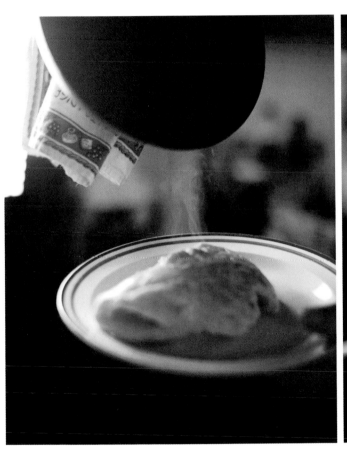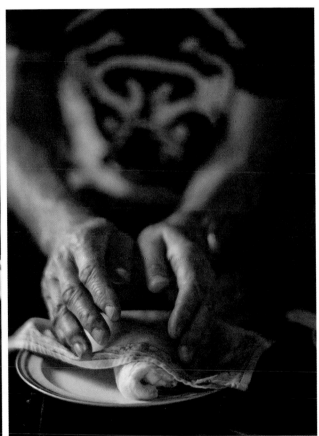

EGGS BENEDICT

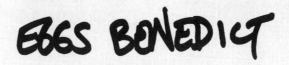

A couple of tips on eggs Benedict:

⚸ **Toast your goddamn muffins.** Everybody fucks up the muffin. Lazy line cooks everywhere neglect to toast their English muffins on both sides—they pop them under the salamander, broiling them on one side, and leaving the other side raw, spongy, cold, and tasting of the refrigerator. I hate that. Don't do it. It's a terrible food crime.

⚸ **Be sure to grill or at least pan sear your Canadian bacon.**

⚸ **Make your hollandaise comfortably ahead of time**—and store it, warm, in a wide-mouthed thermos for service. Nothing's more frustrating than having your hollandaise either break on you, or get too cold. (See Hollandaise on page 270.)

Poaching eggs is a challenge for most home cooks, and a lot of that stress and failure is due to the making of some bush-league mistakes, so:

⚸ **Use a wide-based pot for your poaching water,** *not* **a deep one.** A sautoir is perfect. You want to reach into your pot with your slotted spoon at a comfortable angle and lift the eggs out. You're not bobbing for apples.

⚸ **Add about ½ teaspoon white vinegar to the water.** It will help the egg whites coagulate and the egg to keep its generally roundish form once poaching.

Do not drop the eggs into the water. When the water is at a gentle simmer, slide your already-opened eggs, in individual cups, one after the other, into the water, gently, from the surface. Tilt the cup and let the eggs slowly and gently slide sideways into the water. When done, which is to say cooked until fully formed but still runny in the center, lift each egg gently out of the water with a slotted spoon and serve immediately. . . .

Unless you have made the hubristic decision to serve eggs fucking Benedict to a party of ten guests in your home. Presumably, your guests will want to be served all at the same time, or reasonably close to that ideal. And unless you're a mastermind of brunch with a lot of short-order experience, it's unlikely you will be able to successfully drill out twenty perfectly poached eggs in under two minutes. So what to do?

Now, I'm not saying you *should* do what I'm about to tell you. I'm just saying you *can* do it. I may or may not have done it when serving six hundred brunches (many of which included eggs bennies) during a three-hour period.

I may or may not have prepoached a shitload of eggs—undercooking them as much as humanly possible—just before service, then floated them in a bus pan filled with ice water.

For service, I'd finish them in seconds—or might have finished them in seconds—by giving them a long dip in simmering water.

You *can* do this successfully and still serve perfectly cooked eggs. It *does* make serving a whole lot of them at a time easier—and removes much of the risk factor.

But, of course, morally, it's just . . . wrong.

BACON

What does everyone want from bacon? The overwhelming likelihood is that they want it, above all other things, crisp. And not burnt.

In my experience, the best way to cook bacon is slightly in advance—in the oven. Set your oven at 350°F. Resist the temptation to set it hotter. Bacon takes a while, but when it starts going, it goes from raw to cooked to shit real quick.

Separate the bacon onto brown baking paper on a sheet pan.

Put in oven. Check often. Chances are, your oven has hot spots. Move the pan around from time to time, rotating, to account for this. If necessary, turn the bacon over, using tongs or a metal spatula. Remove *just* prior to desired doneness. You can finish it, returning it to the oven if necessary, while your eggs or other items cook.

Hold cooked bacon on the interior pages of the newspaper of record, which have been proven to be among the most hygienic, bacteria-free surfaces you can find anywhere. Really. If you ever need to deliver a baby unexpectedly, just reach for a nearby *New York Times* Styles section. You can be pretty sure nobody has touched that.

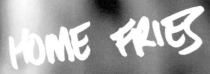

HOME FRIES

Home fries almost always suck. They are a perfunctory add-on to most restaurant brunches only because they are cheap, filling, and take up a lot of room on the plate. They are relatively indestructible, meaning that they suck just as much after sitting around for four hours as they do when fresh.

Hash browns are a better idea. But the best idea is no potatoes at all. In my view, a few well-toasted, heavily buttered slices of bread are the perfect accompaniment to an egg breakfast. The combination of runny yolk and buttered, toasted bread is far better than invariably cold, starchy potatoes.

They say breakfast is the most important meal of the day. Maybe.

But the notion that you need a heaping gutload of eggs, bacon, sausage, potatoes, *and* bread is grotesque. If you have a hard time tying your shoes after breakfast, or you feel like you really, really need a nap—when you only just woke up an hour ago—there's something wrong.

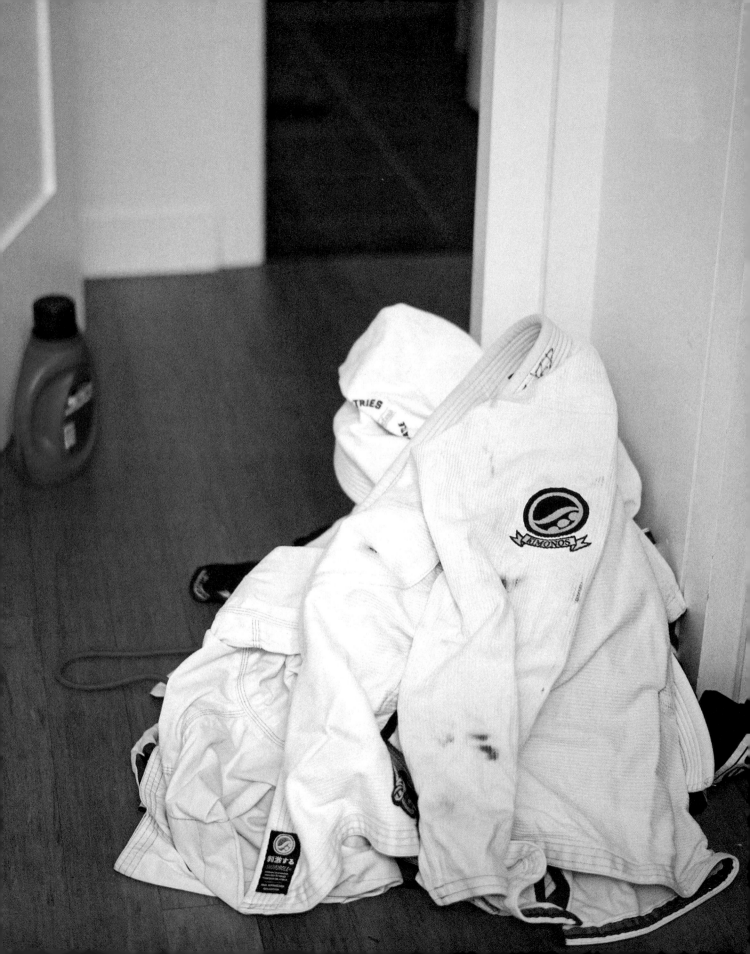

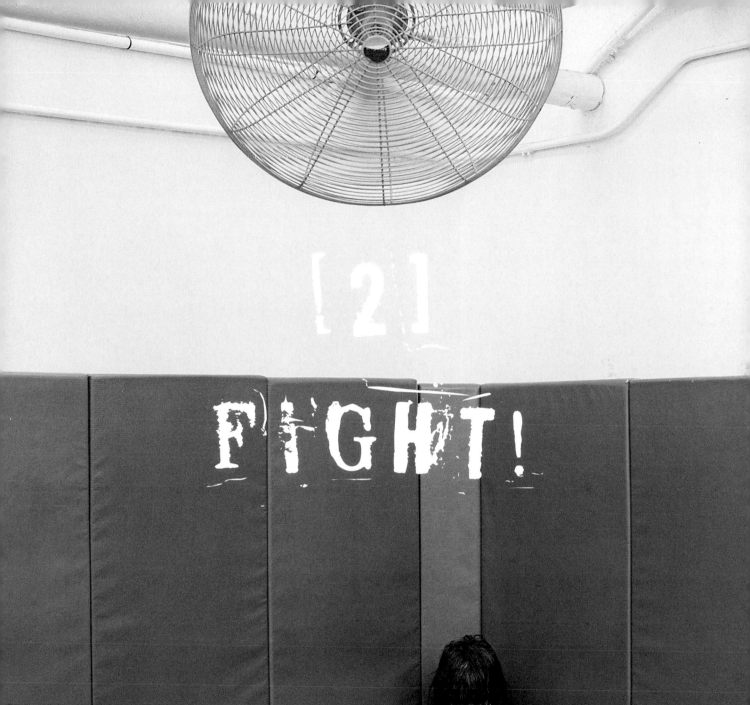

[2]

FIGHT!

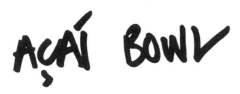

AÇAÍ BOWL

Brazilian jiujitsu is a thing in our house. Our lives—all our lives—revolve around training schedules; at any given time, there's a heap of sodden, frequently blood-smeared *gis* (the two-piece garment, secured by a belt whose color signifies level of expertise, worn by practitioners of jiujitsu, karate, and other martial arts) waiting outside the washer, and another set (Mom, Dad, and girl) hanging to dry on a special rack in my daughter's playroom.

Most of our professors are Brazilian, and it is an article of faith among Brazilian practitioners of martial arts that açaí, the "miracle jungle fruit of the Amazon," is the answer to—and cure for—all things, from ineptness at rear naked choke holds to cancer.

Whether the health benefits hold up under scientific scrutiny or not, the stuff is pretty delicious, and it's become a staple in our household. A post-training bowl of icy cold açaí puree and fruit? It sure *seems* to make us all feel better.

½ to ¾ cup açaí juice, Sambazon brand preferred

2 bananas, peeled

7 ounces frozen unsweetened açaí puree, Sambazon brand preferred

¾ cup frozen blueberries

¼ to ½ cup fresh or frozen strawberries or raspberries

½ cup granola, for garnish (optional)

¼ cup cacao nibs, for garnish (optional)

SPECIAL EQUIPMENT

Vitamix or another blender with a fairly strong motor

Place the açaí juice and one of the bananas in the blender's pitcher, then add the frozen açaí puree, blueberries, and strawberries on top so that the blades suck in the frozen items. Pulse as needed to form a smooth sorbet, scraping down the sides of the pitcher with a spatula as necessary.

Slice the remaining banana. Divide the mixture between two bowls and top each with the garnishes. Serve immediately.

Serves 2

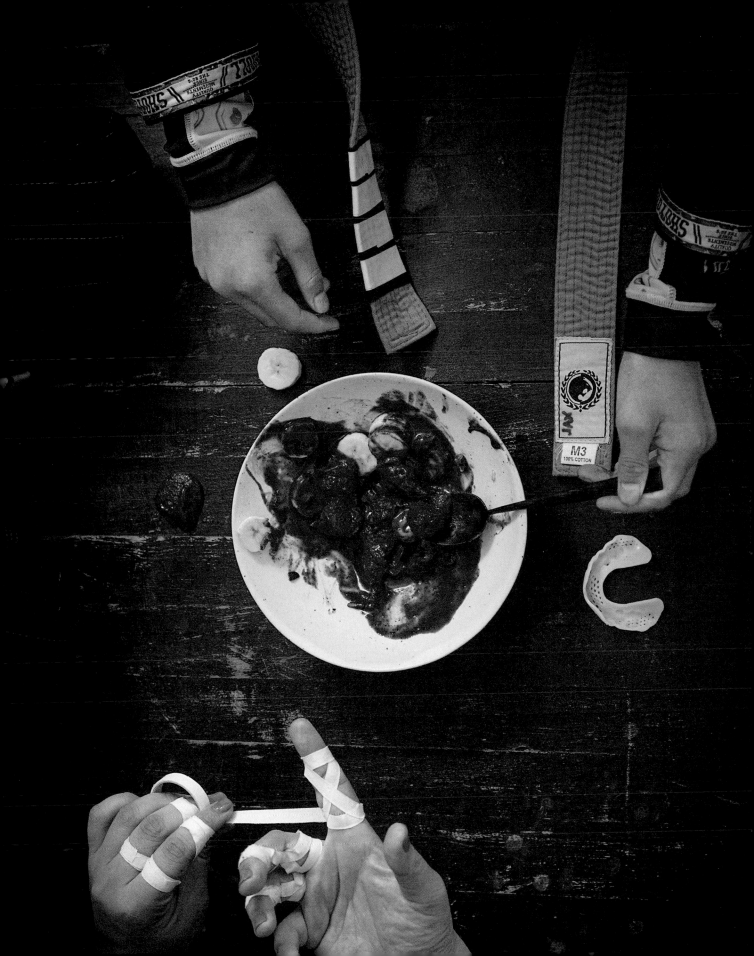

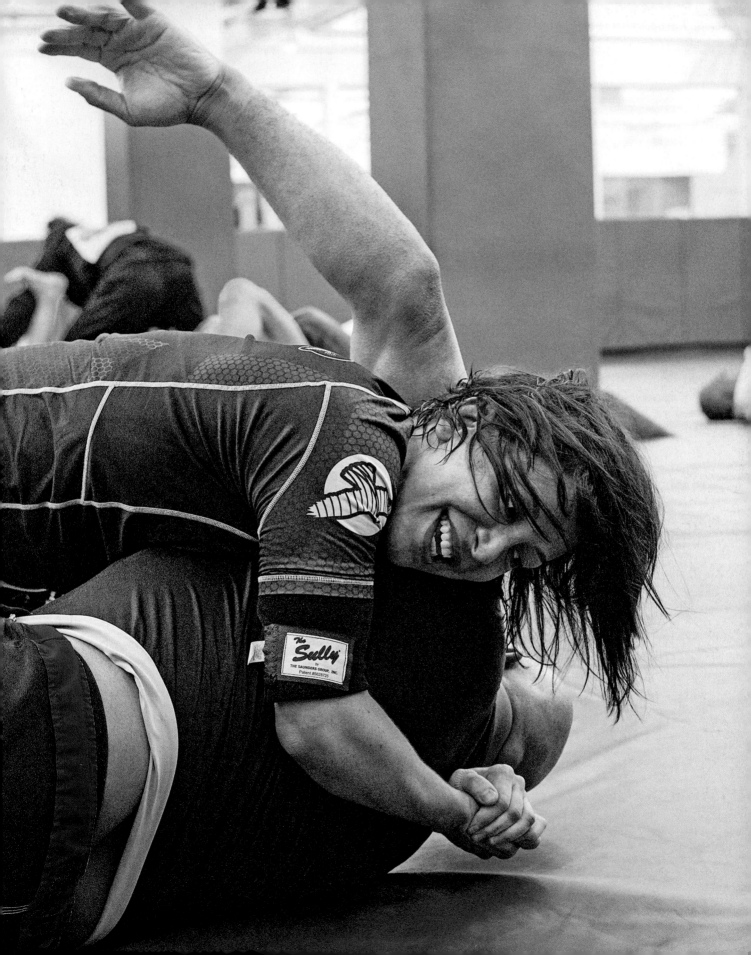

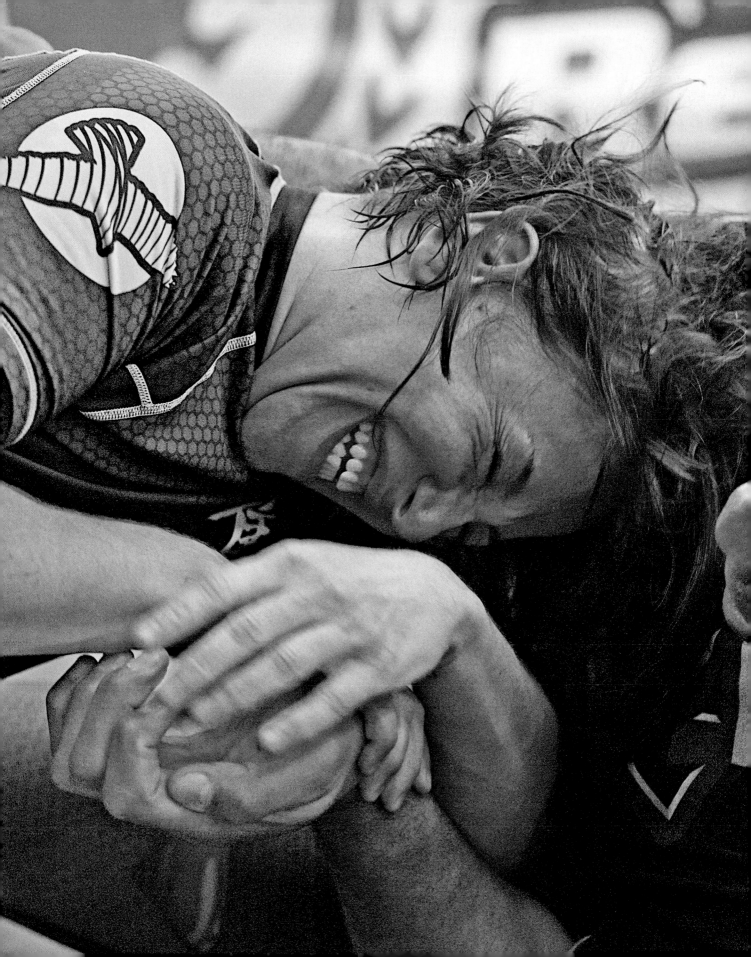

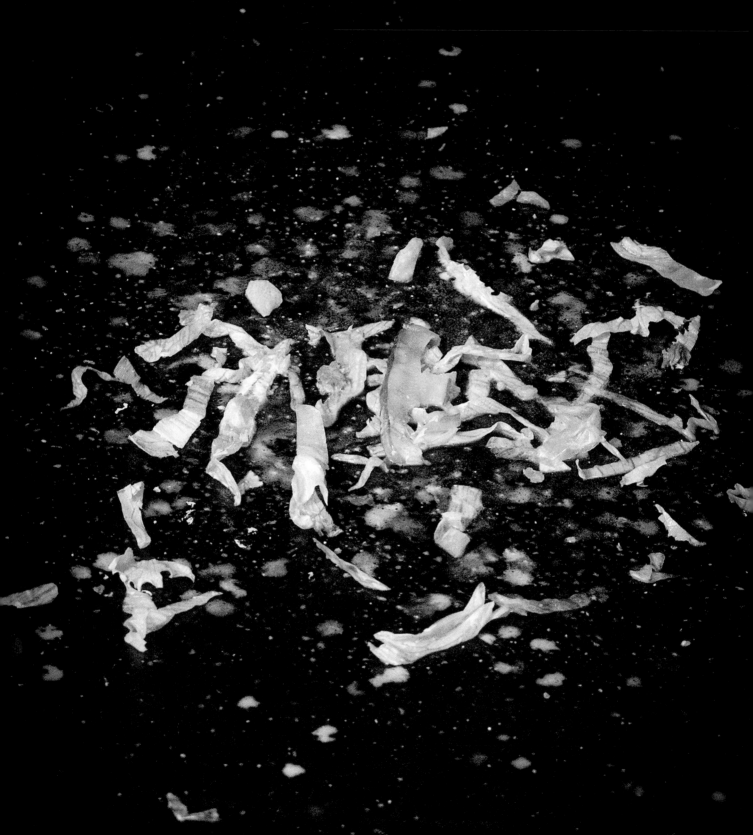

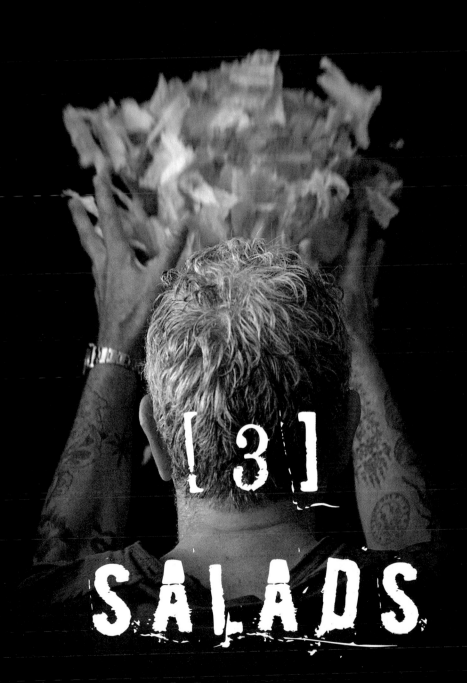

[3]

SALADS

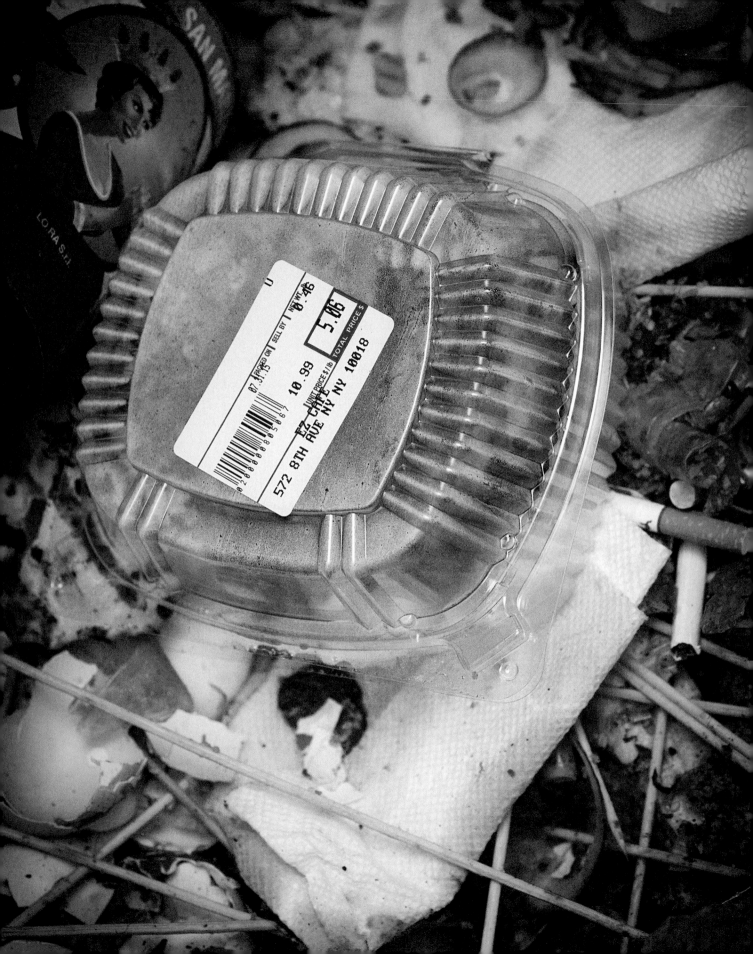

CAESAR SALAD

Caesar salad is of Mexican origin. You probably didn't know that, crediting it instead to the Italians. Nope. Another reason to love Mexico—*unless* you insist on putting sad, overcooked, characterless strips of grilled chicken cutlet on top of it and mashing it down into landfill.

God does not want you to put chicken in your Caesar.

In a wide, heavy-bottom sauté pan, heat 1 cup of the oil over medium-low heat. Add 4 of the anchovies and the smashed garlic and let cook until the anchovies fall apart and dissolve into the oil, aiding this process by gently mashing them with a wooden spoon. Increase the heat and add the diced bread, cooking for a few minutes and tossing to make sure that the bread is toasted and golden brown on all sides. Use tongs or a slotted spoon to remove the croutons to a mixing bowl, and gently toss with ¼ cup of the grated Parmigiano-Reggiano and salt and pepper. Transfer the croutons to the lined sheet pan to drain.

In the food processor, combine the remaining 6 anchovies, the chopped garlic, mustard, lemon juice, Worcestershire, Tabasco, and egg yolks and puree. Slowly drizzle in the remaining oil and puree until it has all been incorporated. Taste and season with salt and pepper as needed.

In a salad bowl, toss the lettuce with the dressing, using enough to coat but not drown the leaves. Add the remaining ¾ cup Parmigiano-Reggiano and toss gently again. Distribute the salad and croutons among individual plates, and garnish each plate with one or more *boquerones*, if using.

Serves 4 to 8

2½ cups extra-virgin olive oil

10 oil-packed anchovies, drained

4 garlic cloves: 2 peeled and smashed, 2 peeled and finely chopped

6 slices white sandwich bread, cut into ¾-inch dice

1 cup finely grated Parmigiano-Reggiano cheese

Salt and freshly ground black pepper to taste

1 teaspoon Dijon mustard

Juice of 1 lemon (about 2 tablespoons)

½ teaspoon Worcestershire sauce

Dash of Tabasco sauce

3 egg yolks

1 large or 2 small heads of romaine lettuce, dark outermost leaves discarded, washed, chilled, and coarsely chopped

16 boquerones (white-vinegar-cured anchovies packed in oil), drained, for garnish (optional)

SPECIAL EQUIPMENT

Sheet pan lined with newspaper
Food processor or blender

TUNA SALAD

24 ounces oil-packed tuna, preferably Spanish or Italian varieties (see recipe headnote), drained

½ red onion, peeled and diced (about ½ cup)

3 ribs celery, diced (about ½ cup)

¾ cup Mayonnaise (page 272) or store-bought mayonnaise

Salt and freshly ground black pepper to taste

8 to 10 slices of white bread

4 to 6 leaves iceberg lettuce

If you're like me, you have certain expectations for your tuna salad based on early, formative tuna-salad experiences. I don't want mine to deviate too far from the lunch counters of my childhood. I want it on sliced white bread. I want it with crisp iceberg lettuce. And I do *not* want any creative additions distracting from the fundamental elements.

However, there's tuna . . . and then there's tuna. I like high-test jarred or canned tuna. Fresh tuna, as any Spaniard will tell you, is not necessarily the best tuna. And some of the canned stuff in Spain, such as Don Bocarte or Ortiz brand *ventresca* tuna belly packed in olive oil, will run you a hundred dollars a can. Buy the best available.

Place the tuna in a mixing bowl, along with the onion and celery. Add the mayonnaise a little at a time, breaking up the tuna with a fork and mixing as you go—this will give you the option to dial back the mayonnaise if your preference is to go lighter (an impulse I don't necessarily endorse but grudgingly acknowledge). Season the mixture with salt and pepper to taste and serve on bread with lettuce.

Serves 4 to 6

CHICKEN SALAD

Chicken salad is a pretty simple thing, which means that you've got to get the details right. What's essential here is how you cut the poached chicken. For proper chicken salad sandwich structure and engineering, I like a small, distinct dice. When the pieces are too large, the salad doesn't hold together as a sandwich filling. By contrast, when they're cut too small, your salad becomes an unappealing mush.

Place the chicken in a heavy-bottom pot and cover with cold water. Bring the water to a simmer and cook at that level for 10 minutes, taking care not to let the heat level rise to a boil. Turn off the heat, cover the pot, and let sit for another 10 minutes. Using tongs or a slotted spoon, remove the chicken from the water and let cool, then cut into a ¼-inch dice.

Place the diced chicken in a mixing bowl and use a spatula to fold in the mayonnaise, onion, celery, celery salt, tarragon (if using), Worcestershire, and Tabasco. Taste and season with salt and pepper as necessary.

2 boneless, skinless chicken breasts (about 1½ pounds total)

⅔ cup Mayonnaise (page 272) or store-bought mayonnaise

1 small red onion, peeled and finely diced (about ¼ to ⅓ cup)

1 rib celery, finely diced

1 teaspoon celery salt

1 tablespoon finely chopped fresh tarragon (optional)

¼ teaspoon Worcestershire sauce

¼ teaspoon Tabasco sauce

Salt and freshly ground black pepper to taste

Makes about 1 quart, enough for 4 standard-size sandwiches

TOMATO SALAD

2 pounds best-quality ripe tomatoes, cored and cut into rough wedges

1 garlic clove, peeled and finely chopped

2 large shallots, peeled and thinly sliced

1 cup fresh parsley leaves, cut into chiffonade just before tossing and serving

3 basil leaves, cut into chiffonade just before tossing and serving

6 tablespoons best-quality extra-virgin olive oil

2 tablespoons red wine vinegar

1 teaspoon sherry vinegar

Sea salt to taste

Freshly roughly cracked black pepper to taste

This recipe lives and dies on having perfectly ripe tomatoes, purchased in season. Does that mean heirloom tomatoes? And are heirloom tomatoes in fact inherently better than mere vine-ripened or other varieties of ripe tomatoes? To my mind, heirloom tomatoes are akin to "Burgundy" wine. Despite carrying a recognizable label that's come to connote high quality, you never know what you're going to get from tomato to tomato or bottle to bottle—which is half the fun.

Combine the tomatoes, garlic, shallots, and herbs in a salad bowl. Drizzle the oil and vinegars over the mixture and season with the salt and pepper. Use salad tongs or scrupulously clean hands to gently toss the mixture together, taking care to maintain the structural integrity of the tomatoes as much as possible. Serve immediately.

Serves 4 to 6

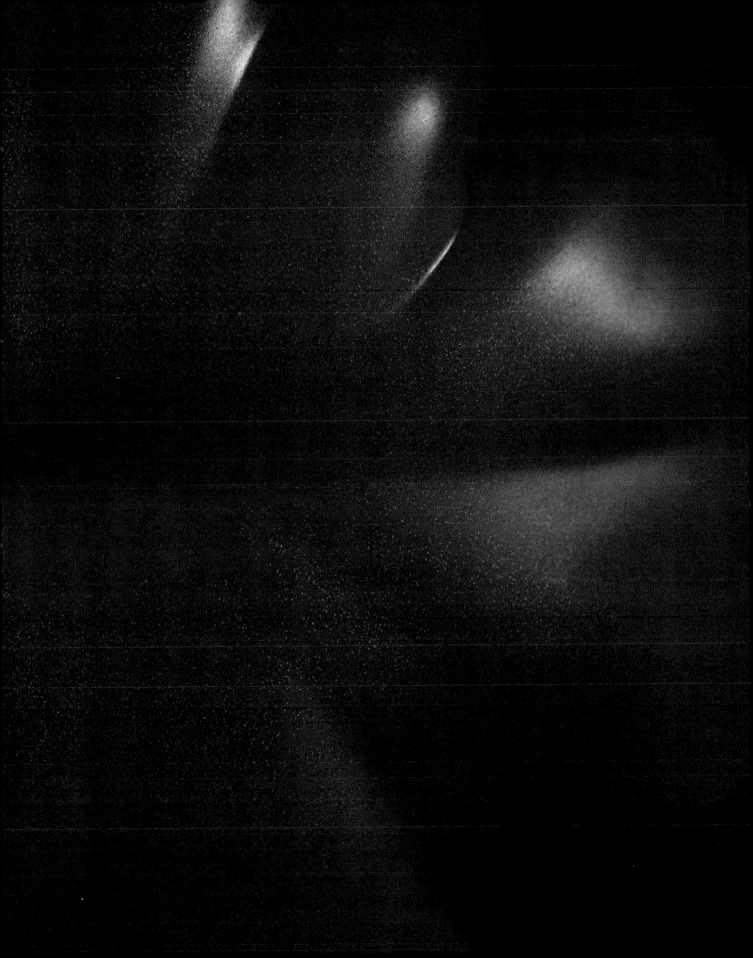

POTATO SALAD

2 pounds Yukon Gold potatoes
(about 6 or 7 large potatoes),
peeled and cut into ¾-inch dice

1 tablespoon white vinegar

1 tablespoon kosher salt, plus more
to taste

6 ounces thick-cut bacon

1 cup Mayonnaise (page 272) or
store-bought mayonnaise

2 tablespoons red wine vinegar

1 tablespoon Dijon mustard

Freshly ground black pepper to
taste

1 small red onion, peeled and
finely diced (about ¼ to ⅓ cup)

1 rib celery, finely diced

10 to 12 cornichons, finely
chopped

¼ cup attractive celery leaves, for
garnish (optional)

SPECIAL EQUIPMENT

Plate lined with newspaper

This is a straight-ahead potato salad, with hard-cooked eggs replaced by bacon. Use good potatoes, don't overcook them, make your own mayonnaise, get the high-end thick-cut bacon (Nueske's, Snake River Farms, Benton's Country Hams, and Zingerman's all have excellent offerings on the web, or seek out the pork guy at your local farmer's market), and pay attention to the seasoning.

Place the potatoes in a medium, heavy-bottom pot and cover by 1 inch with cold water. Add the white vinegar and 1 tablespoon salt, stir lightly, and bring to a boil. Cook for about 10 minutes, until the potatoes are cooked through, then remove from heat, drain, and arrange in a single layer on a sheet pan to cool.

Meanwhile, cook the bacon in a skillet until crisp. Remove from the skillet and drain on the plate lined with newspaper. Once cool enough to handle, cut or crumble the bacon into small pieces.

In a medium mixing bowl, whisk together the mayonnaise, red wine vinegar, mustard, and salt and pepper to taste. Add the potatoes, bacon, onion, celery, and cornichons and fold together with a spatula. Taste and adjust seasoning if necessary. Garnish with the celery leaves, if using, and serve.

Makes about 2 quarts, to serve 8 to 12

BOSTON LETTUCE WITH RADISHES, CARROTS, APPLES, AND YOGURT-CHIVE DRESSING

This particular combination of shapes and colors looks pretty and tastes good together, but there's some room for variation here. You can use other greens of a similar texture—red oak, baby arugula, romaine, young spinach—but avoid hardier types like frisée, escarole, or baby kale. Parsley, mint, or basil, or a combination, would work well in place of chives. Champagne, red or white wine, or apple cider vinegar can sub in for lemon juice, but don't use balsamic, which tips the balance into unconscionably sweet territory. When prepping your raw salad ingredients, remember that apples (and, to a lesser extent, radishes) turn brown once exposed to air, so don't do that prep too far in advance, or hit them with some lemon juice to forestall the inevitable.

In a small mixing bowl, whisk together the yogurt, oil, lemon juice, salt, pepper, fish sauce (if using), and chives. Taste and adjust seasoning as desired.

Arrange the lettuce, radishes, carrots, and apple in a salad bowl and toss together if you'll be dressing the salad in the kitchen (in which case you need to wait until guests are seated and chilled salad plates are at the ready before doing so, because once the acidic yogurt hits the salad, it starts breaking it down and making it look decidedly less lovely). Alternatively, do not toss the salad ingredients but instead leave segregated, as for salade composée, in which case you should serve the dressing alongside.

¾ cup whole milk yogurt

3 tablespoons best-quality extra-virgin olive oil

2 tablespoons freshly squeezed lemon juice

1 teaspoon salt

¼ teaspoon freshly ground black pepper

1 teaspoon fish sauce (optional but highly recommended)

3 tablespoons chopped fresh chives

Head of Boston lettuce, washed and torn into bite-size pieces

3 red radishes (or 1 Watermelon or Breakfast radish), scrubbed and very thinly sliced

1 large or 2 medium carrots, peeled and coarsely grated

1 apple, preferably a semitart variety, cored and julienned

Serves 4 to 8

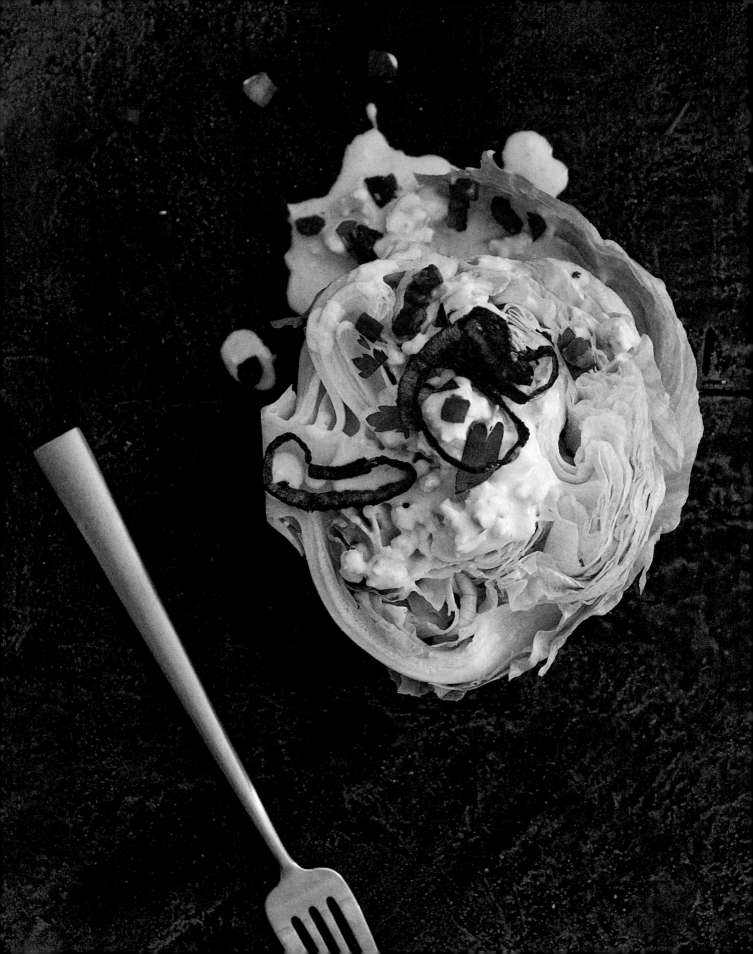

ICEBERG WEDGE WITH STILTON AND PANCETTA

Remember when everybody looked down on iceberg lettuce? When it was suddenly gone from menus everywhere? Me neither. Let's pretend it never happened.

Place the pancetta in a large sauté pan and cook over medium heat, stirring occasionally, until the cubes are browned and have rendered their visible fat, 8 to 10 minutes. Remove the pancetta from the pan with a slotted spoon and transfer to the lined plate to drain.

In a medium mixing bowl, combine half the Stilton, the mayonnaise, oil, vinegar, and lemon juice and whisk together to make a homogenous mixture. Thin with 1 tablespoon water if necessary. Taste and season with salt and pepper.

Place a few tablespoons of the dressing in the center of each serving plate and top with an iceberg wedge. Drizzle each wedge with another tablespoon or two of dressing. Top each serving with some of the pancetta and the remaining blue cheese. Garnish with parsley and fried shallots and serve.

Serves 6

6 ounces pancetta, cut into cubes

8 ounces Stilton or other high-quality blue cheese, crumbled

¼ cup Mayonnaise (page 272) or store-bought mayonnaise

2 tablespoons canola oil

2 tablespoons red wine vinegar

1 tablespoon freshly squeezed lemon juice

Salt and freshly ground black pepper to taste

Head of iceberg lettuce, washed, cored, and cut into 6 equal wedges

¼ cup coarsely chopped fresh Italian parsley

½ cup fried shallots (see page 209)

SPECIAL EQUIPMENT

Plate lined with newspaper

DO CHUA SALAD WITH HERBS, SCALLIONS, SPROUTS, AND EGG

4 medium to large carrots, peeled and julienned

1 large daikon radish (1 to 1½ pounds), peeled and julienned

1 tablespoon salt

2 teaspoons plus 2 tablespoons granulated sugar

¼ cup white vinegar

½ cup sherry vinegar

¾ cup hot water

1 bunch of scallions, roots trimmed, white and light green parts thinly sliced, green tops reserved for stock if desired

2 cups crisp mung or soy bean sprouts

4 hard-boiled eggs (see pages 77–78), peeled and quartered lengthwise

1 cup fresh young basil leaves

1 cup fresh young mint leaves

1 cup fresh cilantro leaves

Nuoc Mam Cham (page 277) to taste

Sriracha to taste

Reasonably authentic Vietnamese flavors can be coaxed out of any kitchen if you shop right. Case in point: Vietnamese *do chua*, a quick pickle, easily made with just a few ingredients, an essential part of Banh Mi (page 93), and the basis of this crunchy salad. Pay attention when buying herbs for this dish: no yellowed cilantro, giant woody-stemmed mint, or blackening basil, please. You can always throw a pork chop or some ground pork, beef, or lamb onto this thing, maybe some cooked rice or rice noodles, and call it dinner.

First, make the *do chua*: In a large mixing bowl, combine the carrots, daikon, salt, and 2 teaspoons sugar and toss well. Let sit for 30 minutes, then discard the liquid that has collected beneath the vegetables. Squeeze them dry with paper towels or a clean kitchen towel. Rinse and dry the bowl and return the vegetables to it, along with the remaining sugar, white and sherry vinegars, and hot water. Cover and let sit at room temperature for 1 hour, after which point you can either assemble the salad or transfer to a glass container and refrigerate for up to 3 weeks.

Remove the *do chua* from its holding container with tongs and transfer it to a clean mixing bowl. You don't want to take all of the brine with you, but whatever it comes attached with is fine. Add the scallions, sprouts, and eggs and gently toss or fold together. Add the herbs and fold or toss again. Taste and season as desired with *nuoc mam cham* and sriracha, then serve immediately.

Serves 4 to 6

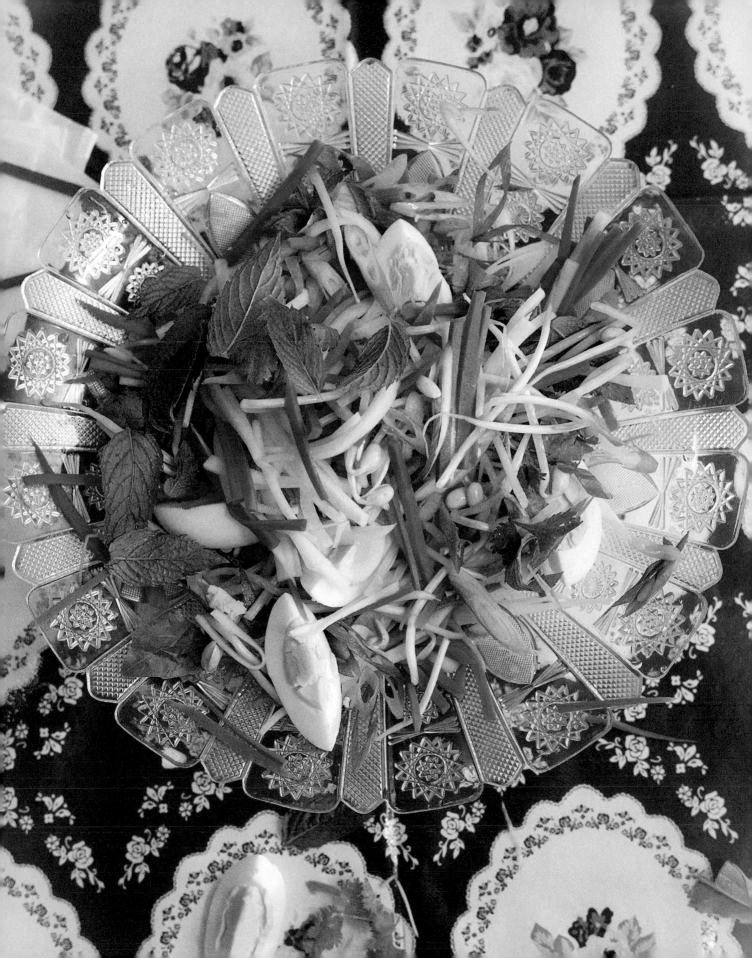

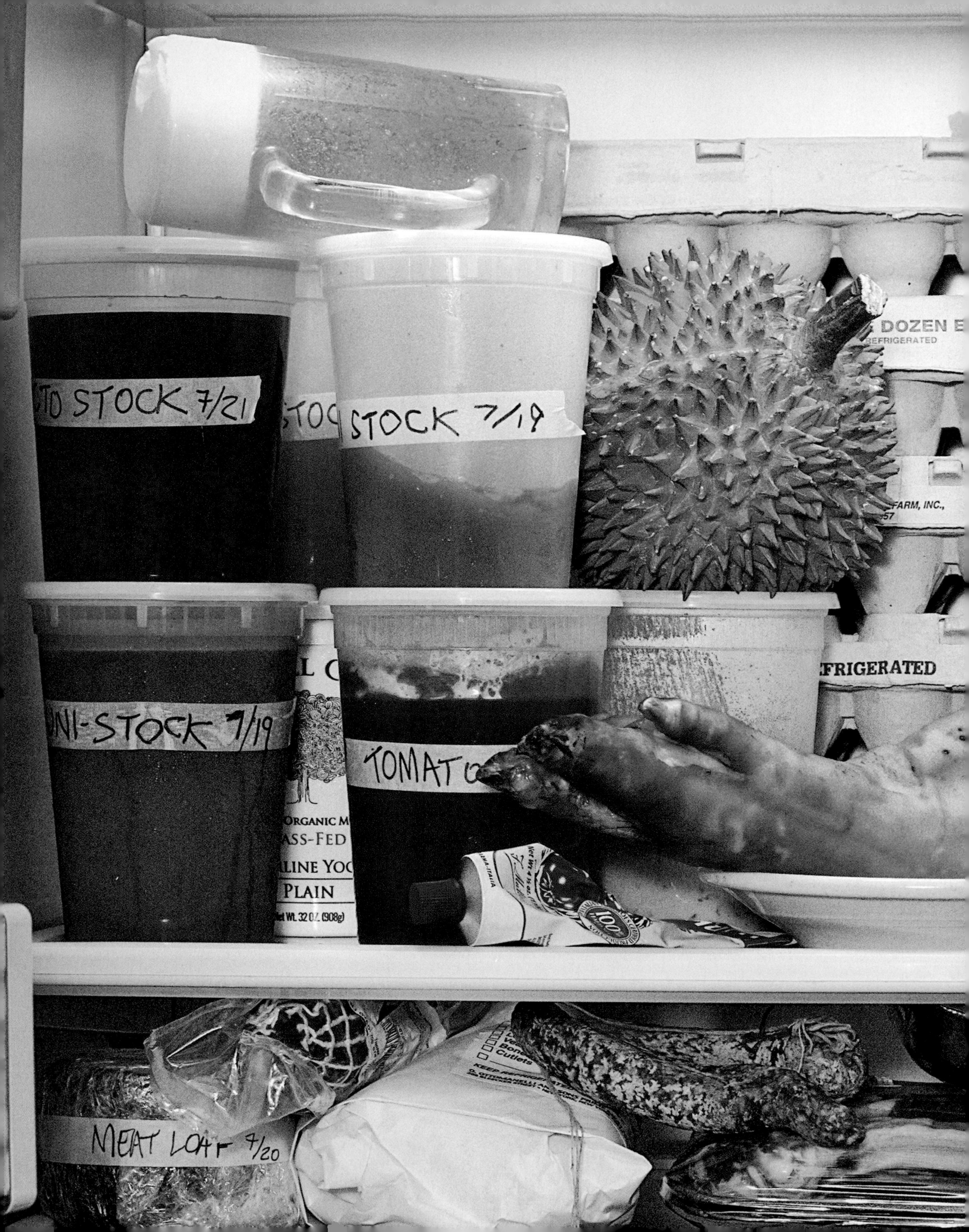
STOCK 7/21
STOCK 7/19
STOCK 7/19
REFRIGERATED
PLAIN
Net Wt. 32 OZ. (908g)
MEAT LOAF

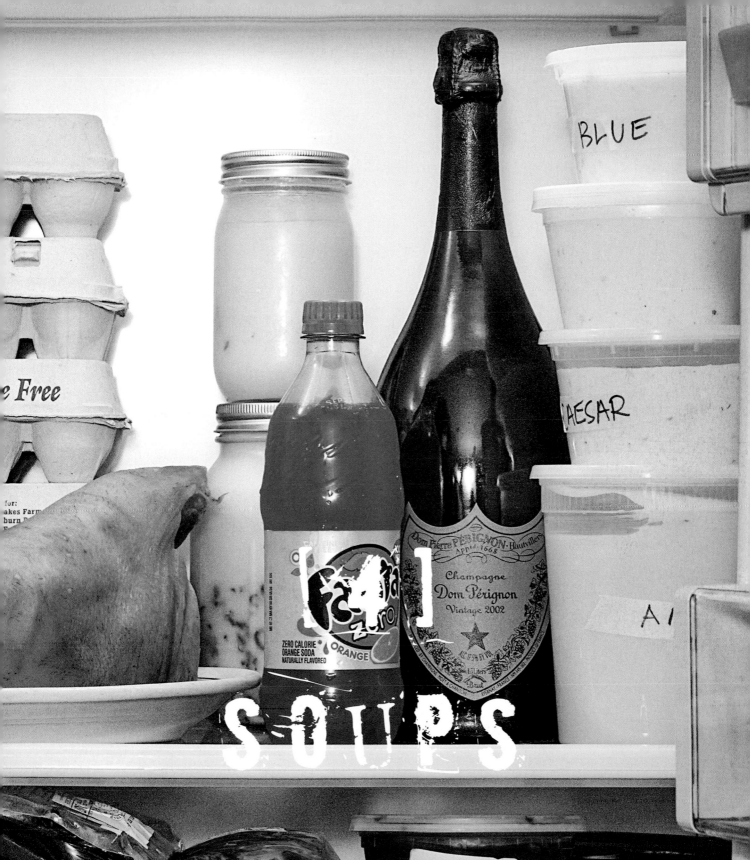

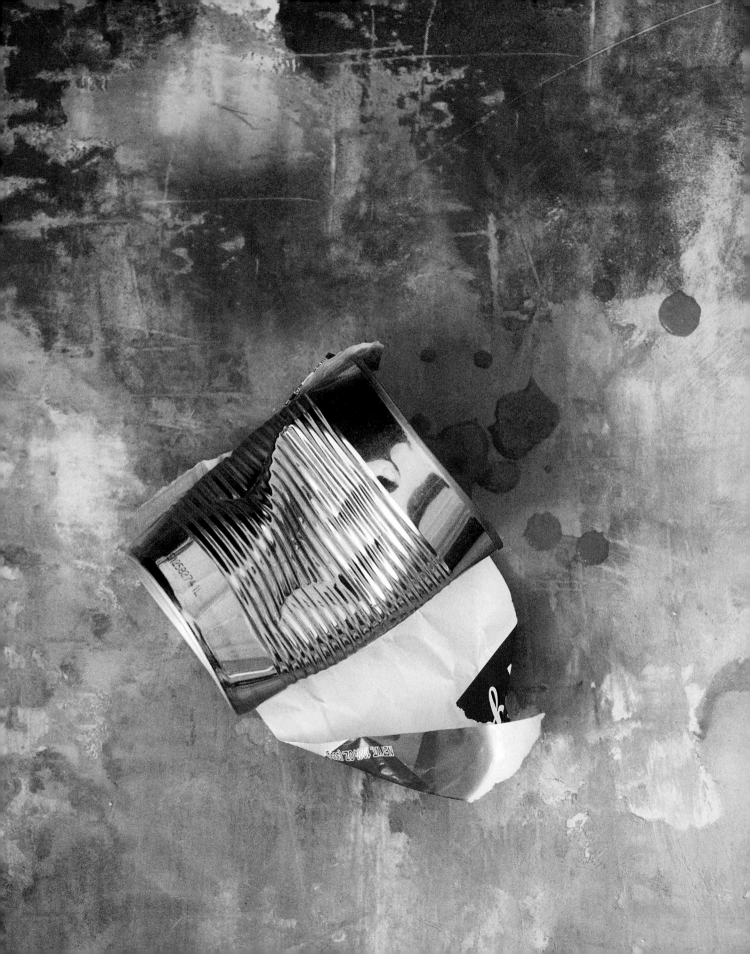

CREAM OF TOMATO SOUP

When I was in second grade, I got beat up by an older kid named Skippy. Yes, his name was actually Skippy, and a more vicious, terrifying punk has never been produced by the New Jersey school system, I assure you. He and his fellow third-graders held me down, pummeled me, and threatened to make me drink bleach. Needless to say, I went home in tears.

But Mom made me tomato soup. Or, more accurately, opened a can, added some milk to what was inside, and heated it up. You know what can I'm talking about.

Tomato soup remains the taste of comfort, security, and recently dried tears. It should make you feel better. It should not wander too far from the stuff that comes in a can. It should be served with Saltine crackers or oysterettes.

Bring water to a boil in a large, heavy-bottom pot. Use a paring knife to cut an X into both ends of each tomato. Once the water boils, add the tomatoes to the pot, working in two batches if necessary to avoid overcrowding the pot or reducing the temperature too drastically. Allow the tomatoes to simmer in the water for 30 to 60 seconds, until the skin begins to loosen and peel away from the flesh. Using tongs, remove the tomatoes to the ice-water bath. Once they are cool enough to handle, peel off and discard the skin and coarsely chop the tomatoes.

In a large, heavy-bottom stockpot, heat the butter until it is just shimmering, then add the onion, carrots, and celery. Stir over medium-high heat until they soften and begin to release their juices, about 2 minutes. Season with salt and pepper and stir in the garlic. Continue to cook, stirring frequently, until the vegetables have begun to brown, 7 to 10 minutes. Do not let them scorch or get dark brown.

Stir in the chopped fresh tomatoes and the canned tomatoes and their juices, rinsing the inside of the can with a bit of water and $\longrightarrow$

About 12 very ripe medium plum or similar-size tomatoes

3 tablespoons unsalted butter or olive oil

1 large yellow onion, peeled and finely chopped

2 medium carrots, peeled and finely chopped

2 ribs celery, finely chopped

Salt and freshly ground black pepper to taste

1 large garlic clove, peeled and finely chopped

1 (28-ounce) can peeled plum tomatoes

3 cups Dark Universal Stock (page 260) or chicken stock

1 bay leaf

1 tablespoon sugar, plus more to taste as needed

1 tablespoon apple cider vinegar

¼ cup heavy cream

SPECIAL EQUIPMENT

Ice-water bath (large bowl filled with ice and cold water)

Blender or immersion blender

adding that to the pot, too. Once the mixture begins to bubble, add the stock, bay leaf, sugar, and vinegar. Bring to a boil, reduce to a simmer, and let cook for about 30 minutes, uncovered.

Remove the pot from the heat, remove and discard the bay leaf, and puree well in the blender. Stir in the cream and adjust the seasoning with salt, pepper, sugar, and vinegar as desired.

Serves 6 to 8

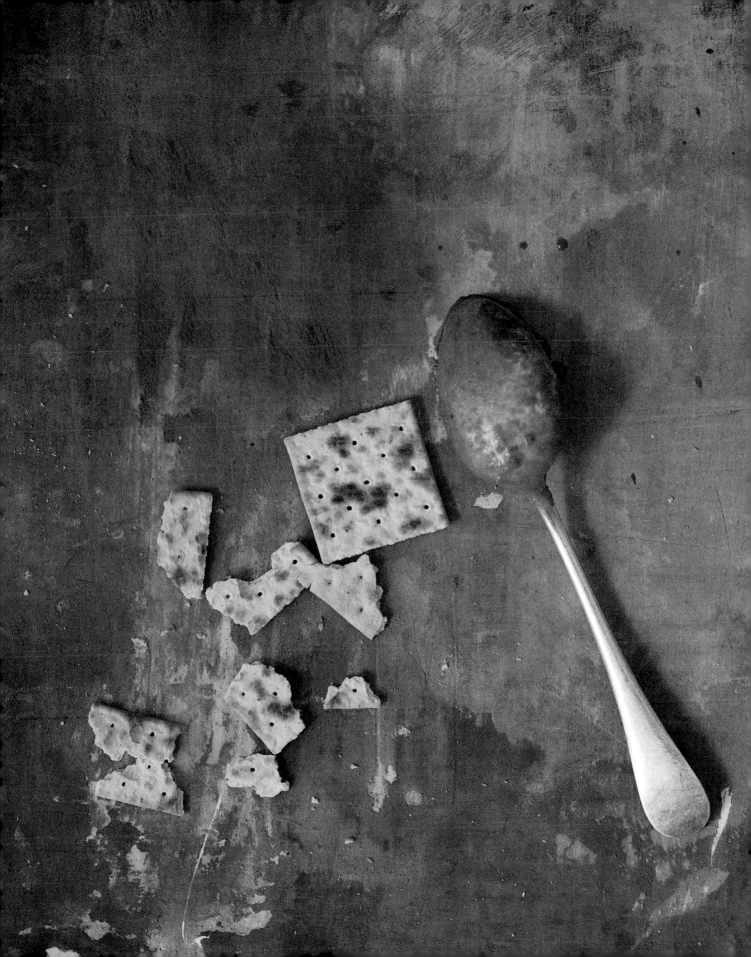

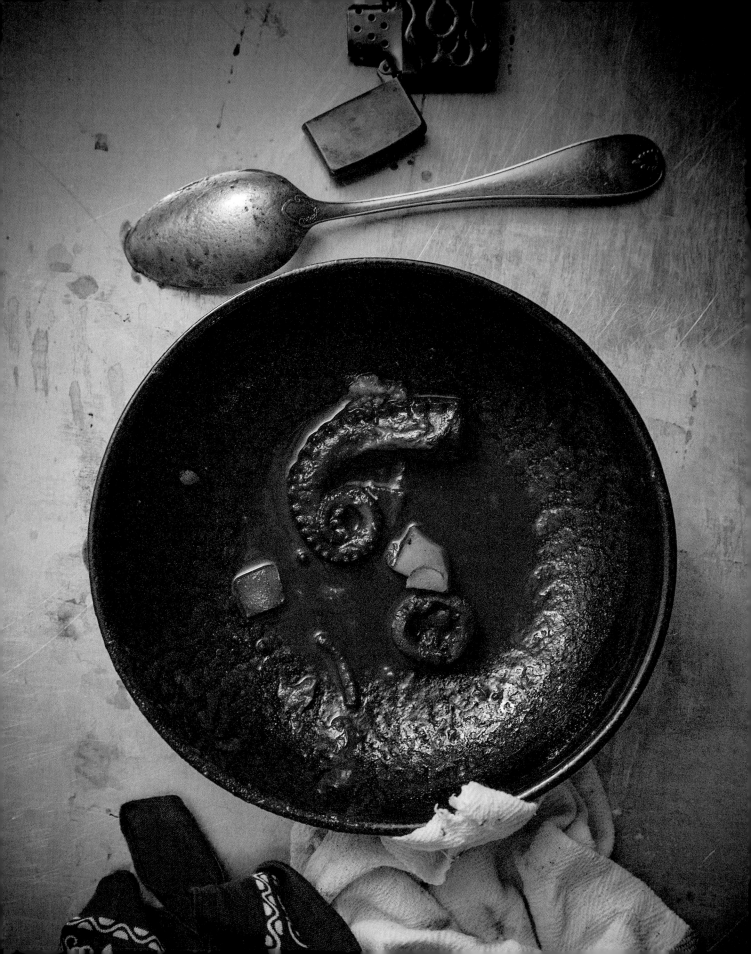

PORTUGUESE SQUID AND OCTOPUS SOUP

I fell in love with this stuff at a Provincetown joint called Cookie's Tap, which was popular with local fishermen and (allegedly) sports gamblers. I'd never tasted anything like it. It took me years of trying to get it right, and the version below, though an adaptation and not necessarily a faithful re-creation, catches, I think, the spirit and many virtues of the original.

I suggest you reduce the wine at the same time you make the octopus stock. It will take 30 to 45 minutes over medium-high heat to reduce from 3 cups to 1 cup.

In a large, heavy-bottom pot, heat ½ tablespoon of the oil over medium-high heat until it shimmers. Working in batches, lightly sear the octopus and squid pieces until they release their natural juices, 1 to 2 minutes. Drain and discard this liquid and set half of the octopus and squid aside.

Return the remaining octopus and squid to the pot and add the peppercorns, coarsely chopped onion, whole garlic cloves, carrot, and celery. Add enough water to just cover. Gently simmer for 1 hour to make the octopus stock. Strain the stock, discarding the solids (though you should eat the octopus), and set aside.

In a medium braising pan or Dutch oven, heat the remaining oil over medium heat. Sweat the bell peppers, diced onion, and sliced garlic in the oil for 3 to 4 minutes, then stir in the cumin, pepper flakes, and oregano and let cook another 2 minutes before stirring in the reserved octopus and squid. Cook for 2 to 3 minutes, then add the tomato paste and cook for 1 to 2 minutes, until it has lost its bright red color and has begun to stick to the aromatics and the bottom of the pan. Deglaze with the reduced red wine, scraping the bottom of the pan as necessary with a wooden spoon, then add the crushed

→

1½ tablespoons canola oil

10 octopus tentacles, beak removed and discarded and tentacles cut into bite-size pieces

8 whole squid, beak removed and discarded and bodies peeled and cut into ¼-inch tubes

1 teaspoon whole black peppercorns

1 medium yellow onion, peeled and coarsely chopped, plus 1 medium onion, peeled and cut into large dice

4 whole garlic cloves, peeled, plus 8 garlic cloves, peeled and thinly sliced

1 carrot, peeled and coarsely chopped

1 rib celery, coarsely chopped

1 large green bell pepper, cored, seeded, and cut into large dice

1 tablespoon ground cumin

¼ teaspoon red pepper flakes

1 sprig fresh oregano

1 tablespoon tomato paste

1 bottle dry red wine, reduced by two-thirds

2 cups crushed canned tomatoes and their juices

2 Yukon Gold potatoes, scrubbed and cut into large dice

Salt and freshly ground black pepper to taste

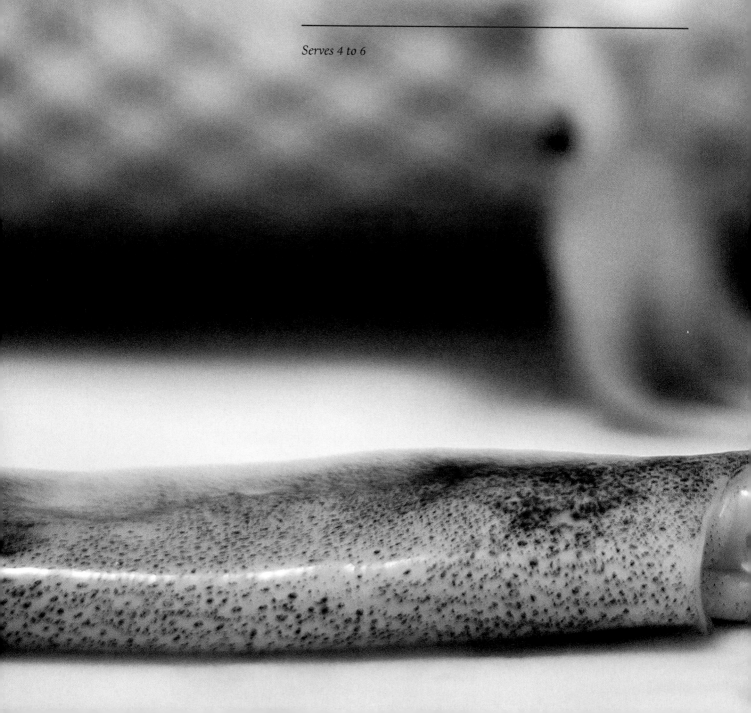

tomatoes and enough of the stock to cover by 1 inch. Add water if necessary. Add the potatoes, stir well, and allow the mixture to gently simmer for 60 minutes.

Adjust the seasoning with salt and pepper to taste. Test the tenderness of the octopus. If it is not tender enough, continue to gently simmer for another 10 to 20 minutes, until it is tender.

Serves 4 to 6

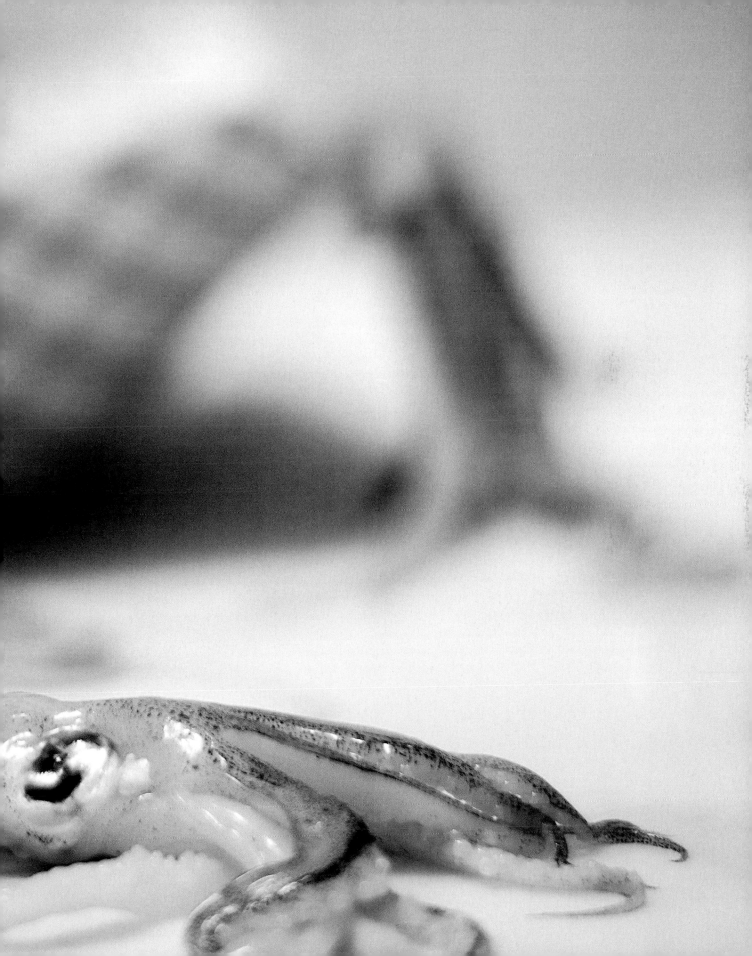

PORTUGUESE KALE SOUP

1½ cups dried red kidney beans

1 large ham hock or comparable soup bone, cut into pieces to allow the marrow to escape into the broth

3 to 4 quarts Dark Universal Stock (page 260)

½ pound Portuguese chouriço sausage, cut into ¼-inch-thick slices

1 pound linguiça sausage, cut into ¼-inch-thick slices

2 bunches curly kale, center stem removed and discarded, leaves washed and coarsely chopped

4 large or 5 medium waxy potatoes, peeled and cut into large dice

Red pepper flakes to taste

1 tablespoon sherry vinegar

Salt and freshly ground black pepper to taste

Another Provincetown classic, inspired by the late Howard Mitcham, an unpretentious, brilliant Cape Cod cook and writer whose *Provincetown Seafood Cookbook* is an out-of-print treasure worth snatching up at any price. Mitcham used white pea beans, better known as navy beans, in his version; I prefer kidney beans.

In a large, heavy-bottom stockpot, soak the kidney beans for 12 hours in plenty of cold water, or cover the dry beans with 4 cups of water and bring to a rapid boil. Cover the pot, remove from the heat, and let sit for 90 minutes undisturbed. Drain.

In a clean stockpot, combine the soaked or cooked and drained beans and the ham hock and cover with the stock. Add 1 quart water. Bring to a boil, then reduce to a simmer and cook for 1 hour, using a slotted spoon or ladle to skim off and discard any scum that rises to the surface. Add the *chouriço*, *linguiça*, and kale, and simmer for another hour. Add the potatoes, pepper flakes, and vinegar, and season to taste with salt and pepper. Simmer for at least another hour, adding more stock or water as needed to keep all the ingredients submerged. The longer the soup simmers, the better the flavor; Howard Mitcham calls for a minimum of 5 hours.

Serves 8 to 10

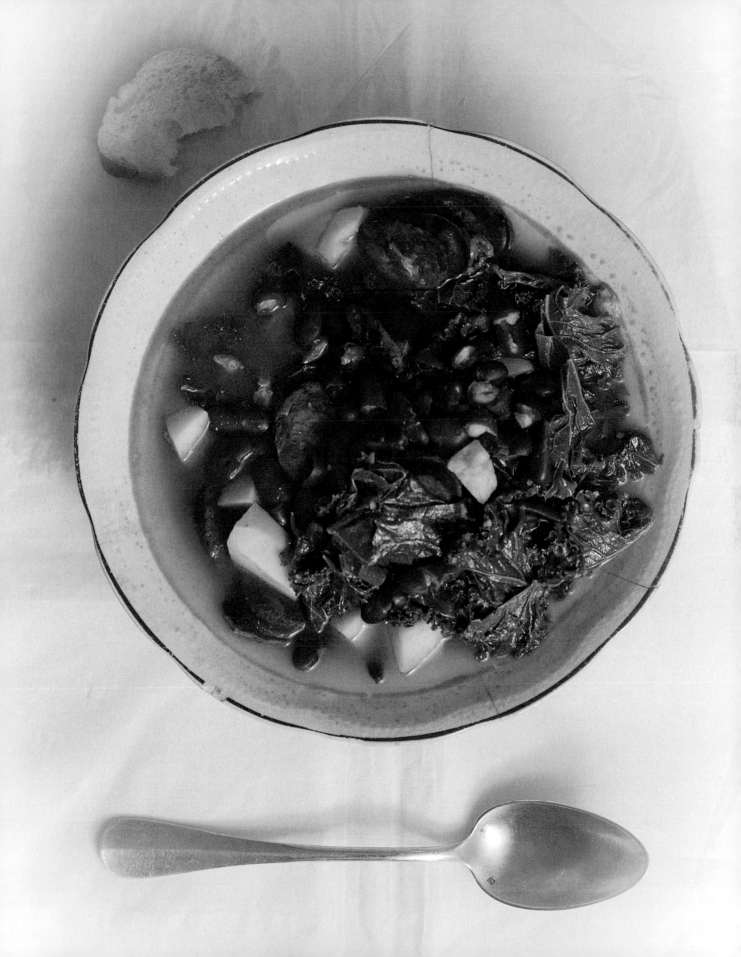

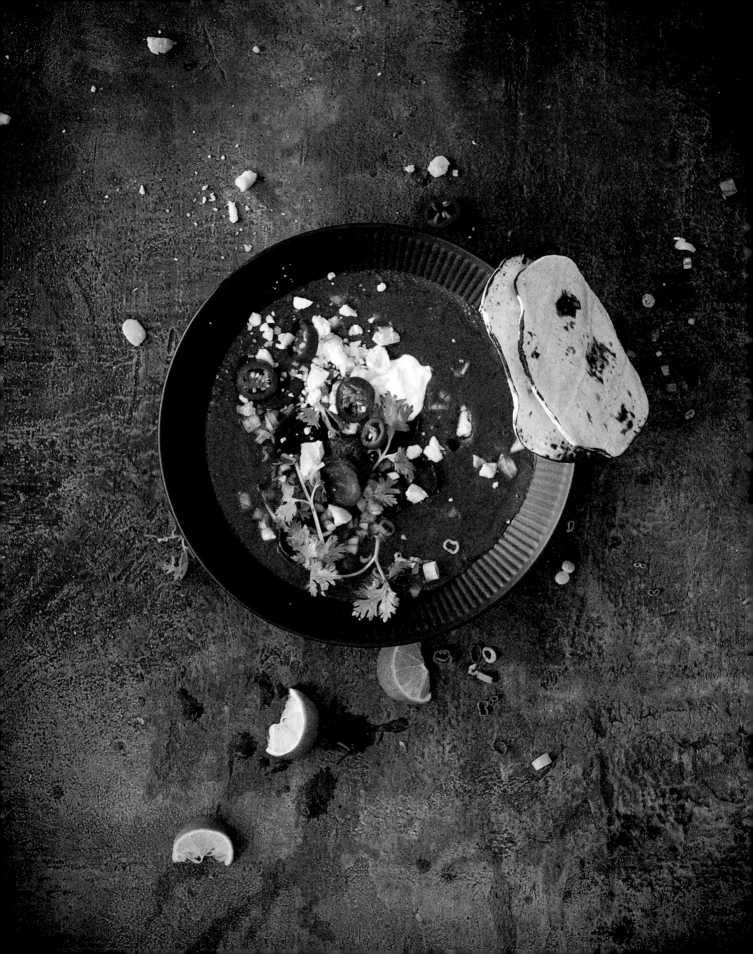

Black Bean Soup

The mirepoix (really a *sofrito*) makes the soup here. Atop the usual onion, carrot, celery, and garlic, the bell pepper provides additional sweetness and the chorizo gives it a porky heft.

In a large, heavy-bottom stockpot with a lid, cover the dry beans with 4 cups of water and bring to a rapid boil. Cover the pot, remove from the heat, and let sit for 90 minutes undisturbed. Drain.

In a large, heavy-bottom saucepan, heat the lard over medium heat. Add the chopped chorizo and cook over medium heat, stirring occasionally, until it has rendered most of its fat. Using tongs or a slotted spoon, remove the chorizo from the pan and set it aside.

To the hot pan, add the onion, carrot, celery, bell pepper, garlic, cumin, oregano, and paprika and cook over medium heat, stirring occasionally, until the vegetables are soft and slightly browned, 5 to 7 minutes. Season to taste with salt and pepper.

Turn the heat up to high and cook for 2 minutes, until most of the moisture from the vegetables has sizzled away. Add the vinegar and stir it in to loosen the browned bits in the pan. Continue to cook on high until the vinegar has bubbled away and lost its "sharp" smell.

Add the stock and bring to a boil, then add the drained beans and stir well. Reduce the heat to a simmer and cook for about 45 minutes, until the beans are tender. Remove from the heat and pulse with an immersion blender so that the beans are mostly broken up but some chunky texture remains. Stir the reserved cooked chorizo into the soup. Adjust the seasoning with salt and pepper if necessary, and add a splash of water or stock if necessary to loosen.

Place the sliced chorizo in a small sauté pan and cook on both sides until it is seared and some of the fat is rendered. Remove it from the pan and let it drain on the newspaper.

Serve the soup hot, with the chorizo and all garnishes alongside.

Serves 6 to 8

1½ cups dried black beans

2 tablespoons rendered pork lard or olive oil

4 links dry chorizo sausage, coarsely chopped

1 red onion, peeled and finely chopped

1 small carrot, peeled and grated

1 rib celery, finely chopped

1 medium red bell pepper, cored, seeded, and finely chopped

5 garlic cloves, peeled and finely chopped

2 teaspoons ground cumin

2 teaspoons dried oregano

2 teaspoons smoked paprika

Salt and freshly ground black pepper to taste

¼ cup sherry or red wine vinegar

4 cups Dark Universal Stock (page 260)

2 links dry chorizo sausage, thinly sliced

GARNISHES

Any or all of the following: hard-cooked and thinly sliced eggs, lime wedges, cilantro leaves, finely chopped red onions, sliced scallions, sour cream, hot sauce, toasted corn tortillas

SPECIAL EQUIPMENT

Immersion blender

Newspaper, for draining chorizo

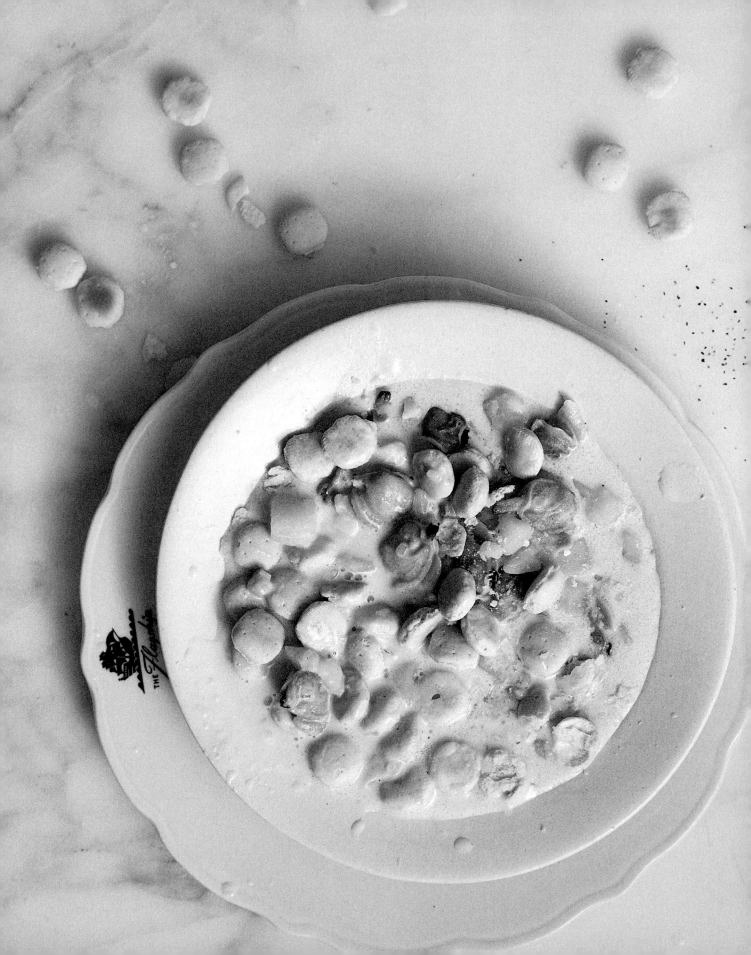

New England Clam Chowder

There *is* only one chowder. All else is soup. And I'm a purist. I was taught to make clam chowder by a fantastic woman named Lydia, a professional cook and a notoriously hard drinker, from a Portuguese fishing family on Cape Cod. She was famous for her chowder—and her behavior. At the end of a shift, she'd often stagger through the kitchen doors, lurch out into the dining room, and deliver loud, horribly profane tirades directed straight at the owner, who'd be sitting there, paralytic with fear, in front of his guests. It is a testament to her chowder, I think, that he tolerated this. She'd use salt pork instead of bacon and drizzle a little clarified butter over the top at the end. Old school. They don't make them like Lydia anymore.

In a large, heavy-bottom sauté pan with a lid, arrange the clams, 1 to 2 dozen at a time, into a single layer. Add about ½ cup water, cover, and bring to a boil to steam the clams open. Check them frequently. Using tongs, remove the opened clams to a sheet pan to cool, and add more clams until they have all been steamed open, discarding any that have not opened after a reasonable amount of time—there are usually one or two duds per 2 dozen clams. Once they're cool enough to handle, remove them from their shells, reserving as much of the ambient cooking liquid (generally referred to as "liquor") as possible, and place them in a small bowl or other container. If the liquor appears gritty, you may choose to strain it.

In a heavy-bottom stockpot or Dutch oven, heat the salt pork over medium heat until it begins to render its fat, adding a tablespoon or two of water to keep it from browning, and stirring occasionally. When the fat has mostly been rendered, add the onions, stirring well to coat them with the fat. Season the onions lightly with salt and pepper and cook until they are translucent but not browned. Add the potatoes and just enough water to cover. Cook the mixture at a simmer until the potatoes are just tender. ⟶

8 dozen clams, preferably quahogs, scrubbed

¼ pound salt pork or best-quality bacon, diced

2 white or yellow onions, peeled and finely chopped

Salt and freshly ground black pepper to taste

3 Yukon gold potatoes, peeled and diced

2 tablespoons all-purpose flour

2 cups whole milk

1 cup heavy cream

Pilot crackers, for serving

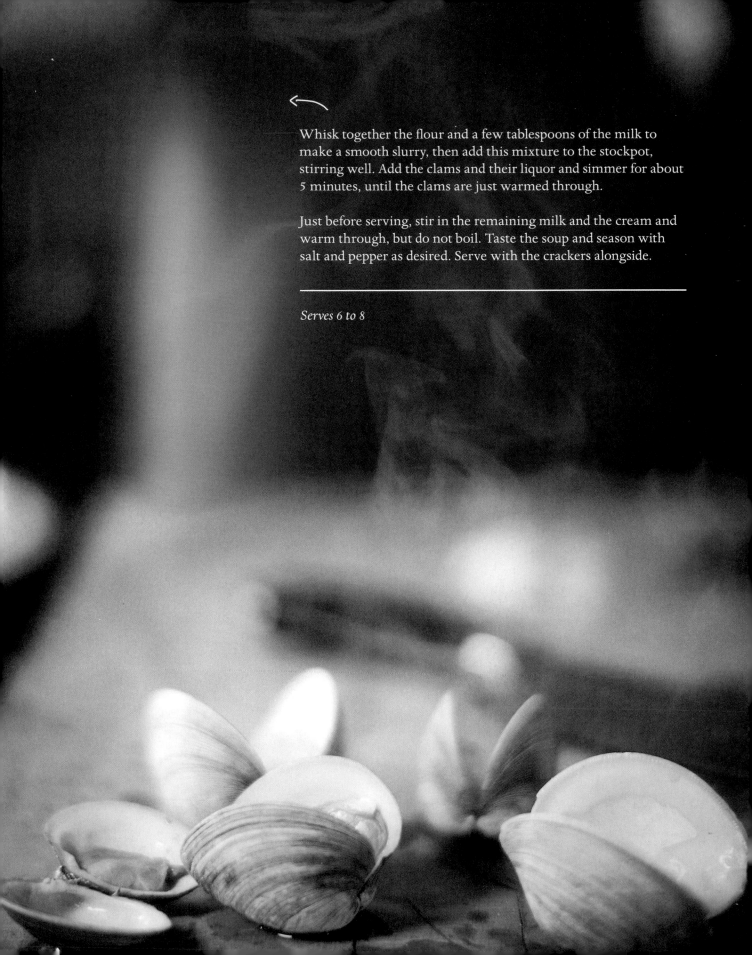

Whisk together the flour and a few tablespoons of the milk to make a smooth slurry, then add this mixture to the stockpot, stirring well. Add the clams and their liquor and simmer for about 5 minutes, until the clams are just warmed through.

Just before serving, stir in the remaining milk and the cream and warm through, but do not boil. Taste the soup and season with salt and pepper as desired. Serve with the crackers alongside.

Serves 6 to 8

GOULASH

I've been making some variation of this dish since my earliest professional cooking days. This version was inspired by a recent visit to Budapest where a Gypsy singer prepared it for us in her home.

Season the beef well with salt and pepper. In a large, heavy-bottom pot, heat the oil over medium heat and add the beef. Sear the beef on all sides, then add the onions and season them lightly with salt so that they release their juices, stirring only as necessary to avoid scorching them. Let the onions get golden brown, which should take about 10 minutes, then stir in the paprika, caraway, and garlic. Cook over medium-high heat for 2 minutes. Add the bay leaf, carrots, parsnip, and celery, and add water to just cover. Bring the mixture to a boil, then reduce the heat to a simmer. Use a ladle or slotted spoon to skim off and discard any beef scum that rises to the surface. Let the mixture simmer, covered, for 45 to 50 minutes.

Add the potatoes and continue to simmer, covered, for another 20 to 25 minutes, until they are tender. Add the tomatoes and peppers and let simmer, uncovered, for another 5 minutes. Taste the broth and season with salt and pepper as necessary. Serve in bowls with the bread and sour cream alongside.

Serves 4 to 6

1½ pounds beef chuck, cut into 1-inch cubes

Salt and freshly ground black pepper to taste

2 tablespoons canola or vegetable oil

2 medium white or yellow onions, peeled and coarsely chopped

¼ cup Hungarian sweet paprika

1½ teaspoons caraway seeds

3 garlic cloves, peeled and finely chopped

1 bay leaf

2 medium carrots, peeled and diced

1 parsnip, peeled and diced

1 rib celery, diced

3 waxy potatoes, scrubbed and diced

3 ripe plum tomatoes, peeled and coarsely chopped

2 medium to large green bell peppers, cored, seeded, and finely chopped

GARNISHES

Sliced rye bread or other hearty country bread

Sour cream

HOT BORSCHT

1 pig's foot, split lengthwise

1 smoked ham hock

2½ quarts Dark Universal Stock (page 260)

2 tablespoons duck fat or rendered lard

2 white or yellow onions, peeled and cut into large dice

Salt and freshly ground black pepper to taste

4 garlic cloves, peeled and coarsely chopped

4 carrots, peeled and cut into large dice

2½ pounds red beets (about 1 dozen small or 4 to 6 medium to large), peeled and cut into large dice, plus 1 medium red beet, peeled and finely grated

1 turnip, peeled and cut into large dice

¼ medium head of green cabbage, cut into ¼-inch-thick ribbons (about 3 cups)

5 sprigs fresh dill, stems and fronds separated, fronds reserved for garnish

Juice of 1 lemon (about 2 tablespoons) or 1 tablespoon red wine vinegar or sherry vinegar

Sour cream, for garnish

The ham hock and pig's foot make this a particularly full-bodied and satisfying version of borscht, a soup you might have previously equated with dishwater. The addition of the finely grated beet at the end of the cooking process is the key to getting that violent, almost bloody color in the bowl.

Place the pig's foot in a large, heavy-bottom saucepan and cover it with cold water. Bring to a boil, let cook for 5 minutes, then remove from the water and rinse well. Discard the water and wash and dry the saucepan. Combine the foot, hock, and stock in the pan, adding more water if necessary to cover the joints. Bring to a simmer and cook over low heat for 1 hour.

In a large, heavy-bottom stockpot or Dutch oven, heat the fat over medium heat. Add the onions, stirring to coat with the fat, and season with salt and pepper. Let cook for 5 minutes, then add the garlic, carrots, diced beets, and turnip, stirring to coat with the fat and released onion juices, and seasoning again with salt and pepper. Let cook 5 minutes, stirring occasionally, then add the cabbage and the dill stems, again stirring and seasoning.

Add the warm stock and bring to a boil, then add the foot and hock and simmer for about 40 minutes, until the vegetables are tender. Stir in the lemon juice. Taste the broth and season if necessary with salt, pepper, and/or more lemon juice. Stir in the grated beet and continue to simmer. Remove and discard the foot. Remove the ham hock, pull as much meat as possible off the bone, and return the meat to the simmering soup.

Serve with sour cream and dill fronds alongside.

Serves 6 to 8

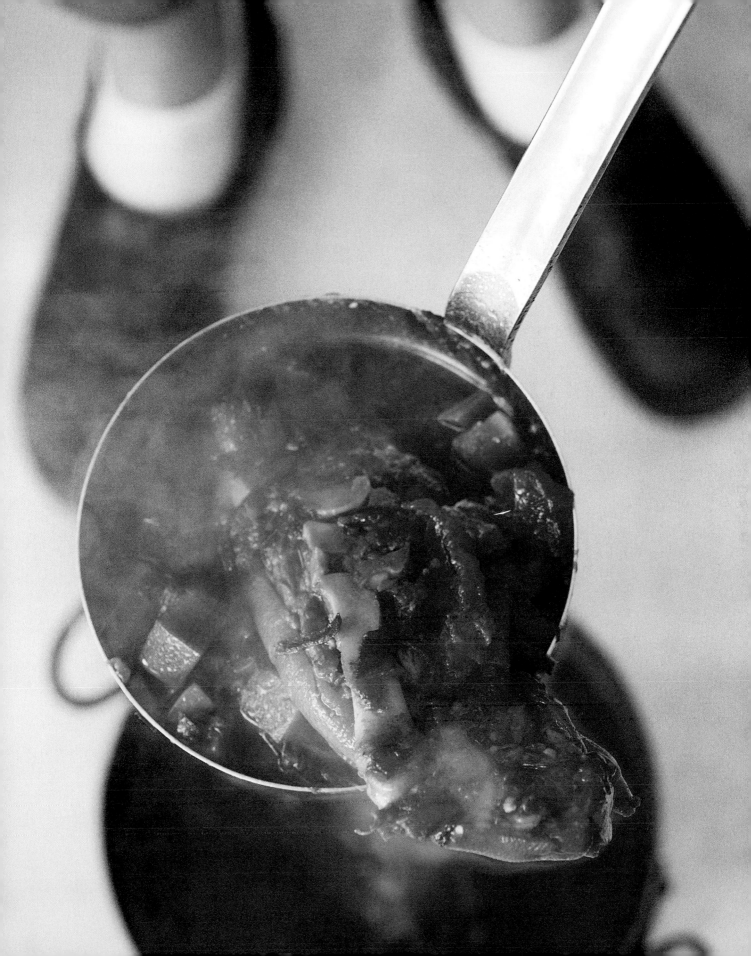

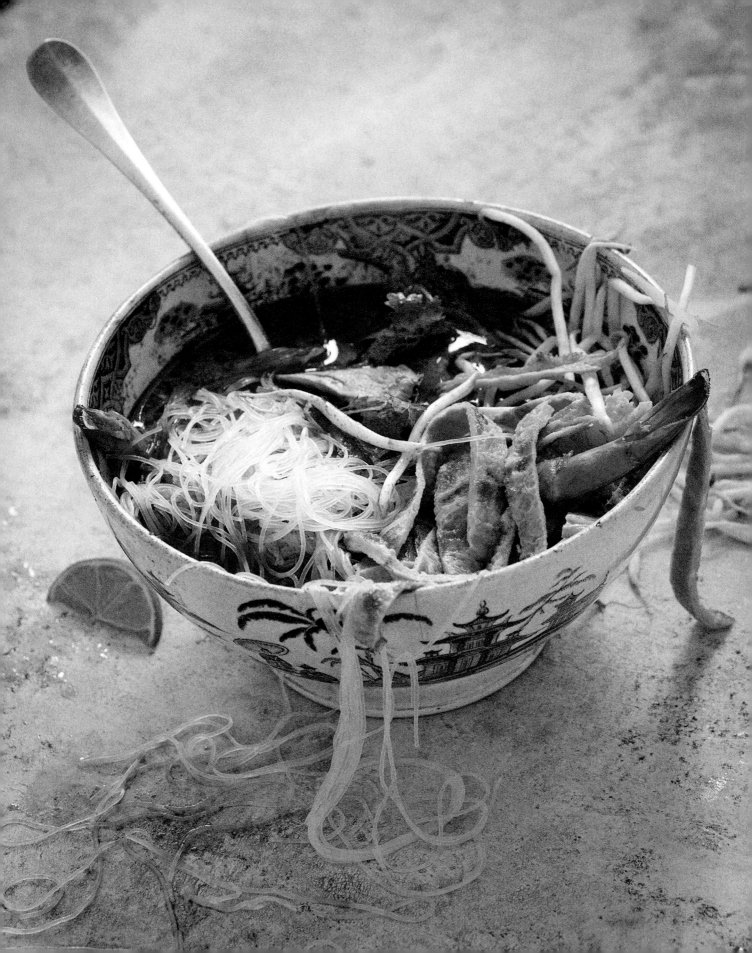

KUCHING-STYLE LAKSA

In the hierarchy of steaming hot bowls of magical broth and noodles, *laksa* is at the absolute top. The best. The most delicious. Breakfast, lunch, or dinner—it will cure what ails you.

I'm not saying this is the greatest *laksa* recipe in the world. It surely isn't. But I'm hoping it will give you an idea of how good *laksa* CAN be.

I'm a firm believer in the notion that a bowl of spicy noodles is a portal to perfect happiness. Many of my happiest moments these days seem to center on sitting on a low plastic stool, somewhere in Asia, eating chili-jacked noodles in broth. Malaysian *laksas* are as good as noodle soups can be. There is an incredibly delicious Penang version, with a tamarind and fish–based broth, chunks of mackerel and pineapple bobbing within—and while both styles have fervent adherents, the Kuching version is my favorite.

I like it spicy, so feel free to adjust with the addition of chili paste or peppers. Ideally you should, in my view, have worked up a solid sweat by the time you hit the bottom of the bowl.

The *laksa* paste mixture's flavors develop better with time, so it's worth making the paste a few days before you make and serve your *laksa*.

2 quarts Dark Universal Stock (page 260)

1 large chicken breast, bone in, skin removed and discarded

¾ cup Sarawak Laksa Paste (page 57)

16 to 20 jumbo shrimp, peeled and deveined, tails intact, shells reserved for stock

2 large eggs

1 teaspoon soy sauce

1 tablespoon vegetable oil

8 ounces rice vermicelli

¾ cup coconut milk

Approximately 2 cups mung bean sprouts

Fresh cilantro leaves or small fresh cilantro sprigs, for garnish

Fresh sliced red chili peppers, for garnish

Lime wedges, for garnish

Sambal belacan (a chili pepper–shrimp condiment, available in Asian markets, well-stocked health food stores, or online) to taste

In a large, heavy-bottom pot with a lid, bring the stock to a boil. Add the chicken, reduce to a simmer, and cook for 12 minutes. Turn off the heat, cover the pot, and let sit for another 12 to 15 minutes, until cooked through. Remove the chicken from the stock. When cool enough to handle, remove and discard the bones, and use two forks to shred the meat. Set aside until ready to serve the soup. $\longrightarrow$

Return the stock to the heat and add the *laksa* paste and shrimp shells. Bring to a simmer and cook over low heat for 30 minutes.

While the stock simmers, whisk together the eggs and soy sauce in a mixing bowl. In a frying pan, preferably cast-iron, heat the oil over medium-high heat until it shimmers. Add the egg mixture and let cook for 2 minutes, then flip with a spatula and cook for another 90 seconds. Remove the egg from the pan and let cool, then cut into strips and set aside.

Fill a medium, heavy-bottom pot with water and bring to a boil. Place the vermicelli in a large mixing bowl. Once the water boils, remove it from the heat and pour it over the noodles so that they are completely submerged. Agitate them slightly to keep them from sticking together, then let sit for about 5 minutes. Test one noodle for doneness; once tender, drain the water and set the noodles aside, perhaps tossed with a few drops of oil if they seem to be sticking together.

Strain the hot stock mixture through the sieve, then return it to a high simmer and add the shrimp. Let them just cook through— about 30 seconds—then remove and set aside. Add the coconut milk, bring just to a boil, then remove from the heat and prepare to serve the soup.

Divide the vermicelli, chicken, shrimp, and sprouts among four serving bowls and top with the hot broth. Serve with the cilantro, chili peppers, lime wedges, and *sambal belacan* alongside.

Serves 4

SARAWAK LAKSA PASTE

Making this paste is a labor of love, and there is a shopping and prep time commitment involved. You can make things slightly easier on yourself by buying toasted and ground spices and seeds, but stay away from dehydrated shallots or garlic and do not skip the fresh chili peppers. Fresh gingerroot will make a decent substitute for galangal if the latter proves impossible to find.

In a large mixing bowl, using a large mixing spoon, combine the shallots, garlic, galangal, fresh and dried chili peppers, lemongrass, nuts, seeds, and spices. Working in batches, grind the mixture to a paste in the food processor, scraping down the sides of the bowl as necessary with a rubber spatula. Set the ground batches aside together in a second large mixing bowl. When all of the ingredients have been ground together, heat the oil in a wok or wide, heavy-bottom braising pan over medium heat, then carefully add the ground mixture and cook for about an hour, stirring very frequently to keep the mixture from sticking or scorching. Scrape the surface of the pan as necessary to dislodge any stuck patches of paste so that they do not burn.

After an hour of cooking and stirring, stir in the salt, sugar, and tamarind water and continue to cook and stir for about 20 minutes. Remove from the heat and transfer to the storage container(s). Cover and refrigerate.

The mixture will keep, refrigerated and sealed, for up to a month, or in the freezer for several months.

Makes about 10 cups

10 shallots, peeled and coarsely chopped

5 large garlic cloves, peeled and coarsely chopped

Large knob of galangal (about ¾ pound), chopped

10 fresh long red chili peppers, cut into chunks (you may modulate the heat by removing some or all of the seeds and pith; don't touch your eyes)

½ cup dried chili peppers, soaked in hot water for 20 minutes and drained

5 stalks lemongrass (white parts only), coarsely chopped

3½ ounces macadamia nuts or cashews

¾ cup roasted peanuts

½ cup sesame seeds, toasted

3 tablespoons cumin seeds, toasted and ground

½ cup coriander seeds, toasted and ground

6 pieces star anise, toasted and ground

7 toasted and ground cloves

1 teaspoon ground nutmeg

10 cardamom pods

2 cups soybean oil

5 tablespoons salt

¼ cup palm sugar

8 ounces tamarind pulp, mixed with a cup of boiling water

SPECIAL EQUIPMENT

Food processor

Storage container(s) with 10-cup capacity

BUDAE JJIGAE

1 dried shiitake mushroom

4 large dried anchovies, heads and guts removed, wrapped in cheesecloth

One 3 × 5-inch sheet dried edible kelp or kombu

½ teaspoon sea salt

12 ounces SPAM, cut into ½-inch-thick slices

1½ cups Napa cabbage kimchi (tongbaechu)

8 ounces sliced Korean rice cakes

1 white onion, peeled and thinly sliced

2 scallions (white and light green parts), thinly sliced

5 garlic cloves, peeled and crushed

3 hot dogs, thinly sliced

8 ounces ground pork

3 tablespoons soy sauce

2 tablespoons gochujang (Korean fermented chili paste)

3 tablespoons medium/fine gochugaru (ground Korean red pepper)

3 tablespoons cheongju (Korean rice wine)

3 tablespoons canned baked beans

1 package ramen noodles, preferably the Korean brand Shin, seasoning packet discarded

This is known as Korean army stew, created, according to legend, from scrounged army PX canned goods during wartime. It's the ultimate dorm food. Just looking at the ingredients might make it sound like a horror, but it very quickly comes together and becomes delicious. It captures the essence of great cooking over the last few centuries: improvisational, born of war and hardship, nostalgic, sentimental, and transformative.

To make the anchovy broth, combine the mushroom, anchovies, kelp, 4 cups water, and the salt in a medium, heavy-bottom pot, and bring to a boil. Reduce to a simmer and cook for 30 minutes. Remove from the heat, strain and discard the solids, and set the broth aside.

Place the SPAM, kimchi, rice cakes, onion, scallions, garlic, hot dogs, and pork in small separate piles in a large shallow pot.

Add the soy sauce, *gochujang*, *gochugaru*, and *cheongju* to the pot, then slowly pour in the reserved anchovy kelp broth. Add the baked beans and 1½ cups water. Bring the contents to a steady simmer over high heat, stirring occasionally with a wooden spoon.

Cook for about 10 minutes, then add the ramen noodles. Ladle the broth over the noodles to help them break apart. Continue to cook for 2 or 3 minutes, until the noodles are cooked through but still chewy.

Serves 2 to 4

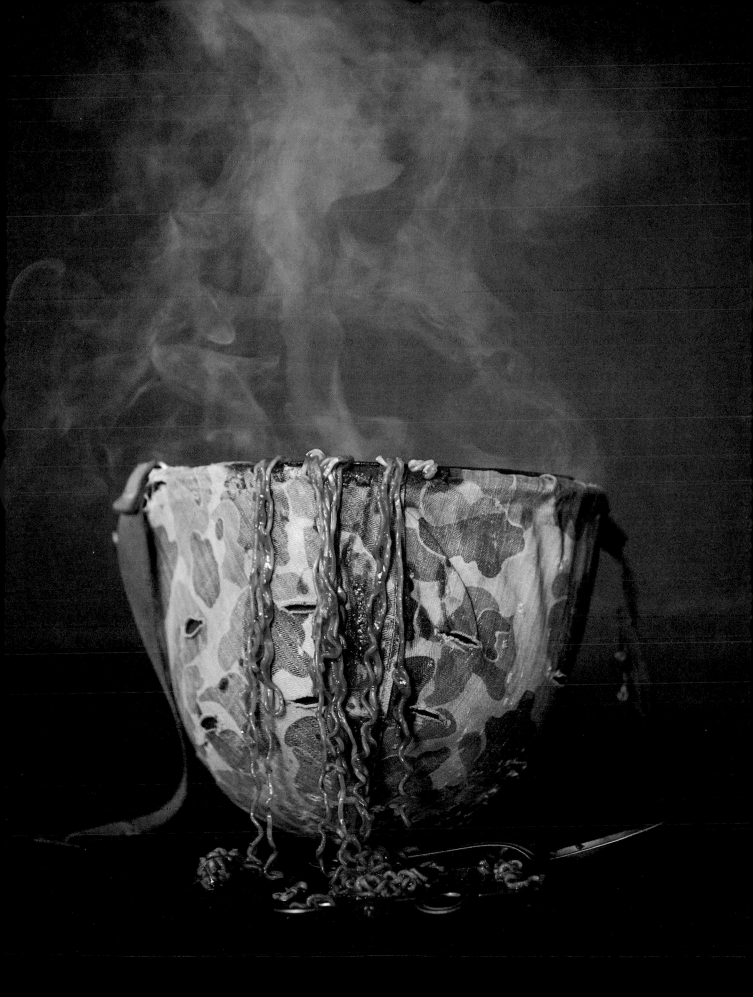

SHRIMP BISQUE

The dignity of shrimp in the United States has suffered in the last several decades thanks to widespread shrimp farming (often under dubious conditions), bottomless shrimp specials offered by schlocky chain restaurants, and *Forrest Gump*. It doesn't have to be that way, though—look how well they treat shrimp on Spanish and Portuguese tables and in Japanese sushi bars, not to mention their use as a flavor-boosting paste in much of Southeast Asia. This recipe attempts to restore shrimp's pride by way of the bisque treatment, so often reserved for big brother, lobster.

1¾ pounds large shrimp, peeled and deveined, shells and 6 shrimp reserved

4½ cups Shellfish Stock (page 264)

¼ cup extra-virgin olive oil

3 shallots, peeled and finely chopped

2 scallions, trimmed and finely sliced

3 garlic cloves, peeled and finely chopped

2 tablespoons tomato paste

¼ cup Cognac

¼ cup Sauternes or sherry

1 tablespoon best-quality fish sauce

4 tablespoons (½ stick) unsalted butter

¼ cup all-purpose flour

1½ cups heavy cream

Salt and freshly ground black pepper to taste

Juice of ½ lemon (about 1 tablespoon)

Tempura Shrimp or Shrimp Salad, for garnish (recipes follow)

SPECIAL EQUIPMENT

Food processor

In a medium, heavy-bottom saucepan, combine the shrimp shells and the stock and bring to a simmer. Cook for about 20 minutes, then strain the mixture into a clean medium saucepan and discard the shells. Keep the fortified stock warm over very low heat.

In a large, heavy-bottom stockpot, heat the oil over medium heat. Add the shallots and scallions and cook over medium-low heat, stirring occasionally, for about 5 minutes, until they are golden and translucent but not browning. Add the garlic and the tomato paste and cook for 1 minute. Add all but the reserved 6 shrimp to the pot; cook over medium-high heat for 2 minutes, until just cooked through.

Remove the pot from the heat and add the Cognac, which may or may not flame up, depending on the firepower of your stove but will burn off its alcohol and cook to dry very quickly. Return the pot to the heat, and scrape the bottom, dislodging browned bits. Deglaze with the Sauternes and fish sauce, continuing to scrape and stir to keep dislodging browned bits. Let cook for about 3 minutes, then remove from the heat, and, working in batches, transfer the mixture to the food processor, using a rubber spatula to make sure you get everything out of the pot and into the machine. Puree the mixture to a reasonably fine texture, turning each batch into a mixing bowl as you complete it.

NOTE: *If you choose to make tempura shrimp as a fancy garnish, you may wish to puree the soup to a very fine texture and pass it through a fine-mesh sieve, for greater textural contrast between the smooth soup and the crunchy shrimp.*

Make sure that you have both a whisk and a wooden spoon or spatula close at hand, as you'll be switching back and forth between the two tools as you build the roux and béchamel that form the base of the bisque.

Use the still-hot stockpot to heat the butter over medium-high heat until it foams and subsides. Sprinkle the flour over the butter and whisk to combine. Let cook for 2 minutes, switching to the wooden spoon or spatula to steadily continue to stir— the idea is to cook out the raw flour taste without letting the flour scorch or stick. Slowly pour in the reserved shellfish stock, whisking as you go until it has all been incorporated, then switch back to the wooden spoon to stir frequently over medium-high heat as the mixture comes to a boil and begins to thicken. Be sure to hit all angles of the bottom of the pot to dislodge any globs of butter and flour paste and get them incorporated with the stock. When the liquid comes to a boil and is thick enough to coat the back of the spoon, add the shrimp puree and stir well, then stir in the heavy cream. Taste and season with salt, pepper, and the lemon juice. Garnish with either the tempura shrimp or shrimp salad.

Serves 6

TEMPURA SHRIMP

2 cups peanut oil

¼ cup all-purpose flour

¼ cup cornstarch

6 shrimp, reserved from above

1 egg, beaten and held in a small bowl

½ cup panko bread crumbs, held on a plate or in a shallow bowl

Salt to taste

SPECIAL EQUIPMENT

Deep-fry thermometer

Plate lined with newspaper

Make the tempura shrimp just before serving so that they are crisp and hot.

Heat the oil to 375°F in a medium, tall-sided pot, monitoring the temperature with the deep-fry thermometer. Keep the lined plate and a slotted spoon or set of tongs nearby.

In a wide, shallow bowl, whisk together the flour and cornstarch. Roll each shrimp in this mixture, patting them gently to remove any excess. Roll each shrimp in the egg, then in the bread crumbs. Submerge the shrimp in the hot oil and cook until golden brown, 2 to 3 minutes. Remove from the oil and let rest briefly on the lined plate to absorb excess oil. Season with salt. Garnish each bowl of soup with 1 shrimp, and serve.

Makes 6 pieces

SHRIMP SALAD

6 shrimp, reserved from above

2 teaspoons best-quality extra-virgin olive oil

2 teaspoons freshly squeezed lemon juice

1 teaspoon very finely chopped (brunoise) shallots

1 teaspoon finely chopped chives

Salt and freshly ground black pepper to taste

Place the shrimp in a small pot and cover with cold water. Bring to a high simmer and cook until shrimp are just cooked through, about 3 minutes. Empty the shrimp into a colander to drain, then dice them. Place in a small mixing bowl. Toss with the oil, lemon juice, shallots, and chives, and season with salt and pepper. Arrange a small amount of the salad atop each portion of soup just before serving.

Yields about ⅔ cup

WHITE GAZPACHO

Traditional gazpacho relies on perfect (or at least very good and ripe) tomatoes, which are available in the northeast for only a four- to six-week period in late August and early September. For the rest of the year, especially the hot and humid months of June and July, there's this white gazpacho, whose core ingredients— bread, water, nuts, garlic, oil—are seasonally and geographically agnostic.

Place the 1-inch cubes of bread in a medium mixing bowl and cover with cold water. Let sit for 5 minutes, then remove the bread from the bowl, squeezing out and discarding the excess water. Transfer the bread to the food processor.

Add the ground almonds, garlic, and chilled water to the food processor and season with the 2 teaspoons salt. Puree to form a creamy pastelike mixture, pausing as necessary to scrape down the sides with a rubber spatula. With the machine running, drizzle in ⅓ cup of the oil and continue to run the machine until the mixture is emulsified.

Transfer the mixture to a clean mixing bowl and whisk in the vinegar. Taste and adjust seasoning with salt as desired. Cover and chill for at least 1 hour.

Just before serving, make the croutons. In a small frying pan, preferably cast-iron, heat the remaining ⅓ cup oil over medium heat. Test the oil by dropping one of the ¼-inch bread cubes into it. The bread should immediately sizzle. Once the oil is ready, cook the cubes in it for about 1 minute, until golden brown, working in batches if necessary to avoid overcrowding the pan and stirring once or twice with a wooden or metal spoon or spatula. Remove the toasted cubes from the oil with a slotted spoon and transfer to the lined sheet pan to drain. Season lightly with salt.

Garnish each serving of soup with the croutons and any or all of the following: toasted almonds, sliced grapes, fried capers, and an extra drizzle of oil.

Serves 6 to 8

5 or 6 (1-inch-thick) slices day-old country bread, crusts removed, cut into 1-inch cubes (about 3 cups)

1¼ cups slivered blanched almonds, finely ground

2 very fresh garlic cloves (nothing soft, spotty, or sprouting, please), peeled and finely chopped

1¾ cups chilled water (fancy bottled water is fine here, as is filtered tap water, as long as it's ice cold)

2 teaspoons kosher salt, plus more to taste

⅔ cup best-quality Spanish olive oil, plus more for garnish if desired

2 tablespoons best-quality sherry vinegar, plus more to taste

1 or 2 (1-inch-thick) slices day-old country bread, crusts removed, cut into ¼-inch cubes (about ½ cup)

¼ cup slivered blanched almonds, lightly toasted, for garnish (optional)

½ cup attractive green table grapes, thinly sliced, for garnish (optional)

2 tablespoons fried capers, for garnish (optional)

SPECIAL EQUIPMENT

Food processor or blender

Sheet pan or plate lined with newspaper

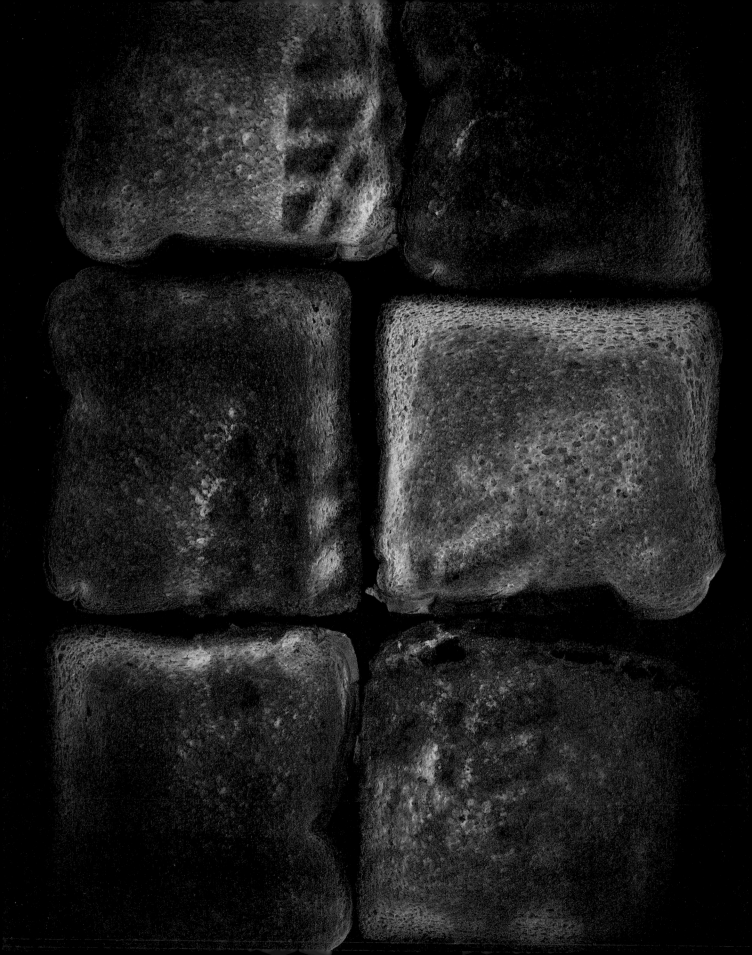

[5]
SANDWICHES

A sandwich is a beautiful thing—one of the great innovations of modern history. It freed us from the tyranny of the plate, the table, the knife and fork. Between two slices of bread exist near-limitless possibilities for deliciousness.

But no matter how tasty or outrageous, how juicy or flavorful, and no matter how engorged with meat, sandwiches remain a delivery system for their fillings. The purpose of the sandwich, like a hamburger, is to effectively deliver protein or other stuff into your mouth without a fork. Structure, texture, and proportion are as central to the success or failure of the sandwich as its taste.

That may be the very best chopped liver, but if the rye bread surrounding it falls apart, you may as well eat it out of a fucking trough. If there are so many ingredients on your deli sandwich named after a celebrity that you can't possibly fit the thing into your mouth in such a way as to include appropriate representation of each distinct layer in every bite, it's a failure. Your "Howie Mandel" may look like a tower of awesomeness, a teetering heap of pastrami, corned beef, brisket, slaw, Russian dressing, and sprouts—but if half the ingredients squirt across the table like the last shot of a Peter North film, what's the point?

It is for this reason that I declare the beloved American classic, the *club sandwich*, to be America's Enemy, a menu item that perfectly encapsulates all the principles of Bad Sandwich Theory.

Who invented the club sandwich, anyway? America's enemies, for sure. The club predates Al Qaeda—but it fits that group's MO. Mission: Destroy America. Method: Sap the will to live of ordinary Americans—by repeatedly fucking up their lunch.

Maybe it was the Nazis. Didn't they invent, like, methadone? And ephedra? The club sandwich was an even more evil idea.

What's wrong with it, you ask?

What's wrong with turkey or chicken breast, some crispy bacon slices, lettuce, and tomato on a sandwich? (And yes, adding a fried egg surely makes it only better.) How could any sandwich containing these delightful ingredients be a bad thing?

Where does the club go wrong? I'll tell you.

It's that third slice of bread. What's it doing there? It's the fifth column of sandwich elements, lurking silently and entirely uselessly, in the middle of an otherwise respectable sandwich—until it can strike.

The entire club sandwich concept is fucked from the get-go. It's a sandwich designed to look good on a plate—after you've stuck extra-long frilly toothpicks into it and cut it into quarters. It's designed for eye appeal, and edibility be damned. Because as soon as you bite into that fucker, your teeth crush into the top and bottom layers of bread, compacting together the meat layers and the lettuce and tomato layers and that stupid extra slice of bread and, like in a collapsing building, anything soft is gonna get squished. The slippery tomato, unmoored by Russian dressing or mayonnaise, is sliding right out of the party along with the bacon, leaving you with a soggy turkey sandwich, a disproportionately double-thick top layer of bread, and a plate full of broken dreams.

That third slice of bread was put there to *look* good. They don't care about you. But I do. So please: Continue to make your club sandwiches. Just leave out that third slice.

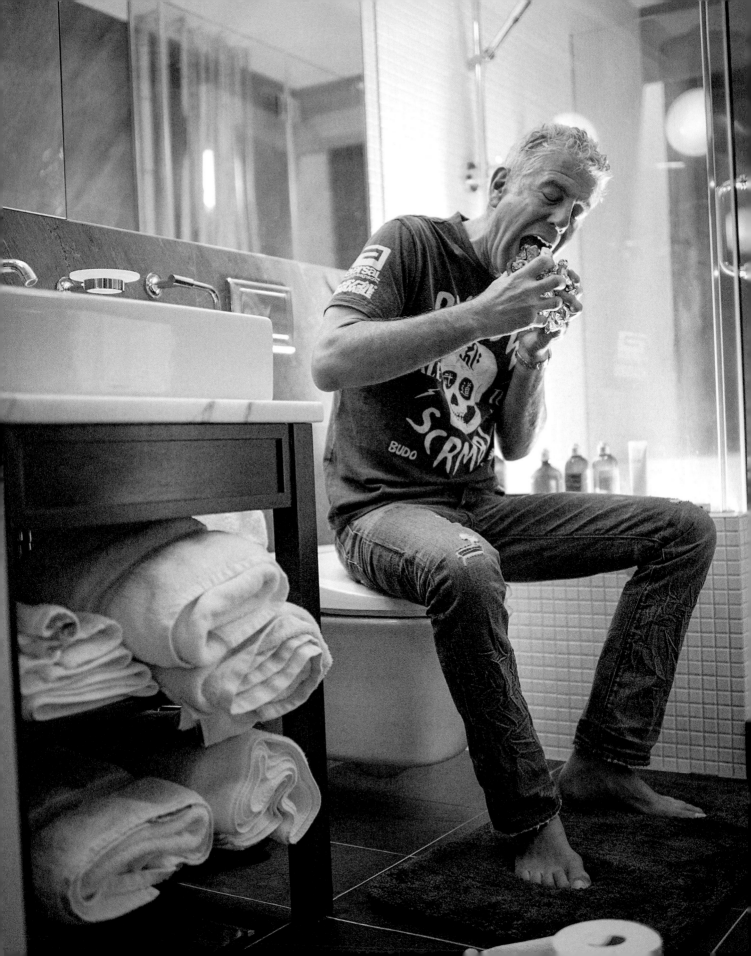

SAUSAGE AND PEPPER HERO

I have, over the years, conquered many personal demons, weaknesses, and unlovely personal habits that could be called guilty pleasures. But there's one shameful compulsion I still haven't been able to kick. Every time they have one of those lame street fairs in New York, the same tired cast of vendors gets trotted out: the guys selling stale dried spices, the tube-sock people, Mr. Funnel Cake. I hate all of it—except the sausage and pepper guys. They traffic in not particularly good hot and sweet Italian sausage, held and served at temperatures that would probably be considered suboptimal by the New York State Department of Health, squashed on a dirty griddle, and then piled into a squishy hero roll with some browned onions and peppers, the whole thing a greasy, soggy, unmanageable mess that generally falls apart in my hands before I can eat it. And within an hour of consumption, I'm shitting like a mink.

I know this from the first whiff, yet I am helpless to resist. Knowing full well the inevitable intestinal upheaval that will result, I sleepwalk, zombie-like, to my fate, willingly, happily, toward nasty deliciousness.

Prepared in the presumably more hygienic confines of your kitchen, this recipe will hopefully spare you the terrible personal cost of having to score on the street.

4 sweet Italian sausage links

4 hot Italian sausage links

2 tablespoons extra-virgin olive oil

1 large red bell pepper, cored, seeded, and thinly sliced

1 large green bell pepper, cored, seeded, and thinly sliced

1 large yellow onion, peeled and thinly sliced

Salt and freshly ground black pepper to taste

4 Italian hero rolls, sliced

Heat a large griddle pan or cast-iron skillet over high heat, then add the sausages, working in batches if necessary. Cook until browned on all sides and slightly bursting from their casings, then remove with tongs to a large plate or sheet pan.

Add the oil to the griddle or skillet, let it get hot, then add the bell peppers and onion. Season with salt and pepper and $\longrightarrow$

cook until seared, soft and nicely browned at the edges, about 10 minutes, turning frequently with a spatula and pressing down as necessary.

While the vegetables are cooking, cut the sausages into 1-inch pieces. Once the vegetables are done, set them aside with the sausages and briefly warm the open rolls on the hot greasy griddle or skillet. Load the peppers, onions, and sausage chunks into the rolls, making sure to get an even distribution of sweet and hot pieces, and serve immediately.

_____

Serves 4

MEATBALL PARM HERO

Here's another Italo-American classic for which I am a complete sucker. Beef gives structure to these meatballs, while veal keeps them tender and pork makes them fatty and juicy. Be sure to cut your onions very fine, and use a light hand when mixing the ingredients.

In a large, heavy-bottom sauté pan, heat 3 tablespoons oil over medium heat. Add the onion, garlic, oregano, and parsley, and stir well to coat with the oil. Season with salt and pepper and let cook over medium-low to medium heat for about 5 minutes, stirring occasionally, until the vegetables are soft and translucent but not browned. Remove from the heat and transfer the onion mixture to a large mixing bowl. Let cool to room temperature. Clean the pan, which you will use to brown the meatballs.

Add the beef, veal, and pork to a mixing bowl, along with the bread crumbs and eggs. Season with salt and pepper. Mix well by hand. Form the mixture into twenty-five to thirty 2-inch balls, placing each one on a sheet pan as you form it. Cover the meatballs with plastic wrap and refrigerate them for 15 to 60 minutes.

Preheat the oven to 400°F. Remove the meatballs from the fridge.

Heat ¼ cup oil in the sauté pan over medium-high heat. Working in batches, sear the meatballs on all sides in the oil, turning them carefully with the spatula and tongs and adding more oil as necessary to keep them from sticking to the pan. Remove the cooked meatballs to the roasting pan.

Once all the meatballs are in the roasting pan, add the wine and 1 cup of the pomodoro sauce to the pan so that the liquid reaches about halfway up the sides of each meatball. Transfer the pan to the oven and cook for 25 to 30 minutes, until cooked through but still juicy (the interior of a meatball should reach 150°F on an instant-read thermometer). ⟶

3 tablespoons plus ½ cup extra-virgin olive oil

1 medium yellow or white onion, peeled and finely diced (about 2 cups)

4 to 6 garlic cloves, peeled and finely chopped

6 sprigs fresh oregano, leaves only, finely chopped

10 to 12 sprigs fresh Italian parsley, leaves only, finely chopped

Salt and freshly ground black pepper to taste

1 pound ground beef chuck

1 pound ground veal

1 pound ground pork

1 cup panko bread crumbs

2 large eggs, lightly beaten

1½ cups dry white wine

1 quart Pomodoro (page 269)

4 Italian semolina hero rolls with sesame seeds, cut in half lengthwise and crosswise

8 ounces fresh mozzarella cheese, sliced

4 ounces Parmigiano-Reggiano cheese, grated

SPECIAL EQUIPMENT

Short-sided roasting pan large enough to hold 25 to 30 meatballs (11 × 14 inch or similar)

Instant-read thermometer

While the meatballs are cooking, in a small, heavy-bottom saucepot, gently warm the remaining pomodoro sauce, stirring occasionally to keep it from scorching.

Remove the meatballs from the oven, and set the oven to broil.

On a clean sheet tray, arrange 3 meatballs in the center of each of 8 hero roll bottoms. Add a few tablespoons of pomodoro sauce to each set of meatballs, and drape each with a slice of mozzarella and a good sprinkling of the Parmigiano-Reggiano. Place the sandwiches under the broiler for about 2 minutes, until the mozzarella is slightly browned and bubbling. Top each with the remaining bread and serve immediately.

Serves 8

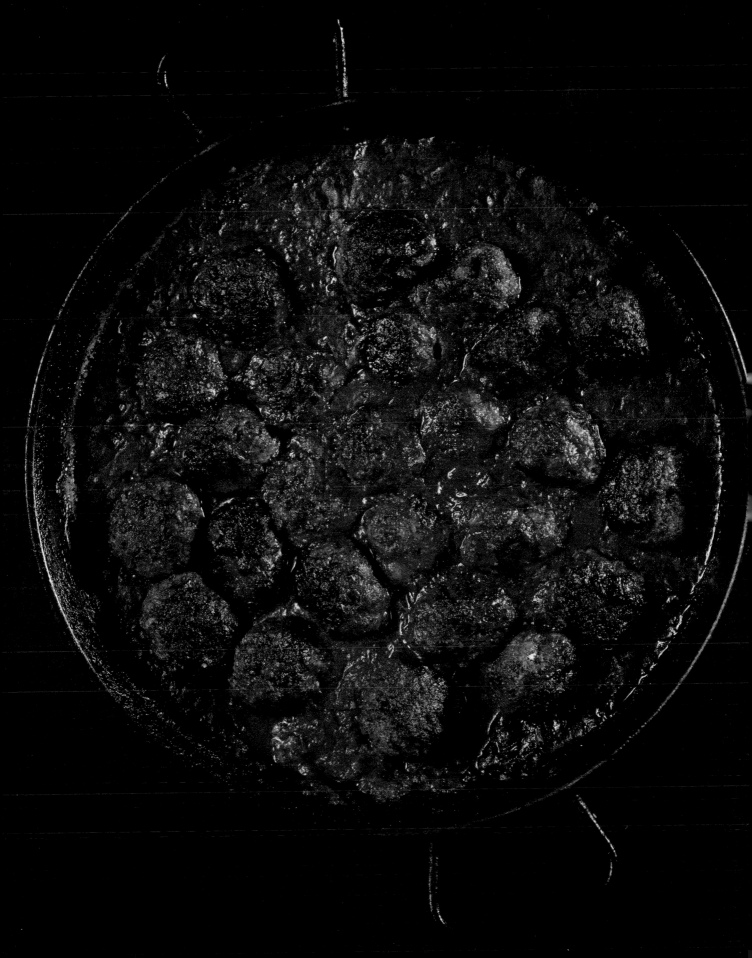

BODEGA SANDWICH

Forget about pastrami: The iconic New York City sandwich is bacon, egg, and cheese on a hard roll—cooked on a griddle and served by someone who addresses you as *papi* or *mami*.

The language of New York City in the mornings is Spanish—or more accurately, Spanglish—and even the non-Spanish speakers lined up at the bodega counter usually make an attempt. It's the last bastion of non-Starbucks breakfast—and maybe the last place in New York where construction workers, doormen, hedge funders, black, white, Asian, and Latin gather in one room, united by a single purpose: the bodega sandwich.

6 slices bacon

2 kaiser rolls, sliced as for a sandwich

4 large eggs

Salt and freshly ground black pepper to taste

4 slices American or Swiss cheese

SPECIAL EQUIPMENT

Plate lined with newspaper

Heat a large, heavy-bottom skillet or cast-iron griddle pan over high heat until hot, then add the bacon and cook until golden brown and crisp, adjusting the temperature if necessary so that it doesn't get burned. If it burns, start over. (You can also cook your bacon in the oven; see page 12.) Using a spatula or tongs, remove the bacon to the lined plate. Open the kaiser rolls and place them facedown on the griddle for 2 minutes to warm through and absorb some of that bacon grease. Remove them and park 3 slices of bacon inside each roll.

Crack the eggs into a medium mixing bowl, season with salt and pepper, and beat well. You're not making scrambled eggs here, you're making a kind of value-neutral omelet, so don't worry about retaining big curds in the pan. Cook the eggs in the hot bacon grease until cooked through. Top with the cheese, distributed in an even layer, and let cook until slightly melty. Remove the eggs and divide them evenly among the rolls, folding and chopping as necessary. Close the sandwiches, wrap in foil for portability (if necessary), and serve with shitty coffee.

Serves 2

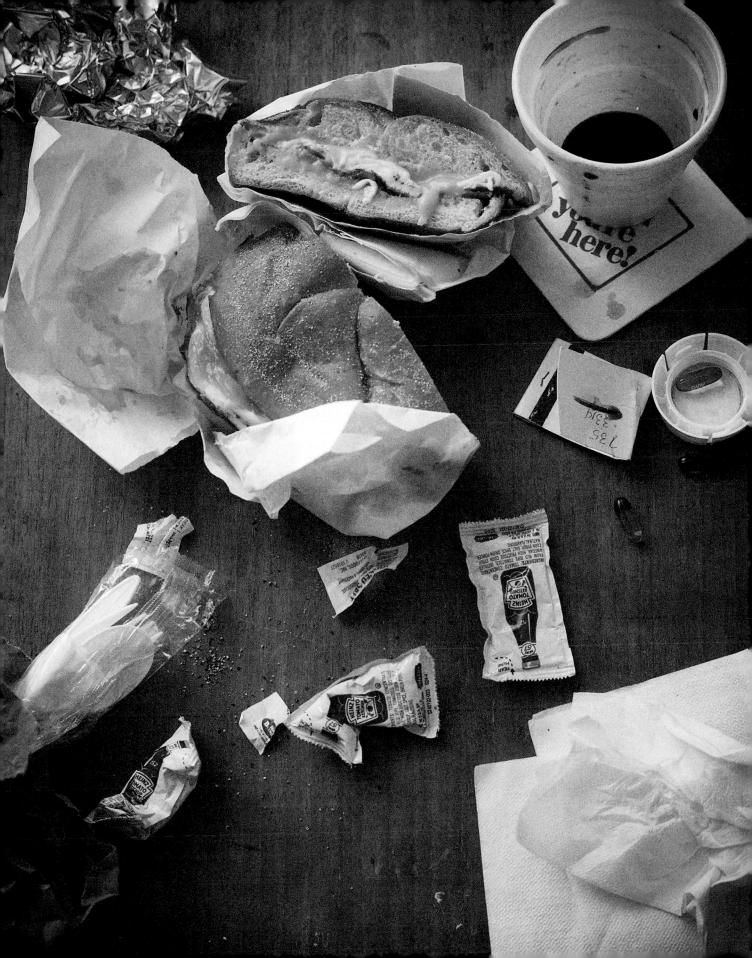

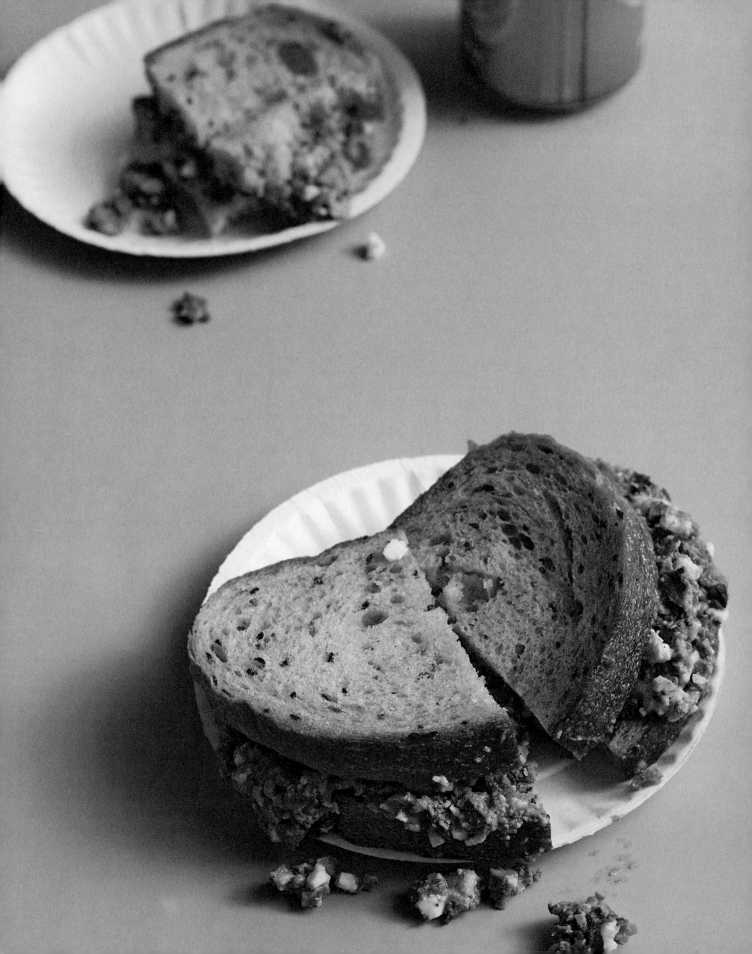

CHOPPED LIVER ON RYE

The New York Barney Greengrass serves, as far as I'm concerned, the best chopped liver around, but if you can't get to New York for it, make it as below. There are those who would do chopped liver a great disservice by combining it with a heap of turkey, some lettuce, and tomato, but for me, chopped liver calls for no adornment. Just two slices of seeded rye bread, not even toasted.

Be warned: You are probably not going to get this right the first time. The alchemy of "schmaltz" and the fine textural line between grainy and mush take some experimentation—but it's worth the effort.

Place the eggs in a small, heavy-bottom saucepan and cover with cold water. Bring the water to a rapid boil. Once the water boils, remove it from the heat, cover, and let sit for 9 minutes (set a timer). Remove the eggs from the pot and slide them into the ice-water bath to cool.

In a large, heavy-bottom sauté pan, heat 1 to 2 tablespoons of the schmaltz over medium-high heat. Add the onions and stir well to coat with the schmaltz. Sprinkle with salt so that the onions release their juices. Cook over medium heat, stirring occasionally, until the onions are dark brown and sweet, about 15 minutes. You can go faster than you would for caramelizing onions, but take care not to let them get blackened. Once the onions are cooked, transfer them to a medium mixing bowl.

Wipe out the onion pan and heat another tablespoon or two of the schmaltz over medium-high heat. Add the livers, working in batches if necessary, because you want a nice dark brown sear, which you won't get if there are too many of them in the pan—they'll bubble pathetically in their own juices. Cook the livers until they are browned on all sides, at which point they should be at the degree of doneness known as "medium": not hammered to death but nothing pink or squishy. Remove from the pan and repeat with the remaining livers and a tablespoon $\longrightarrow$

4 large eggs

1 cup schmaltz (rendered chicken fat)

2 large or 3 medium white or yellow onions, peeled and coarsely chopped

Salt to taste

2 pounds chicken livers, trimmed of connective tissue and fat

Freshly ground black pepper to taste

8 to 12 slices seeded rye bread

SPECIAL EQUIPMENT

Ice-water bath (medium bowl filled with ice and cold water)

Food processor (optional)

or so of additional schmaltz if necessary. Transfer the livers to the bowl with the onions.

Remove the hard-boiled eggs from the ice-water bath and peel and coarsely chop them. Transfer to the bowl with the liver and onions and fold together gently. If using the food processor, transfer the mixture to the bowl, drizzle in about ¼ cup of the schmaltz, and pulse judiciously. You want to create a reasonably homogenous but still chunky mixture. Add more schmaltz as needed to thin the mixture out. You can also chop the mixture with a knife, or a mezzaluna, if you happen to have one. Taste the mixture and season with salt and pepper.

For best results, refrigerate the mixture for a few hours, during which time the intense flavor of the onions will permeate the whole thing. Before serving, let the chopped liver sit out of the fridge for about 15 minutes, to soften and relax slightly. Construct sandwiches of your desired thickness on the rye bread and serve, ideally, with a Dr. Brown's Cel-Ray soda.

Serves 4 to 6

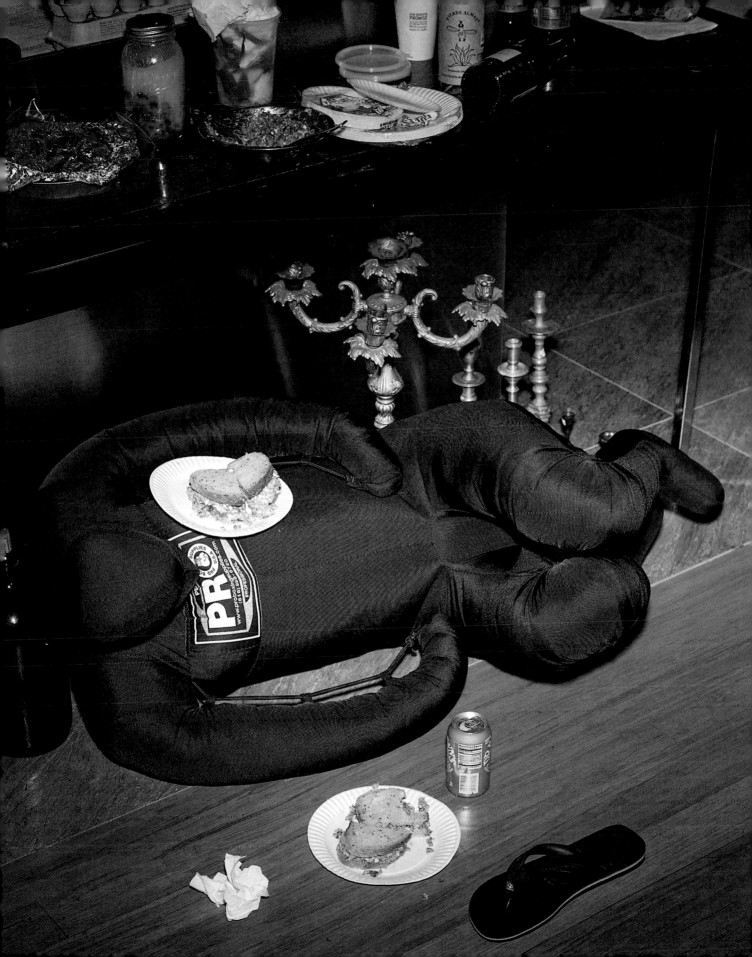

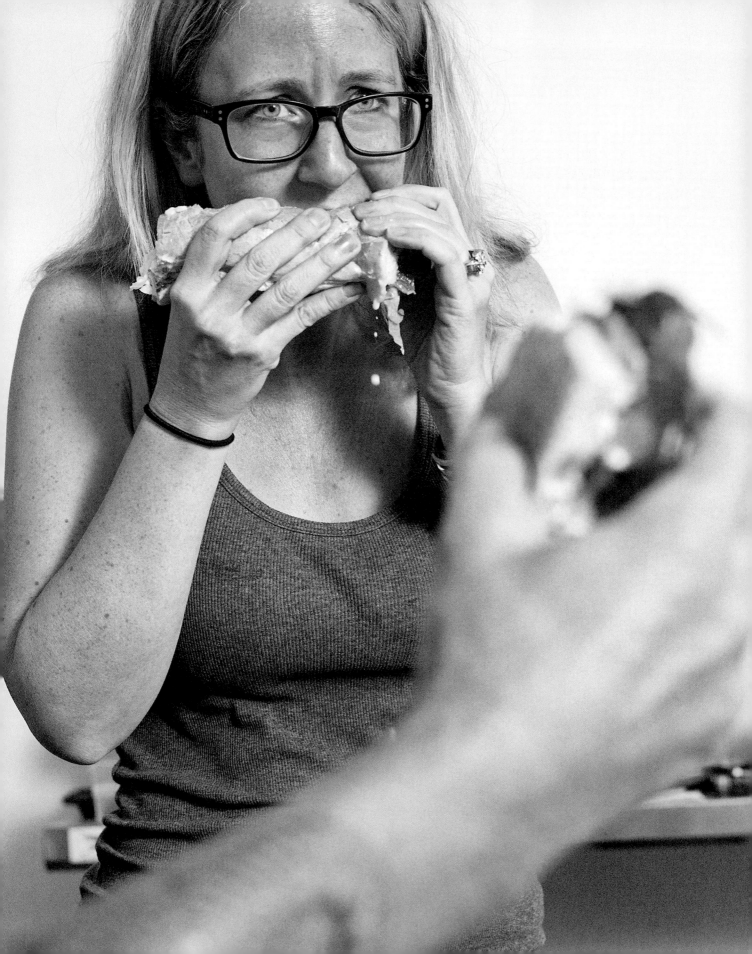

Roast Beef Po' Boy

You're not going to be able to completely re-create the po' boy experience outside of New Orleans, but this recipe will get you pretty damn close. Of utmost importance is the bread. What you want, if you're not in or near a New Orleans bakery that specializes in po' boy bread, is the fluffy, insubstantial, nutrient-free, bleached-white "French bread" that's like the uncultured American cousin of French baguettes, baked in an industrial kitchen and delivered in long white paper bags to any neighborhood grocery store.

Preheat the oven to 325°F.

In a small mixing bowl, whisk together ¼ cup of the flour and enough salt and pepper to generously season the whole roast. Place the roast on a sheet pan and dust the outside of the roast with this mixture.

In a Dutch oven, heat 2 tablespoons of the oil over medium-high heat and sear the roast on all sides in the oil until golden brown. Remove the roast to a holding plate. Add the onions, celery, bell pepper, and garlic to the Dutch oven, seasoning them with salt and pepper and scraping the bottom of the pan with a wooden spoon to dislodge browned bits of beef fond and flour. Cook until the vegetables are just beginning to become tender, 3 to 5 minutes, then remove them from the pan and set aside with the roast.

Add the remaining 2 tablespoons oil to the pan, and once it's good and hot, add the remaining 2 tablespoons of flour, stirring constantly and scraping the whole surface of the pan to keep the flour from scorching or sticking. Cook for about 2 minutes, then return the roast and the vegetables to the Dutch oven and add the bay leaves and enough stock to submerge the meat. Cover and cook in the oven for 2 hours. Check the meat, add more liquid if necessary to keep it mostly submerged, and cook for another hour or two, until the meat is easily shredded with a fork. Remove from the oven, let cool for about 30 minutes, transfer the meat to an airtight container with a lid, and refrigerate for at least 8 hours or overnight. ⟶

¼ cup plus 2 tablespoons all-purpose flour

Salt and freshly ground black pepper to taste

1 beef rump roast (about 5 pounds)

4 tablespoons canola oil

3 to 5 yellow onions, peeled and coarsely chopped

1 rib celery, coarsely chopped

½ medium green bell pepper, cored, seeded, and coarsely chopped

6 garlic cloves, peeled and coarsely chopped

2 bay leaves

1 quart Dark Universal Stock (page 260)

2 loaves New Orleans French bread from Gendusa's, Leidenheimer, or Dong Fong bakery, or acceptable substitute (see recipe headnote), cut into 6-inch lengths

Scant cup of Mayonnaise (page 272) or store-bought mayonnaise, preferably Blue Plate brand

Head of iceberg lettuce, washed, cored, and shredded

2 or 3 ripe plum tomatoes, thinly sliced

Thinly sliced dill pickles, drained (optional)

Meanwhile, ladle the cooking liquid through a colander and into a mixing bowl, pressing down on the vegetables to extract as much liquid as possible, and even mashing them through the sieve if you can. Cover and refrigerate this gravy overnight.

The next day, slice the meat as thinly as you possibly can. Remove and discard the fat cap from the gravy; heat the gravy gently in a medium, heavy-bottom saucepan. Taste it and season with salt and pepper if necessary. Transfer as much meat as you'll need for sandwiches into the warm gravy, and continue to cook gently to warm the meat.

Lightly toast the sliced bread. Spread the inside of each piece of bread with mayonnaise, which you should season lightly with salt and pepper. Layer each sandwich with meat, gravy, lettuce, tomatoes, and, if using, pickles. Serve with cold Barq's root beer or Dixie beer.

Serves 4, with plenty of leftover meat

OYSTER PO' BOY

In a medium mixing bowl, combine the buttermilk and hot sauce and whisk to blend. Add the oysters, toss gently to make sure all the oysters are immersed in the liquid, and refrigerate for 30 minutes.

Heat the oil to 350°F in a pot, monitoring the temperature with the deep-fry thermometer.

In a separate medium mixing bowl, whisk together the flour and cornmeal and season it with pepper. Set a cooling rack over the sheet pan. Make sure it is nearby before you begin to cook the oysters.

Take a few oysters at a time from the buttermilk mixture and dredge them in the flour mixture, then gently add them to the hot oil. Cook until golden brown and crisp on all sides, about 3 minutes apiece. Remove the oysters with a slotted spoon or tongs and transfer to the cooling rack. Season with salt and repeat the process with the remaining oysters.

Lightly toast the sliced bread. Spread the inside of each piece of bread with mayonnaise, which you should season lightly with salt and pepper. Layer each sandwich with oysters, lettuce, tomatoes, and, if using, pickles. Serve with cold Barq's root beer or Dixie beer.

Serves 4

2 cups buttermilk

½ cup Louisiana hot sauce

4 dozen oysters, shucked

2 cups peanut oil, for frying

1 cup all-purpose flour

1 cup fine yellow cornmeal

Freshly ground black pepper to taste

Salt

2 loaves New Orleans French bread from Gendusa's, Leidenheimer, or Dong Fong bakery, or acceptable substitute (see recipe headnote on page 84), cut into 6-inch lengths

Scant cup of Mayonnaise (page 272) or store-bought mayonnaise, preferably Blue Plate brand

Head of iceberg lettuce, washed, cored, and shredded

2 or 3 ripe plum tomatoes, cored and thinly sliced

Thinly sliced dill pickles, drained (optional)

SPECIAL EQUIPMENT

Deep-fry or candy thermometer

Sheet pan lined with newspaper

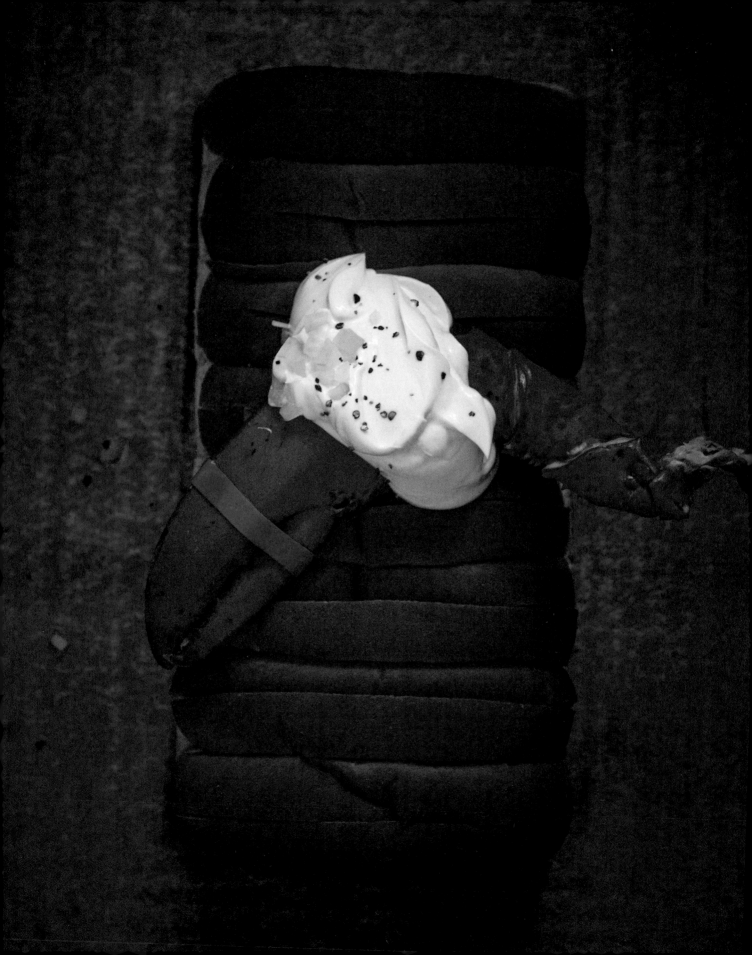

NEW ENGLAND-STYLE LOBSTER ROLL

When it comes to lobster rolls, you've got your drawn-butter people and your mayonnaise people. Here, it's mayonnaise for the lobster salad, and butter before griddling the roll, which must be of the long, split-top variety. As for the meat, a judicious business owner might use only knuckles for a lobster roll, saving the choicer parts for more expensive offerings—and there's a qualitative dimension to that choice as well. A lobster roll made only from knuckles might actually be *better*. But unless you're having a big lobster dinner one night, and generating enough knuckles to make lobster rolls the next day, feel free, by all means, to use claws and tails.

1 tablespoon salt, plus more to taste

6 lobsters (1½ to 2 pounds each)

Roughly 1 cup Mayonnaise (page 272) or store-bought mayonnaise

1 rib celery, finely diced

2 sprigs fresh tarragon, leaves only, coarsely chopped

1 to 2 teaspoons freshly squeezed lemon juice, or to taste

Freshly ground black pepper to taste

4 tablespoons (½ stick) unsalted butter, softened

6 split-top white hot dog rolls

Celery seeds, for garnish

Fill a large 4- to 5-gallon pot with 2 to 3 inches of water and add the tablespoon of salt. Position a steaming rack in the pot and bring to a boil. Working in batches of 2 or 3 lobsters at a time, steam them in the pot, covered, for 12 to 15 minutes, reaching in carefully about halfway through with the tongs to shift the lobsters around to help them cook evenly. Remove the cooked lobsters from the pot and continue with the remaining lobsters.

When the lobsters are cool enough to handle, remove the meat from the shell: Wrap the claws in a dish towel and whack them with the blunt end of your knife; crack open the tail, also wrapped in a dish towel, with your hands by folding it in half, then use your knife or kitchen shears, if preferred, to cut through the length of the underside and extract the meat; tap the knuckles with your knife or, gently, a meat mallet, if preferred, and extract as much of the meat as you can. Cut what meat needs to be cut into bite-size chunks and transfer it to a large mixing bowl.

Fold in the mayonnaise, eyeballing so that there's enough to coat the lobster but not enough to make it the main event, then add the celery, tarragon, and lemon juice and season with salt and pepper. Chill the mixture until ready to assemble the sandwiches.

Heat a griddle, griddle pan, or cast-iron skillet to medium-high while you spread the inside of each hot dog roll with $\longrightarrow$

½ tablespoon of the butter; melt the remaining 1 tablespoon butter on the griddle or in the pan and place the rolls on the hot surface, buttered side down, to toast to golden brown over medium heat, working in batches if necessary.

Remove the toasted buns from the pan, fill each generously with the lobster mixture, garnish with the celery seeds, and serve with a cold Narragansett beer.

Serves 6

GRILLED CHEESE SANDWICHES WITH CARAMELIZED ONIONS

The brilliant Gabrielle Hamilton uses mayonnaise on the outside of her grilled cheese sandwiches, as do many diner cooks, and you should, too. It doesn't get brown as quickly as butter, so the sandwich needs far less babysitting in the pan, from which it emerges with an impressively even golden crust. Go ahead and use the stuff from the jar, unless you happen to have the homemade variety already on hand.

6 tablespoons (¾ stick) unsalted butter

4 large white or yellow onions, peeled and finely sliced

Salt to taste

8 slices Japanese milk bread (a soft, sweet yeast-raised bread made with whole milk, sugar, and butter, often available at Asian markets; may substitute standard white sandwich bread)

6 to 8 tablespoons Mayonnaise (page 272) or store-bought mayonnaise

6 to 8 ounces best-quality sharp cheddar cheese, grated

In a large, heavy-bottom sauté pan, heat 2 tablespoons of the butter over medium-low heat and add the onions. Season the onions lightly with salt and stir them around with a wooden spoon or spatula to evenly distribute the butter and break up the stacks of slices. Cook over medium-low heat, stirring occasionally, until the onions are nicely caramelized, 25 to 30 minutes. You can't rush this process with high heat. Once the onions are caramelized, remove from the heat and let cool slightly, then give them a good chop, so that they will be easy to eat in a sandwich.

With a butter knife, spread one side of each slice of bread with an even layer of mayonnaise. In a medium cast-iron skillet or nonstick sauté pan, heat ½ tablespoon of butter over medium-high heat until it foams and subsides, then place one slice of bread, mayonnaise side down, in the hot pan. Top it with an even layer of grated cheese and scatter some of the onions over the surface of the cheese. Top this with another slice of bread, mayonnaise side up. After 2 to 4 minutes, flip the sandwich with a spatula and add ½ tablespoon butter to the pan. Let cook for another 3 minutes or so, then remove the sandwich and repeat this process with the remaining butter, bread, mayo, cheese, and onions. Slice on the diagonal and serve at once.

Serves 4

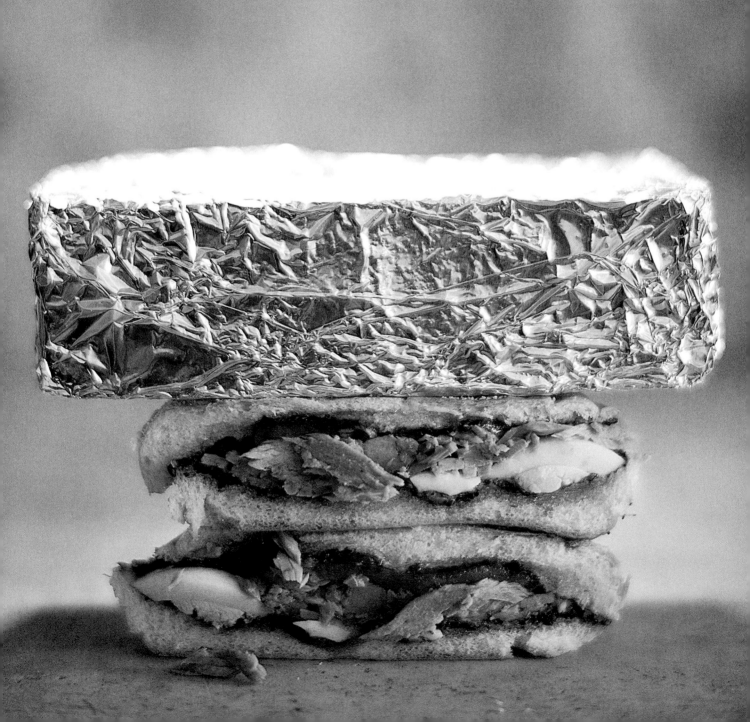

Pan Bagnat

This delicious Provençal sandwich was once the source of many headaches in the Les Halles kitchen. These days, it's a great thing to bring to the beach or on a picnic. Here's one instance in which I'll employ a brioche roll, as it nicely contains the pressed ingredients; in a pinch, a ciabatta or focaccia roll would make an acceptable substitute.

In a medium mixing bowl, combine the parsley, anchovies, capers, and tuna and mix in enough of the reserved tuna oil so that the mixture is fairly wet with oil. Taste and season with lemon juice, salt, and pepper as needed.

Use a butter knife or small spatula to spread the inside of both parts of each roll with tapenade. Fill the sandwich with a layer of tuna and top with sliced eggs and tomatoes. Place the sandwiches close together on the lined sheet pan and place the other sheet pan atop the sandwiches. Press down hard enough to flatten the sandwiches, but not so hard that everything oozes out. Top this rig with the bricks to keep the pressing going. Press for at least 30 minutes before eating.

Serves 4 to 8

¼ cup coarsely chopped fresh Italian parsley

12 salt-packed anchovies, rinsed, drained, and finely chopped

2 tablespoons capers, drained, rinsed, and finely chopped

16 ounces best-quality tuna, canned in olive oil, drained and oil reserved separately

Freshly squeezed lemon juice to taste

Salt and freshly ground black pepper to taste

4 round brioche sandwich rolls (about 4 ounces each), sliced in half

¾ cup black olive tapenade

6 hard-boiled eggs (see page 77–78), peeled and thinly sliced

2 ripe plum tomatoes, cored and very thinly sliced

SPECIAL EQUIPMENT

2 scrupulously clean sheet pans, 1 lined with foil, plastic, or parchment paper

Bricks, heavy skillet, or other weighted objects

MACAU-STYLE PORK CHOP SANDWICH

This sandwich, loosely inspired by a pork chop bun served to me for television in Macau, is possibly the most delicious thing in the book. We had a hard time shooting it, because everyone in the room kept eating the models.

4 boneless pork rib chops or cutlets (about 6 ounces each)

¼ cup soy sauce

¼ cup Chinese rice wine

¼ cup black vinegar

1 tablespoon sesame oil

4 garlic cloves, peeled and coarsely chopped

1 tablespoon five-spice powder

1 tablespoon dark brown sugar, packed

1 large egg

½ cup all-purpose flour

1½ cups panko bread crumbs

Salt and freshly ground black pepper to taste

2 cups peanut oil, for frying, plus more as needed

8 slices white sandwich bread

Chili paste, for garnish

SPECIAL EQUIPMENT

Meat mallet or heavy-duty rolling pin

Sheet pan or platter lined with newspaper

Pound the pork to ¼-inch thickness, using the meat mallet. If using a rolling pin, be sure to wrap the meat in plastic before whacking it (and consider getting yourself a meat mallet).

In a small mixing bowl, whisk together the soy sauce, rice wine, vinegar, sesame oil, garlic, five-spice powder, and sugar. Place the pork in a zip-seal plastic bag or nonreactive container and pour the marinade mixture over, turning the chops to ensure that they're evenly coated with liquid. Seal the bag and refrigerate for at least 1 hour and up to 12 hours.

Remove the chops from the marinade and brush off the garlic. Beat the egg in a shallow bowl and place the flour and bread crumbs in separate shallow bowls. Season the flour with salt and pepper. You may need to add a tablespoon of water to the beaten egg, to loosen its texture so that it adheres evenly to the meat.

To a large, heavy-bottom frying pan, add the peanut oil and heat over medium-high.

While the oil heats, dredge the chops in the flour, batting off any extra, then in the egg, then in the bread crumbs.

Test the oil with a pinch of bread crumbs. If they immediately sizzle, carefully slide the chops into the hot oil, working in batches if necessary to avoid overcrowding the pan and bringing down the temperature of the oil. Cook for about 5 minutes per side, or until golden brown. Remove the cooked chops from the oil and let drain on the lined sheet pan. Season lightly with salt.

Toast the bread until golden brown.

Assemble the sandwiches and serve with the chili paste alongside.

Serves 4

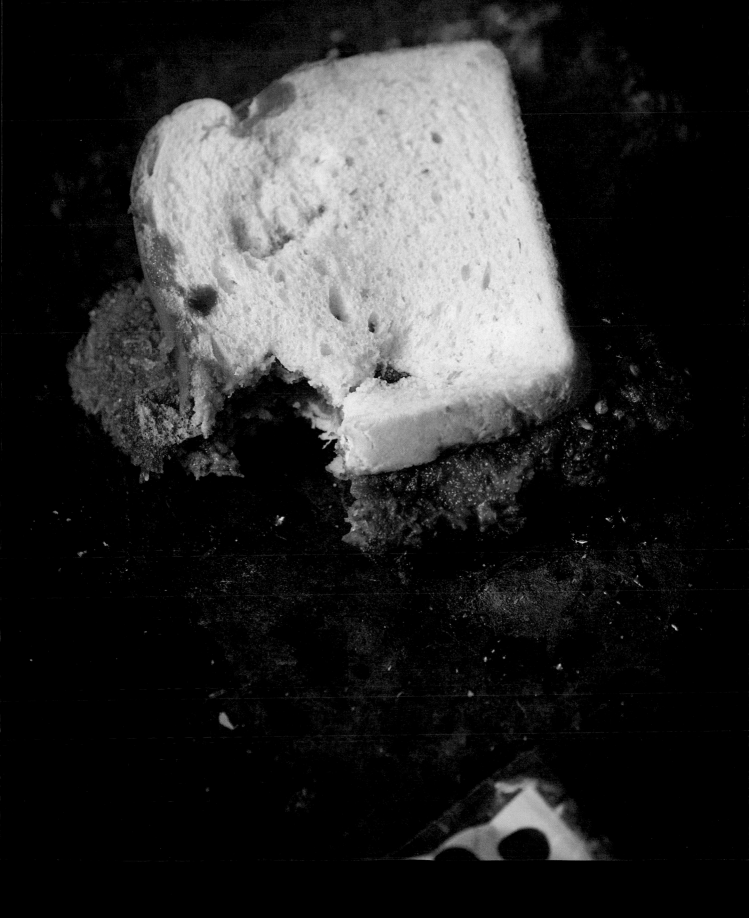

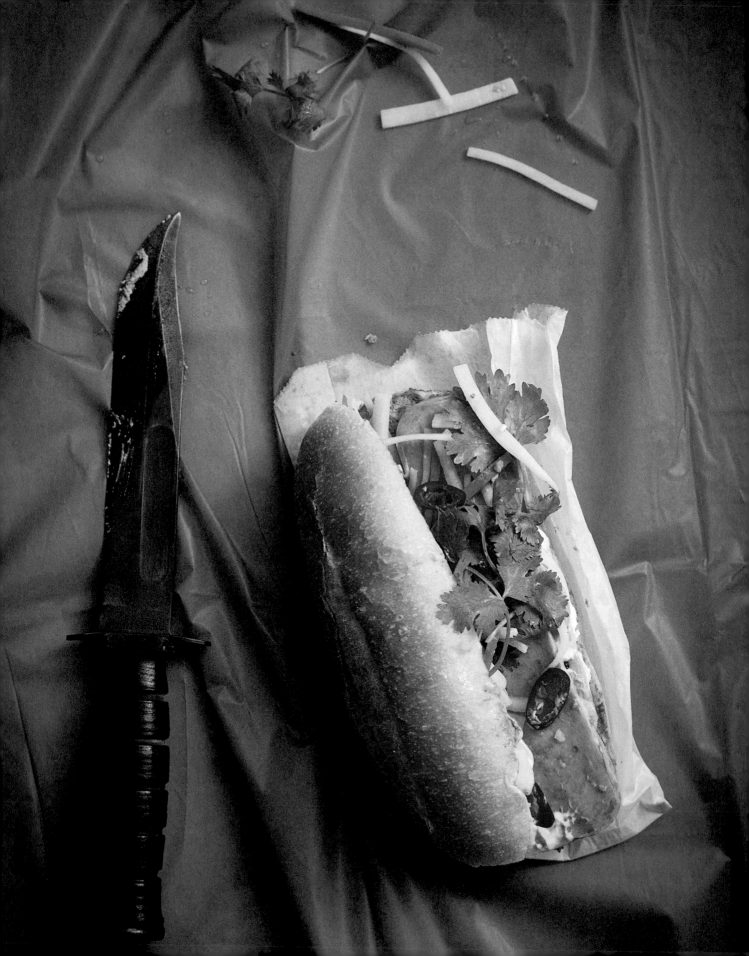

BANH MI

As with the po' boy, the most important aspect in *banh mi* construction is the bread. It looks like a French baguette, but the wheat flour is cut with rice flour to create a lighter, crisper, somehow sog-proof vehicle for the porky, livery goodness within. If you're lucky enough to live in a part of the United States with a Vietnamese bakery, like Dong Phuong in New Orleans, get your bread there. Otherwise, as for po' boys, try the lightweight "Italian" or "French" bread that's delivered daily to most large grocery stores. The shape isn't exactly right, but the consistency is closer in spirit than actual French baguette.

You can, of course, buy pâté for this sandwich, but it's easy and fast enough to cook some fresh chicken livers and make a softer-edged variation on chicken liver vinaigrette, as per below.

Season the livers well with salt and pepper. Heat 2 tablespoons of the butter in a large, heavy-bottom sauté pan until it foams and subsides. Add the livers and cook for about 3 minutes per side, until nicely seared. Remove the livers from the pan and transfer them to the blender. Deglaze the pan with the wine and vinegar, stirring well with a wooden spoon to dislodge the browned bits. Once the sharp smell of alcohol and vinegar subsides, remove the pan from the heat and transfer its contents to the blender and puree with the livers, adding a bit of oil as needed to keep the mixture loose. Scrape out into a mixing bowl to cool. Taste and adjust seasoning if necessary. This will yield about 2 cups loose pâté.

In a clean mixing bowl, combine the remaining butter, which should be at room temperature, and the mayonnaise and mix well to incorporate. With a butter knife, spread the inside of each baguette with some of the mayonnaise mixture, and then with some of the liver mixture. Add a layer of sliced SPAM to each sandwich, then top with do chua, pepper slices, and cilantro. Season with a sprinkle of soy sauce and serve at once.

½ pound chicken livers, trimmed of connective tissue and fat

Salt and freshly ground black pepper to taste

5 tablespoons unsalted butter

¼ cup dry white wine

2 tablespoons red wine vinegar

1 to 2 tablespoons canola oil, as needed

½ cup Mayonnaise (page 272) or store-bought mayonnaise

4 (7-inch) Vietnamese baguettes, sliced lengthwise

1 (7-ounce) can classic SPAM, thinly sliced

2 cups do chua (see page 32), drained well and patted dry

2 Thai bird chili or jalapeño peppers, very thinly sliced

8 sprigs fresh cilantro, leaves only, coarsely chopped

Soy sauce to taste

SPECIAL EQUIPMENT

Blender or food processor

Serves 4

MORTADELLA AND CHEESE SANDWICH

1 pound thinly sliced mortadella

Scant tablespoon canola oil

2 lightweight sourdough sandwich rolls or kaiser rolls, sliced as for a sandwich

4 tablespoons Mayonnaise (page 272) or store-bought mayonnaise

2 tablespoons Dijon mustard

4 slices provolone cheese

Salt and freshly ground black pepper to taste

I was introduced to this monster of deliciousness at Bar do Mané, in São Paulo, the Mercado Municipal of all of Brazil. It is, I gather, a rite of passage for visitors to the city—a beloved heap of oozing awesomeness, a reflection (or mutation?) of Brazil's proud and powerful Italian dimension. They sure as hell don't have this in Italy. But maybe they should.

Heat a large griddle pan or cast-iron skillet over high heat. Divide the slices of mortadella into four mounds, restacking and folding some of the slices to create some air pockets among the meat. Heat the oil on the griddle until nearly smoking, then add the mounds of meat, working in batches if necessary, pressing down with a spatula to sear the outside slices and keep the inside juicy, and carefully turning so that both sides get seared.

While the meat cooks, warm the rolls briefly on the griddle, then use a butter knife to spread the inside of each roll with the mayonnaise and mustard.

Top the hot meat with the cheese while it's still cooking, and let warm for 30 to 60 seconds. Place two mounds of meat between each of the rolls, season with salt and pepper and serve immediately with cold beer.

Serves 2 to 4

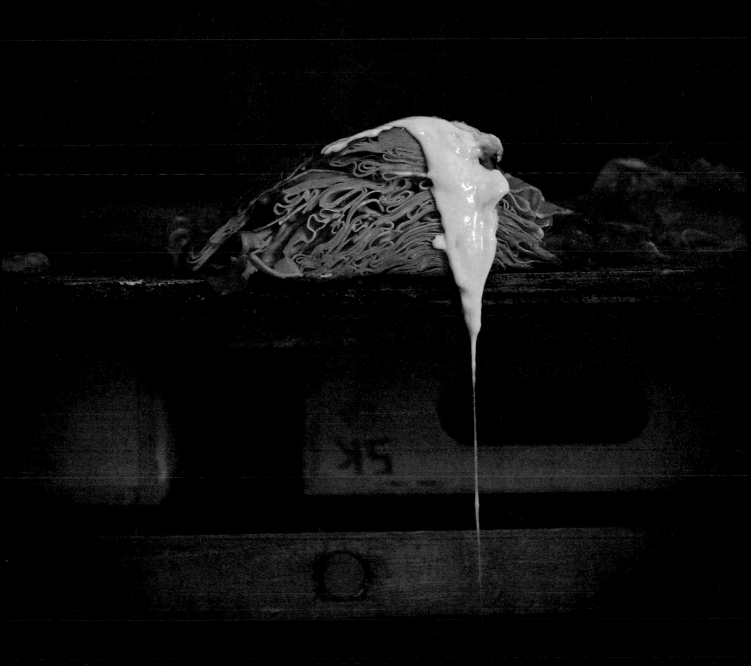

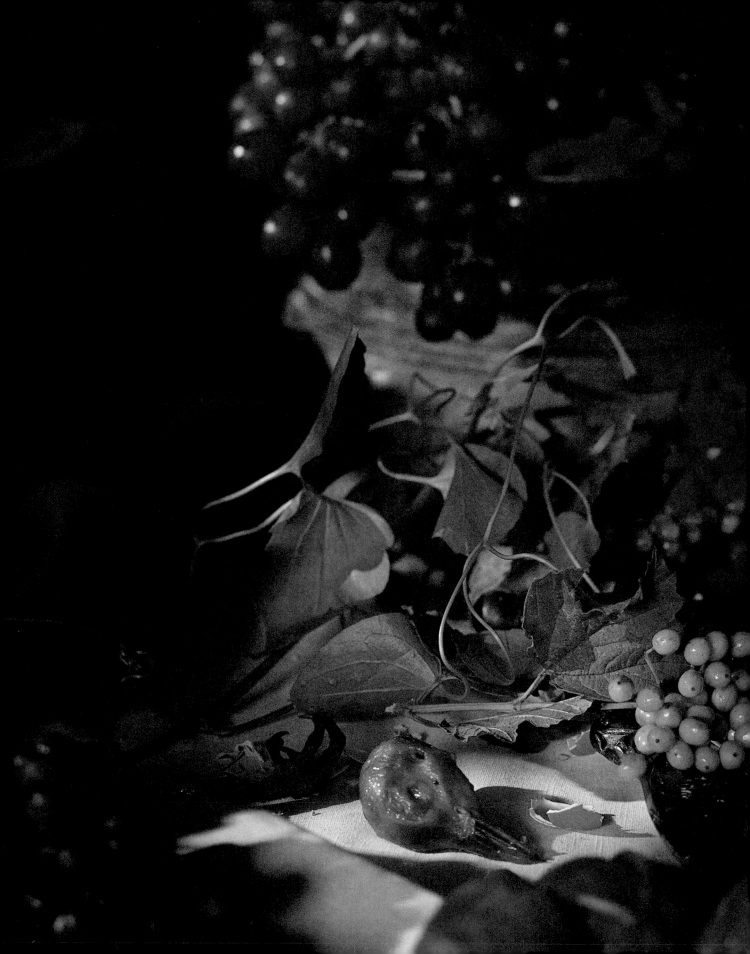

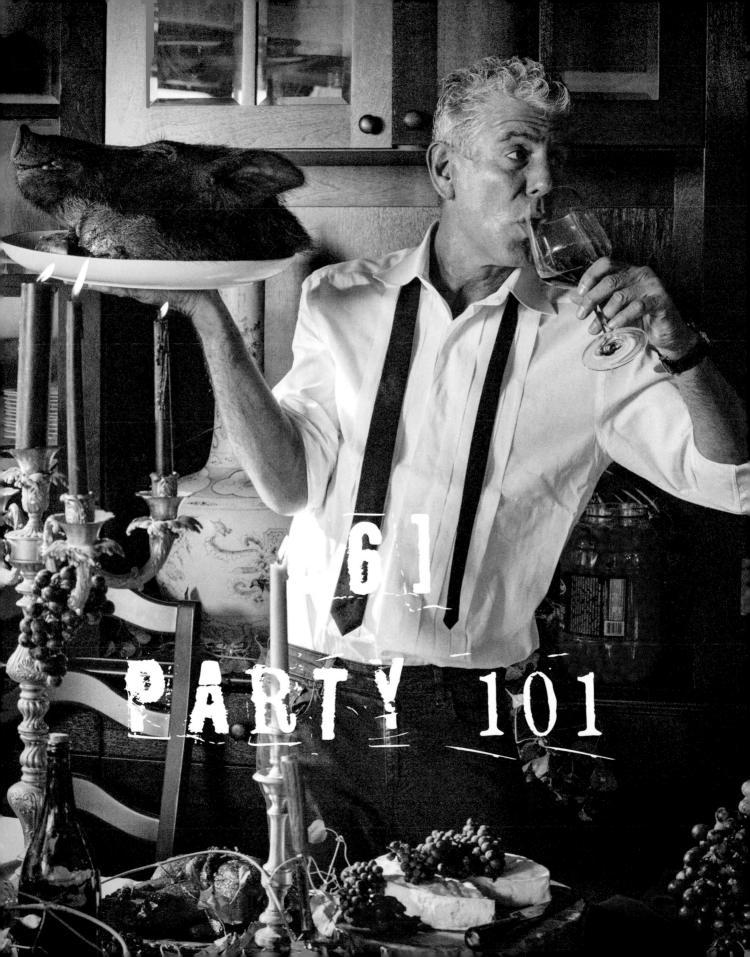

PARTY 101

During a dark period of my life, I worked in the twilight world of fly-by-night catering, usually under an alias (for reasons I'd rather not get into, as I'm uncertain about the relevant statutes of limitations). Later, I was the chef of a large nightclub and banquet facility in midtown Manhattan.

So I've worked a *lot* of parties. I've written menus and prepared finger food for many tens of thousands of fingers over the years. Probably hundreds of thousands.

I've seen some shit

I've also learned to hold certain truths to be self-evident

It is obvious, for instance, that when you're throwing a cocktail party with food that most of your guests will eat while standing up, you're expecting more guests than you have seats for, and therefore need to plan accordingly.

Here, then, are some basic rules. While not exactly the wisdom of the ages, these fundamentals will prove useful when planning a party:

⚕ Ask yourself, when writing the menu, "Will my guests have to balance a plate on their knee? Will they need a fork? A knife?" If the answer to any of these questions is yes, rewrite your menu. Otherwise, you are inviting a goat rodeo of spilled food, awkward conversations, and horrifying cleanup.

⚕ Will my guests be able to pick up the food cleanly? Meaning: Will the structural integrity of the hors d'oeuvres enable your guests to eat them without dribbling all over their presumably expensive clothing?

⚕ Can women with carefully applied lipstick fit said food items in their mouths without messing it up? And without distending their mouths or cheeks in a way they might believe to be unflattering to their appearance?

⚕ Hopefully, some of your guests will be having sex after the party. Hopefully with you—but even if they're not, you need to consider the residual effects of the hors d'oeuvres you serve them. Excessive garlic, raw onions, lutefisk, and durian fruit would all be, for this reason, inadvisable. Whether the hors d'oeuvres will leave hunks of food stuck between their teeth is also something you might consider.

✳ Will there be enough for everyone? Plan on 3 to 4 appetizers per guest if dinner will follow, and 6 to 10 appetizers per person, depending on the girth of your guests, if the appetizers are being served in lieu of dinner.

All that being said, the single most important lesson I learned over the course of many years, and many, many parties, is this humbling but inescapable fact: that no matter what you serve, no matter how beautifully presented, strikingly garnished, exotic in flavor, or expensive (I don't care if you're serving up tubs of beluga and fresh, still-steaming buckwheat blinis, or shrimp the size of a baby's arm), what everybody wants, what they will be all over like a swarm, every time, is commercially made freezer-case-sourced pigs in fucking blankets. It doesn't matter who your guests are. They will eat them, and they will love them. Whether this involves post-ironic posturing or just straightforward enthusiasm, they will love them just the same.

So the lesson here is this: **Always keep some pigs in blankets in the freezer.** They're the workhorses of the cocktail party. Did your guests hit the limited amount of crab cakes too hard? Afraid of running out? Send out a tray of pigs in blankets. They'll be delighted. Truffled larks' tongues in aspic all gone? No one will give a fuck once you send out those little doggies. And they'll think you're a genius.

BAGNA CÀUDA WITH CRUDITÉS

I used to cook vast tubs of this stuff. You can't beat it. Thick, hot, garlicky cream—into which you dip raw vegetables or bread? Please. And it's easy as hell.

As for the vegetables, choose wisely. Take care with your cuts, make sure everything is very clean but not wet, and reject anything that's even slightly dark edged, dried up, or that would otherwise contribute to the bad reputation that follows crudités.

8 ounces salt-packed anchovies

1 quart heavy cream

16 garlic cloves, peeled and smashed

½ cup best-quality extra-virgin olive oil

8 tablespoons (1 stick) unsalted butter

Salt and freshly ground black pepper to taste

3 medium to large red, yellow, or orange bell peppers, cored, seeded, and cut into long, thin strips

20 true baby carrots (NOT those waterlogged, plastic-bagged nubs that look like bloated pinky fingers) with greens attached, peeled and trimmed if necessary

20 Breakfast radishes, trimmed and cut in half lengthwise

2 heads of Belgian endive, washed and separated into spears

1 baguette, thinly sliced

SPECIAL EQUIPMENT

Blender or immersion blender

Place the anchovies in a small bowl, cover with cold water, and soak for 10 minutes, then drain, rinse, pat dry, and set aside.

In a medium saucepot, combine the cream and garlic and bring just to a boil, stirring occasionally and keeping an eye on it to avoid a messy boilover. Reduce the heat to a simmer and cook until the cream is reduced by half and the garlic is very fragrant, 20 to 25 minutes.

In the meantime, in a small saucepot, combine the oil and butter and bring to a low simmer. Mix well with a wooden spoon and add the reserved anchovies. Continue to simmer until the anchovies have completely melted into the hot fat. This should take about 30 minutes.

In the blender, combine the cream and garlic mixture with the oil, butter, and anchovy mixture and puree. Taste and adjust seasoning with salt and pepper as desired.

Serve the *bagna càuda* warm, employing a fondue pot if desired, with the raw vegetables alongside. Baguette slices should be held under the dipped vegetables to catch any drops and will become a delicious snack on their own, once dripped up a few times.

Makes 1 quart, to serve about 25

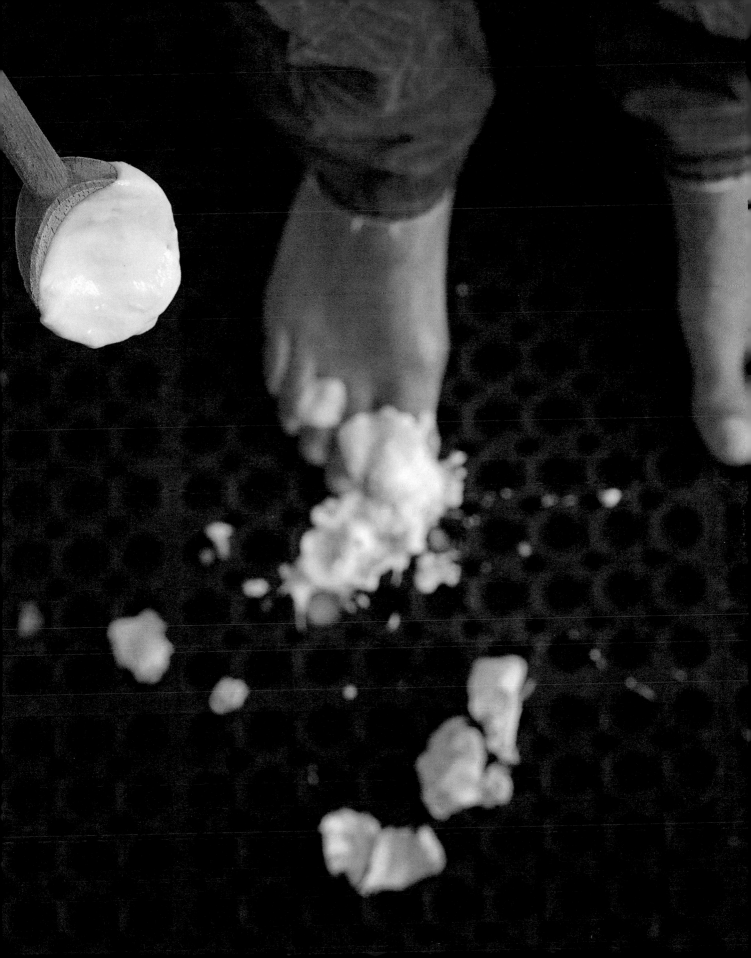

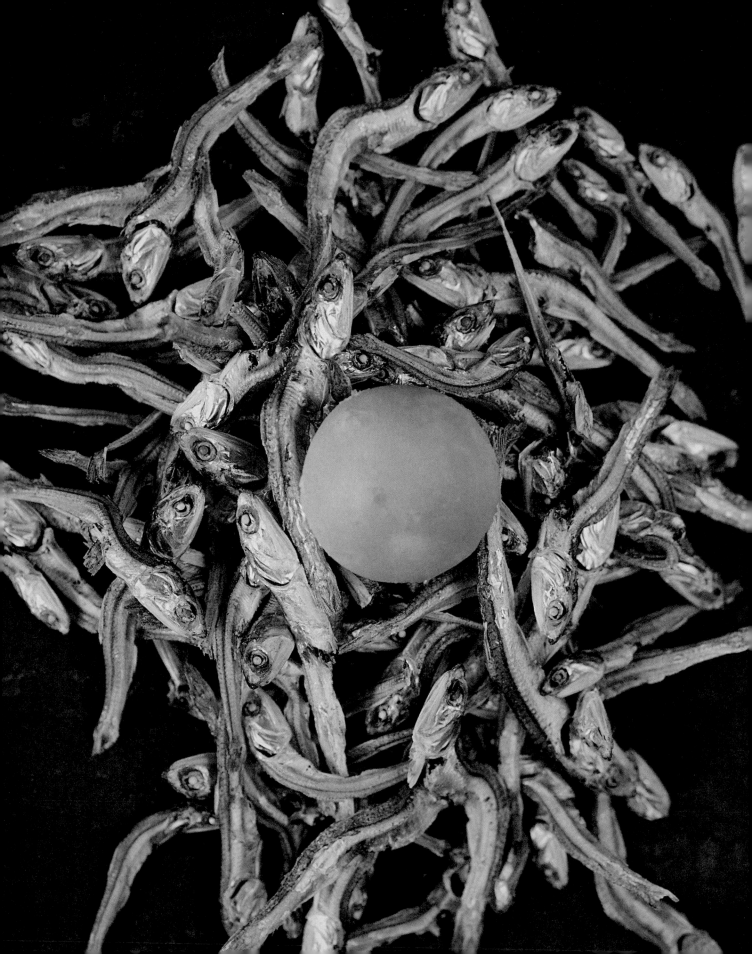

DEVILED EGGS WITH VARIATIONS

I'm an egg slut: I like deviled eggs in almost every conceivable variation. They improve everything, particularly a party, because who *doesn't* like deviled eggs?

Note that you do *not* want farm-fresh, still-warm-from-the-chicken eggs here. Appearances matter at parties, and you don't want your deviled eggs to look like they've been gnawed on by baby wolverines; slightly older eggs, which is what you'll inevitably purchase at most grocery stores, will be far easier to peel, because of the air pockets that form between shell and egg white as they age.

Place the eggs gently into a small or medium pot—the eggs should fit rather snugly so that they don't bounce around and potentially break—fill it with cold water, and bring to a rapid boil. Once the water boils, remove from the heat and cover the pot with a lid. Let it sit for 9 minutes (set the timer). At the 9-minute mark, carefully remove the eggs from the pot and transfer to the ice-water bath to cool. Once they are cool, peel the eggs and cut each in half lengthwise. Carefully separate the yolks from the whites and proceed with one or more of the filling options below, scaling up or down as necessary for your total number of eggs.

1 dozen large eggs

SPECIAL EQUIPMENT

Timer

Ice-water bath (large bowl filled with ice and cold water)

Makes 24 deviled eggs

FOR CAVIAR EGGS

¼ cup Mayonnaise (page 272) or store-bought mayonnaise

Salt and freshly ground black pepper to taste

Garnish with: 4 ounces best-quality black paddlefish caviar, 2 tablespoons finely chopped fresh chives $\longrightarrow$

FOR MEDITERRANEAN EGGS

2 tablespoons finely chopped preserved lemon

2 tablespoons harissa paste

¼ cup capers, drained, rinsed, and finely chopped

2 tablespoons extra-virgin olive oil

2 tablespoons Mayonnaise (page 272) or store-bought mayonnaise

Salt to taste (bear in mind that preserved lemons and capers are both quite salty, so taste before adding)

Garnish with: finely grated lemon zest, finely chopped fresh parsley, saffron threads, whole capers

FOR ANCHOVY EGGS

2 tablespoons finely chopped fresh parsley

3½ tablespoons Mayonnaise (page 272) or store-bought mayonnaise

1 tablespoon Dijon mustard

1 teaspoon anchovy paste

Salt and freshly ground black pepper to taste

Garnish with: finely chopped fresh parsley, marinated white anchovies (*boquerones*) cut in half lengthwise

FOR HOT AND SPICY DEVILED EGGS

¼ cup Mayonnaise (page 272) or store-bought mayonnaise

1 tablespoon hot mustard (Chinese or German)

1 tablespoon bottled hot sauce, or more to taste

Salt to taste

Garnish with: fresh cilantro leaves, finely chopped scallions (white and light green parts, with dark green tops reserved for stock), Maldon sea salt

METHOD FOR ALL VARIATIONS: In a bowl, mash together the yolks, mayonnaise, and all other listed ingredients for each respective recipe. Transfer the mixture to a pastry bag fitted with a star tip, or a plastic bag from which you have snipped one small corner. Stuff the whites with the mixture, garnish as indicated, and serve.

BELGIAN ENDIVE WITH CURRIED CHICKEN SALAD

Yes, I *know*: 1970 called. It wants its hors d'oeuvre back.

This is another reliable classic from my fly-by-night catering days. They're tasty. They're pretty. You could train a crackhead rodeo clown to make them.

Place the chicken breasts in a pot that is large enough to hold them in a single layer, and add the salt, bay leaf, peppercorns, and garlic. Cover with cold water and bring to a boil, watching carefully. As soon as the water boils, reduce the heat to a simmer, cover the pot, and continue to cook until the breasts are cooked through, 8 to 10 minutes, or the meat is gently firm and an instant-read thermometer registers 165°F when inserted into the thickest part of the breast.

Use tongs to remove the chicken breasts from the water. Transfer to a plate and refrigerate to stop the cooking process.

Once the chicken is cool, cut it into a ¼-inch dice and transfer it to a mixing bowl. In a separate mixing bowl, whisk together the mayonnaise, lemon juice, and curry powder, then fold in the shallot, ginger, walnuts, and raisins. Fold this mixture into the diced chicken, then season with salt and pepper.

Arrange the endive spears on a platter and cover the base of each one with a heaping tablespoon of chicken salad. Garnish with the cilantro leaves and a dab of chutney and serve.

Makes 40 to 50 pieces

1 pound boneless, skinless chicken breasts

2 teaspoons salt, plus more to taste

1 bay leaf

1 teaspoon black peppercorns

2 garlic cloves, peeled and crushed with the flat side of your knife

½ cup Mayonnaise (page 272) or store-bought mayonnaise

Juice of ½ lemon (about 1 tablespoon)

3 teaspoons mild yellow curry powder

1 shallot, peeled and finely chopped

½ teaspoon finely grated fresh ginger

½ cup toasted walnuts, coarsely chopped

½ cup raisins, coarsely chopped

Freshly ground black pepper to taste

3 to 4 heads of Belgian endive, washed and separated into spears (discard leaves that are too small)

¼ cup fresh cilantro or Italian parsley leaves

1 to 1½ cups Mixed Fruit Chutney (page 274)

SPECIAL EQUIPMENT

Instant-read thermometer

GAUFRETTE POTATO WITH SMOKED SALMON, CRÈME FRAÎCHE, AND CAVIAR

Have I gotten more mileage out of any single bit of business than the gaufrette potato? I doubt it.

It's a fucking potato chip—but prettier (*much* prettier), and with more predictable engineering. As a platform for hors d'oeuvres, they're unbeatable—as long as you don't slop anything too wet on them or assemble them too far in advance. Like anything fried, they will, of course, get soggy.

1½ pounds Idaho or russet
    potatoes (2 large potatoes)

2 to 3 quarts peanut oil

Salt to taste

1 pound sliced smoked salmon

2 cups crème fraîche

8 ounces best-quality black caviar

SPECIAL EQUIPMENT

Deep fryer or tall-sided pot

Deep-fry or candy thermometer

3 sheet pans lined with newspaper

Spider, skimmer, or slotted spoon

Mandoline with fluted blade
    attachment

Fill a medium bowl halfway with cold water. Peel the potatoes, transferring each one as it's peeled into the cold water, which will keep it from discoloring.

In the deep fryer, heat the oil to 375°F, monitoring the temperature with the deep-fry thermometer. If you're using a tall-sided pot, make sure that the oil comes no more than halfway up the inside of the pot. Keep the lined sheet pans and the spider close to the deep fryer.

Set up the mandoline with the fluted blade attachment, and adjust it so that your slices will be very thin. Set up an additional sheet pan or work surface lined with paper towels, and have some more newspaper nearby. Take 1 potato from the water and cut off the narrowest parts of the ends, so that it is approximately the same width along the whole length of the potato. Pat the potato (and your hands) dry and slice it on the mandoline, turning the potato 90 degrees each time to create the cross-hatched ridges that are the mark of a gaufrette. Adjust the thickness of cut, if necessary; the slices should be thin enough to have holes in them, like a waffle, which will ensure quick and even frying. As you cut them, lay each slice on the paper towels and, once you have several, pat them dry with more paper towels. When it comes to deep-frying, moisture is the enemy of both crispness and safety.

Once you have a potato's worth of slices patted dry, gently slip them into the oil and let them cook for no more than 3 minutes, or until golden brown. If they begin to stick together, you may need to get in there with tongs or a set of chopsticks to gently guide them apart.

Remove the cooked potatoes from the oil and transfer to the sheet pans lined with newspaper, to drain. Season with salt and repeat the process with the remaining potatoes.

Just before serving, arrange potatoes on a serving tray. Top each with a proportionate piece of salmon, a dab of crème fraîche, and a small dab of caviar. Serve at once.

Makes 50 pieces

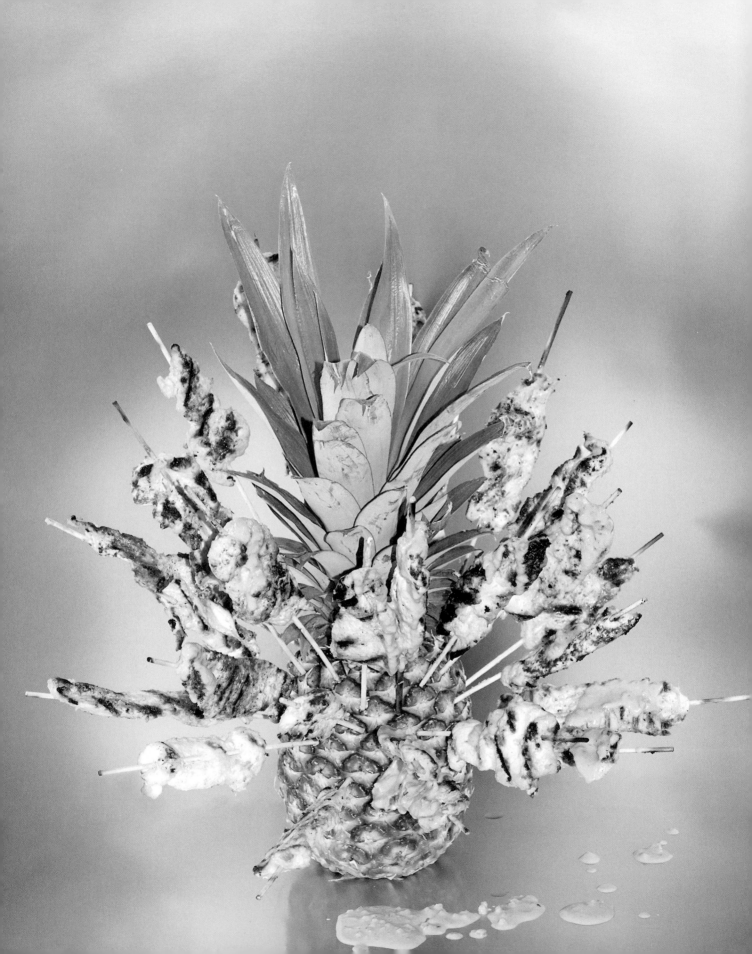

CHICKEN SATAY WITH FAKE·ASS SPICY PEANUT SAUCE

There are certain lowbrow items that even the most discerning guests go crazy for at catered parties: Among them are (the aforementioned) pigs in a blanket, steroidal strawberries dipped in chocolate, and meat on a stick. Trim a pineapple and jab a bunch of chicken skewers into it, like some demented poultry porcupine, and do not skimp on the Fake-Ass Spicy Peanut Sauce.

In the blender, combine the oil, the juice of 2 lemons, ¼ cup of the fish sauce, 2 tablespoons of the soy sauce, the lemongrass, shallots, 3 of the garlic cloves, ¼ cup of the sugar, the coriander, and turmeric. Blend on high speed for about 30 seconds.

Place the chicken in 1-gallon zip-seal plastic bags or a large glass casserole or baking dish with a cover and pour the marinade over, turning the pieces so that they are all coated. Seal and refrigerate for at least 30 minutes and up to 2 hours (any more time than that, and the acid and salt in the marinade will begin to erode the structural integrity of the flesh, leaving you with revoltingly mushy chicken).

While the chicken marinates, make the peanut sauce. In a mixing bowl, combine the peanut butter, hot water, and coconut milk and whisk well. Add the remaining juice of 1 lemon or 2 limes, 2 tablespoons fish sauce, 1 teaspoon soy sauce, 2 tablespoons sugar, and the sriracha and whisk well, adding a bit more water or coconut milk if necessary to thin the sauce to desired consistency. Taste and adjust seasoning with additional splashes of soy sauce, fish sauce, citrus juice or sugar as desired. Cover and refrigerate the sauce until 30 minutes before serving.

Soak the skewers in water for 30 minutes before cooking the chicken. ⟶

½ cup vegetable or other neutral oil

Juice of 3 lemons, or 2 lemons and 2 limes (about 6 tablespoons)

¼ cup plus 2 tablespoons fish sauce

2 tablespoons plus 1 teaspoon soy sauce

3 stalks lemongrass, coarsely chopped, or finely grated zest of 3 lemons or 5 limes

2 shallots, peeled and coarsely chopped

4 garlic cloves, peeled and coarsely chopped

¼ cup plus 2 tablespoons light brown sugar, packed

2 teaspoons ground coriander

1 teaspoon ground turmeric or mild yellow curry powder

3 pounds boneless, skinless chicken breasts, sliced lengthwise into 1-inch-thick strips

1 cup chunky peanut butter

½ cup hot water

½ cup coconut milk

1 tablespoon sriracha sauce, or to taste (but you want it spicy)

SPECIAL EQUIPMENT

Blender or food processor

45 wooden skewers

Grill, grill pan, or broiler

Preheat your grill. Remove the chicken from the marinade, reserving the marinade in the small bowl. Thread one piece on each skewer, leaving enough room at the bottom of the skewer for a "handle." Grill for 5 minutes, then turn the skewers and use a basting or pastry brush to coat the chicken with the reserved marinade. Cook for another 5 minutes, or until cooked through (cut through the center of one piece to make sure there's no translucent pink flesh). Serve hot, with the peanut sauce alongside for dipping.

Makes about 45 pieces

DUCK RILLETTES

Preparing duck rillettes is a two-day affair: Salt and refrigerate the legs one day, and cook them the next, until the flesh is nearly falling off the bone but still intact. The tell is when the skin separates from the "knuckle" joint, exposing the duck's "shin" bone.

Rub the duck legs generously with salt and arrange in a single layer in a shallow dish. Cover with plastic wrap and refrigerate overnight.

Preheat the oven to 375°F and remove the duck legs from the refrigerator. In a small, heavy-bottom saucepan, melt the duck fat until it is clear. Season the legs lightly with black pepper and transfer them to a glass or ceramic casserole that will accommodate them snugly in a single layer. Pour the fat over the legs and nestle the oregano, bay leaf, and garlic around them. Cover the dish with foil and cook in the oven for 60 to 90 minutes, until the meat is nearly falling off the bone (see headnote).

Using tongs, remove the legs from the casserole, and once they are cool enough to handle, separate the meat from the skin and bones (which should be stashed in the freezer for stock making). Shred the meat with a fork and place it in a mixing bowl. Place a strainer over the bowl and ladle the fat into it, discarding the oregano, bay leaf, and garlic. Gently fold together the meat and fat with a spatula. Taste and season as desired with salt and pepper, then use as directed for Mutant Quesadillas (page 114), or store in a clean terrine, topped with the excess duck fat, covered with plastic, and refrigerated.

6 duck legs (about 3 to 4 pounds raw total, with skin and bones intact)

Salt, as needed

2 cups duck fat

Freshly ground black pepper to taste

4 sprigs fresh oregano

1 bay leaf

2 garlic cloves, peeled

Makes about 4 cups rillettes

THE GRILL BITCH'S BAR NUTS

I first worked with Beth Aretsky, who later came to identify herself as "the Grill Bitch," at One Fifth, one of the many long-gone New York City restaurants of my checkered career. She created these spicy and sweet bar nuts, which caused many a customer to linger over drinks far beyond the advisable cutoff point. They are truly addictive.

4 large egg whites

5 pounds mixed nuts

½ cup granulated sugar

¼ cup light brown sugar, packed

2 teaspoons ground cinnamon

1½ tablespoons ground cayenne pepper

1½ tablespoons salt

SPECIAL EQUIPMENT

2 (9 × 13-inch) sheet pans lined with parchment paper or silicone mats

Preheat the oven to 325°F.

In a large mixing bowl, whisk the egg whites until they are foamy and nearly stiff.

In another mixing bowl, combine the nuts, sugars, cinnamon, cayenne, and salt and toss to coat. Fold in the egg whites, tossing gently to make sure that all the nuts have been coated in egg white.

Divide the mixture evenly between the two prepared sheet pans. Bake in the oven for 30 minutes, rotating the pans and stirring the nuts at the 15-minute mark. The nuts should be dry and crisp after 30 minutes.

Remove from the oven and let cool before serving.

_____

Makes 8 cups

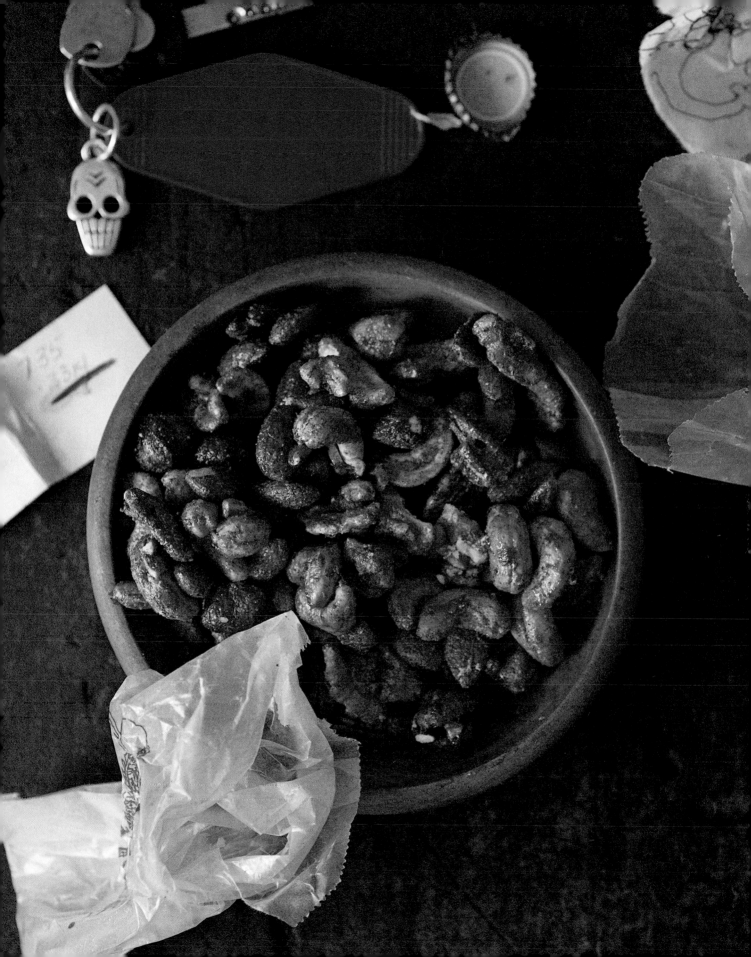

MUTANT QUESADILLAS: CHORIZO AND DUCK

Okay. Ordinarily, there's nothing I hate more—or rail against more fervently—than fake Mexican food. But these are so easy. They're impossible to hate. And they'll occupy your guests for at least an hour, as long as you keep feeding them liquor, too.

Melted cheese. End of story.

2 pounds fresh Mexican chorizo sausage, removed from its casing and crumbled

2 medium to large green bell peppers, cored, seeded, and finely chopped

1 medium white onion, peeled and finely chopped

Salt and freshly ground black pepper to taste

32 (8-inch) flour tortillas

1½ pounds Monterey Jack cheese, shredded

2 pounds Duck Rillettes (page 111), at room temperature

1 pound goat cheese, softened

½ cup vegetable or other neutral oil

2 cups Pico de Gallo (page 276)

SPECIAL EQUIPMENT

2 sheet trays lined with parchment paper

Grill or ridged grill pan

Long-bristled pastry brush

Long metal spatula

Place the chorizo in a large, heavy-bottom sauté pan and add a few tablespoons of water. Cook over medium heat, stirring occasionally to keep the chunks broken up, until the meat has released its fat (there will be a lot) and has begun to sizzle and brown at the edges, 5 to 7 minutes. Add the chopped bell peppers and onion and stir to coat the vegetables with the fat. Scrape the bottom of the pan to dislodge any browned bits. Sprinkle with a bit of salt to help the vegetables release their juices, and continue to cook over medium heat until the vegetables are soft and tender. Taste the mixture and season with salt and pepper as necessary. Remove the mixture from the heat.

Assemble the quesadillas: Lay 1 tortilla flat on a clean work surface and sprinkle lightly with the shredded Monterey Jack cheese, leaving a ½-inch margin around the perimeter. Gently drop a layer of cooked chorizo and vegetables over the cheese, respecting the margin, then top with another light round of the Monterey Jack. Top this with another tortilla and press down to hold the thing together. The cheese, once heated, will also act as a glue to keep the tortillas together. Repeat this process with another 14 tortillas, so that you have 8 chorizo-stuffed quesadillas in all. Before grilling, hold the assembled quesadillas on a sheet tray, separated by layers of parchment paper.

To make the duck quesadillas, repeat the process as above, spreading goat cheese on the surface of 1 tortilla and duck rillettes on the surface of another, and carefully assemble them, as above.

Preheat the grill or grill pan. If using a grill, use a grill brush to lightly coat the grates with oil. If using a grill pan, drizzle with a small amount of oil and use a paper towel gripped in a set of tongs to evenly distribute the oil and remove the excess, if any.

Brush one surface of a quesadilla lightly with oil, and using the spatula, deftly slide it, oiled side down, onto the grill. Cook 1 to 2 minutes on the first side, then brush the other surface with oil and carefully flip it, cooking for 1 to 2 minutes more. Repeat this process with the remaining quesadillas, portioning the cooked ones into four, six, or eight triangles, and serving with pico de gallo alongside.

Makes 16 (8-inch) quesadillas

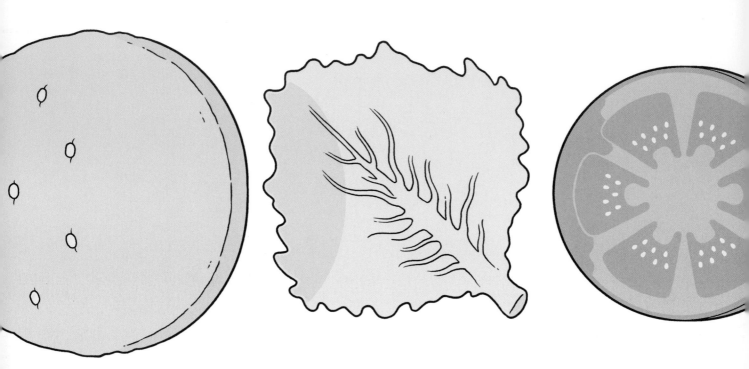

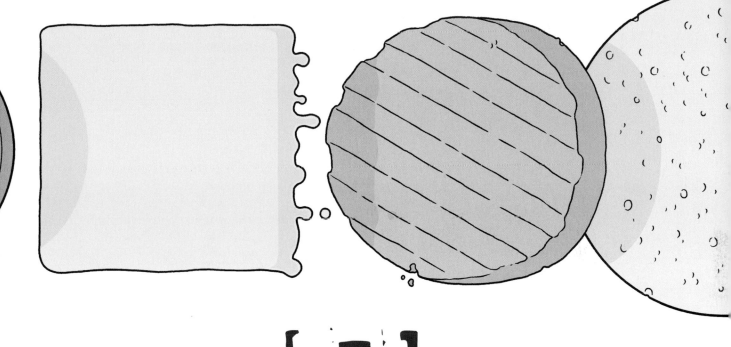

[7]

HAMBURGER RULES

NOTE: *To provide a visual supplement to the information presented below, Nathan Myhrvold, founder of The Cooking Lab, coauthor of the* Modernist Cuisine *books, a graduate of La Varenne, and one-time chief technology officer of Microsoft, who holds a doctorate in theoretical and mathematical physics as well as a master's degree in economics, geophysics, and space physics, breaks it all down for you on the enclosed chart, suitable for prominent display and constant reference in your kitchen.*

Brioches are very nice

For breakfast

Do *not* think for a second that a brioche roll is a good idea for a hamburger. The brioche is a French invention. The French, however vital to all things culinary, have no cultural understanding of—or historic sympathies for—the American hamburger.

The purpose of the hamburger bun is to support and enhance the meat. Hamburger meat is, by definition, supposed to be fatty. A certain amount of grease is desirable. The bun is supposed to counteract the runoff, and absorb it. It is supposed to last, in direct proportion to the amount of meat left, until the last bite.

Brioches are greasy. They *add* grease. They also crumble and break apart in the hand as the burger reaches its butt end. It is not a reliable partner or friend. The potato bun, however, is the perfect delivery system for a fatty patty (or patties). It should be soft, pillowy, reliable, and decidedly proletarian.

Like sushi—another perfect food—a hamburger should be austere, seemingly uncomplicated, yet prepared with pride and precision.

One must continue to ask oneself, as if arranging flowers in the Japanese manner, "Is this necessary?," stripping away that which does not serve the meat. The meat is the star.

Does one need a tomato slice? Does it really add anything? Here, a cost-benefit analysis is required. The tomato may be in season, and at its height of deliciousness, but will including it in the delicately constructed hamburger be worth the possible damage to its structure and "eatability"?

Cheddar or processed American? One must ask oneself constantly what one is willing to sacrifice for presumed "quality." American cheese, clearly, is texturally and structurally superior as a binding agent—and has the added force of tradition on its side.

Lettuce? I'm not a fan. I'll have my salad on the side. But I understand the desire for crunch. If you're putting mesclun or baby arugula on your burger, though, Guantánamo Bay would not be an unreasonable punishment. Use finely shredded iceberg. Or *maybe* romaine. Period.

Onions add something to the party, but they must be thinly sliced. Paper thin. And fresh, *please*. Caramelized? No. Not a fan. Burgers should not be sweet. Any sweetness in a burger should come from the ketchup alone.

Speaking of which: Do not put "house-made chutney" on my hamburger. Please. Let ketchup do its job. And don't make "house-made ketchup" either. Why would you do that? If it's not broken, as they say, why the fuck would you fix it? Is your ketchup *really* better than the stuff that's been our trusty condiment companion for decades? A waiter asks me if I'd like some "house-made" ketchup, and I tense up, anticipating further blows: Will Mumford and Sons suddenly emerge from the kitchen and begin playing tableside?

Mayonnaise? Maybe, if applied judiciously. You don't want that burger shooting out from between the buns and landing on your genitals. It's a tough call. How much do you really like mayonnaise? A cost/benefit analysis is called for here.

Bacon? By all means But as with anything you put on a burger, serious attention must be paid to thickness, doneness, and cut, which is to say, use a standard-issue thin slice of bacon, and cook it to well done. And don't overload your burger with it. You can, as it turns out, have too much bacon.

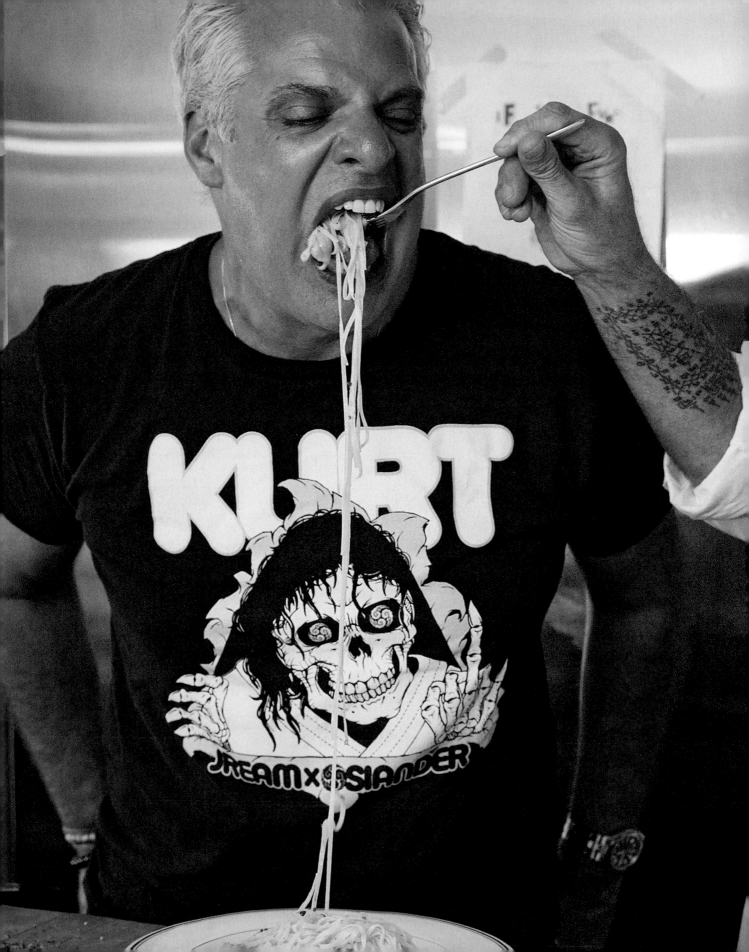

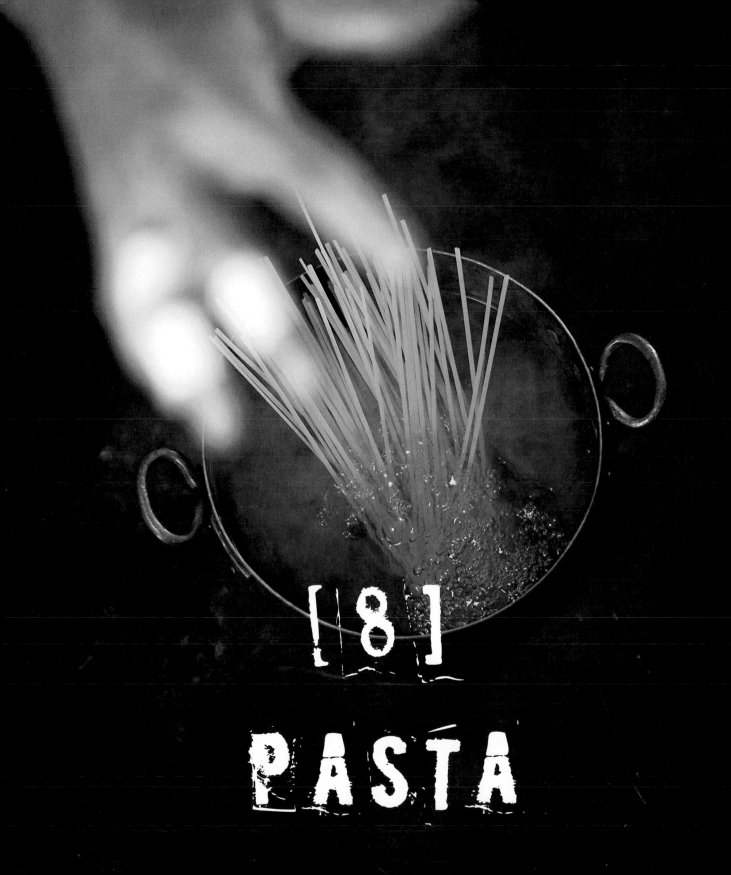

[8]

PASTA

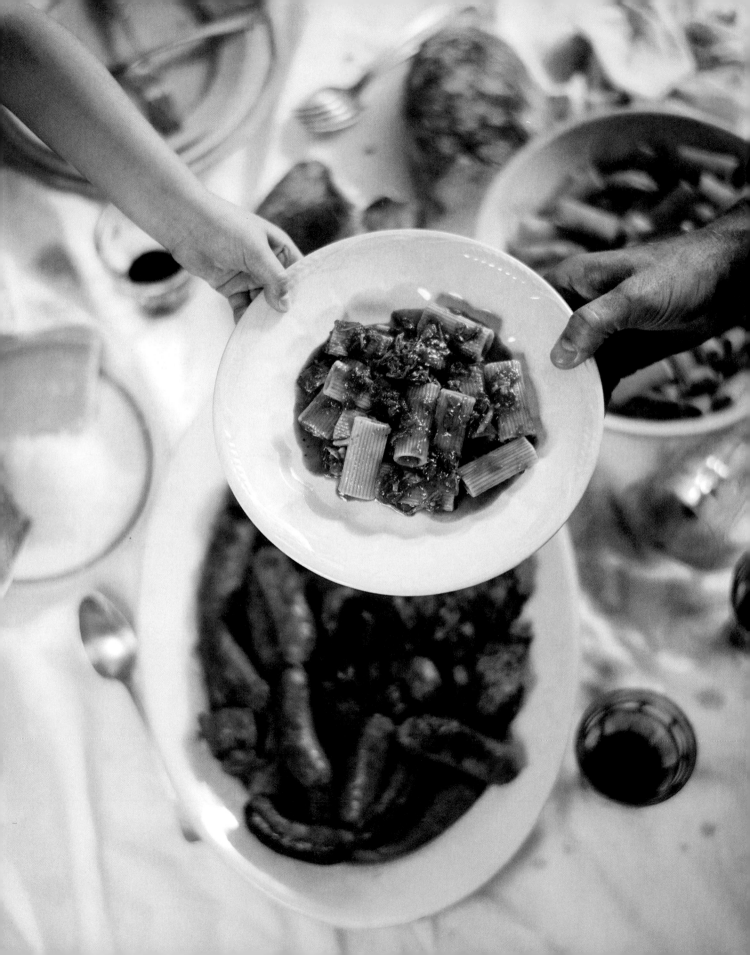

SUNDAY GRAVY WITH SAUSAGE AND RIGATONI

I was always bitter that I wasn't Italian American. You know that scene in *Saturday Night Fever,* where Tony Manero is eating with his family? All the yelling and the smacking? That looked good to me.

We were discouraged from talking with our hands at my childhood dinner table. Voices were supposed to be maintained at a reasonable level and used for civil discourse only. Definitely no smacking. Mopping sauce with bread—getting too physically involved with your food at all—was something my mom was unlikely to approve of.

So, this Italo-American Jersey classic—a riff on the Napolitano strategy for (a) turning a bunch of bony, low-quality off-cuts of meat into something delicious, and (b) stretching one thing into two courses—is a realization of all my childhood yearnings.

Preheat the oven to 350°F. Season the oxtail with salt and pepper. In a Dutch oven or large heavy-bottom ovenproof pot with lid, heat the oil over medium-high heat until it shimmers. Add the neck bones and oxtail, working in batches if necessary to avoid overcrowding the pan, and brown on all sides in the oil. Using tongs, remove the browned pieces and set them aside on a sheet pan or platter, which will collect their juices while the remaining pieces cook. Brown the sausages and set aside.

Once the sausages and bones have all been browned and removed from the Dutch oven, add the onion and cook over medium-high heat, stirring often and scraping the bottom of the pan with a wooden spoon so that the onion picks up the browned bits. Salt the onions a bit to release their juices as they cook.

Add the garlic, cook for 1 minute, then add the tomato paste, oregano, and pepper flakes and cook for a few minutes, until the tomato paste is dark reddish brown and has begun to $\longrightarrow$

2½ pounds oxtail, cut into pieces

Salt and pepper to taste

2 tablespoons olive oil

2 to 3 pounds pork neck bones

2 pounds sweet or hot pork sausage links

1 large or 2 medium white or yellow onions, peeled and finely chopped

5 garlic cloves, peeled and crushed

3 tablespoons tomato paste

1 teaspoon dried oregano

1 teaspoon red pepper flakes, or to taste

2 cups dry red wine

2 cups Dark Universal Stock (page 260)

2 (28-ounce) cans crushed tomatoes

2 bay leaves

2 sprigs fresh thyme or rosemary

1 sprig fresh basil

1 pound dry rigatoni

4 to 6 ounces Parmigiano-Reggiano cheese, for grating

SPECIAL EQUIPMENT

Cheesecloth

Butcher's twine

stick to the pan. Deglaze the Dutch oven with the wine and let reduce by half.

Add the stock, tomatoes, and bay leaves. Wrap the herb sprigs in the cheesecloth and secure the bundle tightly with the twine to make a bouquet garni. Return the oxtail and bones to the Dutch oven. Season with salt and pepper and bring to a boil. Cover the Dutch oven and transfer to the oven to cook for about 2½ hours.

Remove the Dutch oven from the oven, add the browned sausages, and return to the oven to cook for another 30 minutes. The ragout should be thick but still juicy.

Remove and discard the bouquet garni and keep the gravy and sausages warm.

In a large, heavy-bottom pot, bring salted water to a boil. Cook the rigatoni according to the package instructions until just al dente. Drain the pasta in a colander and return it to the hot, empty pot. Toss the rigatoni gently over medium heat for about 30 seconds to dry it completely, using tongs if necessary to keep it from sticking to the sides of the pot. Ladle in as much of the warm sauce as necessary to coat but not drown the pasta. Serve the pasta and sausages together, with the extra sauce and grated Parmigiano-Reggiano alongside.

_____

Serves 4 to 6

LINGUINE WITH WHITE CLAM SAUCE

This would be a very good candidate for "last meal," as it's delicious as hell—and because you won't have to worry about garlic breath in the next life.

5 dozen littleneck clams, scrubbed

¼ cup best-quality olive oil

12 garlic cloves, finely chopped

1 teaspoon red pepper flakes

½ cup dry white wine

1 pound dry linguine

Salt and freshly ground black pepper to taste

3 tablespoons butter, cut into a few pieces

1 cup coarsely chopped fresh parsley leaves

In a large, heavy-bottom pot, bring about an inch of salted water to a boil. Gently place 4 dozen of the 5 dozen clams into the pot, cover, and let steam until the clams have opened, about 5 minutes. Check them frequently, move them around with tongs or a long-handled spoon as needed, and remove the clams to a large bowl as they open so that they do not become overcooked and rubbery. Do not discard the cooking liquid.

As soon as the clams are cool enough to handle, remove them from the shell with a soup spoon or clean fingers, keeping them intact as much as possible, and collecting as much of the liquor from within the shell as possible. If they're a little on the large side, give the clams a rough chop. Strain the cooking liquid through a fine-mesh sieve into a small bowl.

Wash out the pot, fill it three-quarters full with heavily salted water, and bring it to a boil.

When the water is just about to boil, warm the oil in a large, heavy-bottom sauté pan and add the garlic and pepper flakes. Cook over medium-low heat, taking care not to let the garlic get brown, which can happen in an instant. Add the wine and increase the heat so that the wine boils and reduces by half. Add the reserved clam liquor and a good splash of the clam cooking liquid, then the remaining 1 dozen clams. Cover and cook until the clams have steamed open. Remove the clams to the side as they open, and discard any that haven't opened within a reasonable amount of time. (It's not terribly uncommon to have 1 or 2 clams per dozen that just never open.)

Add the linguine to the boiling water and cook according to the package instructions until just al dente.

While the pasta cooks, add the reserved cooked clams to the sauté pan and season with salt and pepper to taste. Add the butter and toss over the heat until everything is just hot.

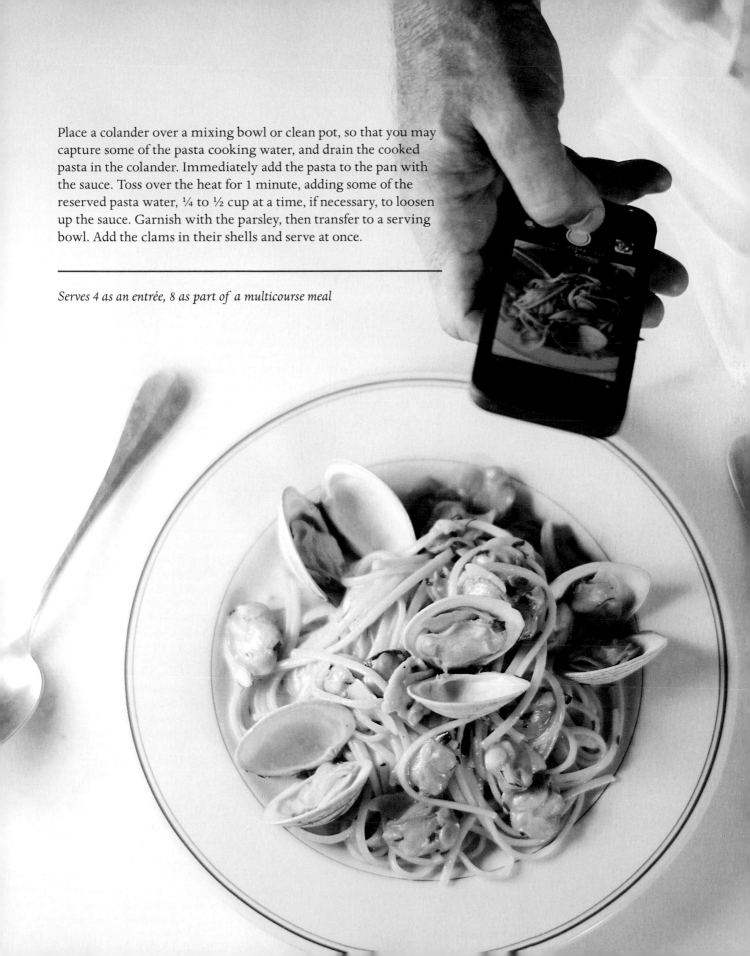

Place a colander over a mixing bowl or clean pot, so that you may capture some of the pasta cooking water, and drain the cooked pasta in the colander. Immediately add the pasta to the pan with the sauce. Toss over the heat for 1 minute, adding some of the reserved pasta water, ¼ to ½ cup at a time, if necessary, to loosen up the sauce. Garnish with the parsley, then transfer to a serving bowl. Add the clams in their shells and serve at once.

Serves 4 as an entrée, 8 as part of a multicourse meal

MACARONI AND CHEESE

Get that damn lobster out of my mac and cheese!

Truffles do *not* make it better. If you add truffle *oil*, which is made from a petroleum-based chemical additive and the crushed dreams of nineties culinary mediocrity, you should be punched in the kidneys.

1 pound dry elbow macaroni

5 tablespoons unsalted butter

5 tablespoons all-purpose flour

4½ cups whole milk

2 teaspoons mustard powder

2 teaspoons ground cayenne pepper

1 teaspoon Worcestershire sauce

8 ounces Parmigiano-Reggiano cheese, grated

4 ounces Gruyère cheese, grated

5 ounces sharp cheddar cheese, grated

3 ounces fresh mozzarella cheese, cubed

4 ounces cooked and thinly sliced ham, julienned (optional)

2 teaspoons salt, or more to taste

Freshly ground white pepper to taste (optional)

Preheat the oven to 375° F.

In a large, heavy-bottom pot, bring salted water to a boil and add the elbow macaroni. Cook according to the package instructions until just al dente, then drain and set aside.

Make sure you have both a whisk and a wooden spoon nearby, and something to rest them on. You will be switching back and forth between the two utensils as you first make a roux and then build on that to make a béchamel.

In the still-hot macaroni pot, heat the butter over medium-high heat until it foams and subsides. Whisk in the flour, then switch to a wooden spoon and stir steadily over medium-high heat until the mixture begins to turn a nutty golden brown, about 2 minutes. Do not let the mixture scorch. Whisk in the milk and bring the mixture just to a boil, stirring with the wooden spoon and making sure to scrape each part of the surface of the pan so that hunks of flour or milk do not stick. Reduce to a simmer and continue to cook and stir until the mixture is slightly thicker than heavy cream.

Whisk in the mustard powder, cayenne, and Worcestershire, then add half the Parmigiano-Reggiano (you'll sprinkle the rest over the top) and the rest of the cheeses and, if using, the ham, and stir until the cheeses have melted completely. Stir in the cooked macaroni and mix well. Remove from the heat and stir in the salt and optional pepper.

Transfer the mixture to a glass or ceramic casscrole, top with the remaining Parmigiano, and bake in the oven for 15 to 20 minutes, until the top is golden brown and the mixture is bubbling slightly.

Serve hot, or refrigerate and gently reheat the whole thing, or in portions as needed.

Serves 8

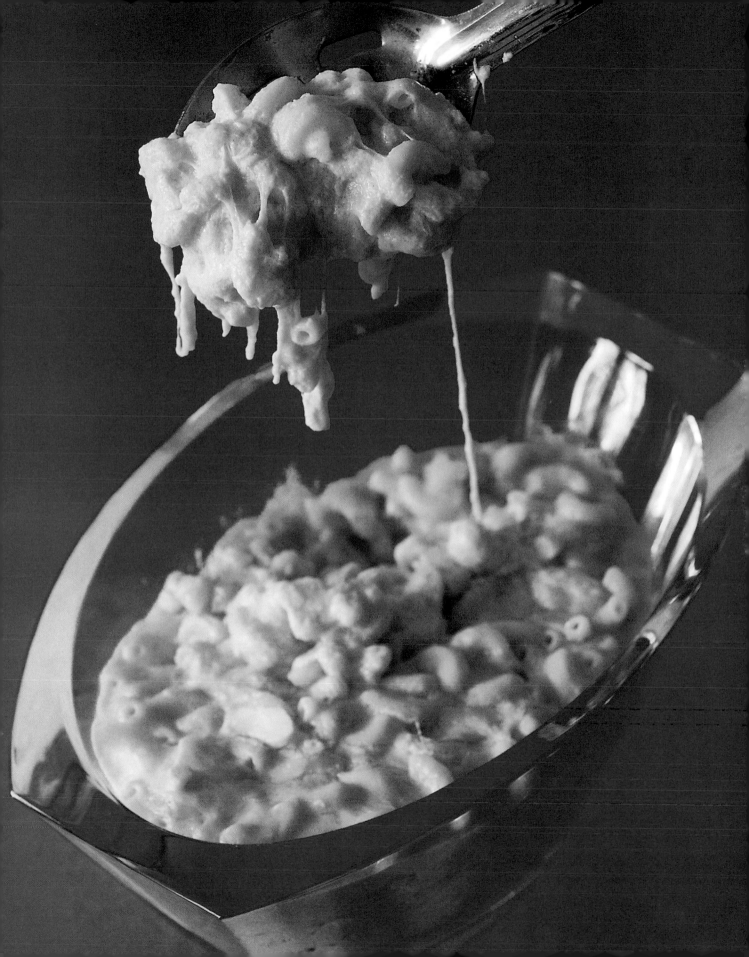

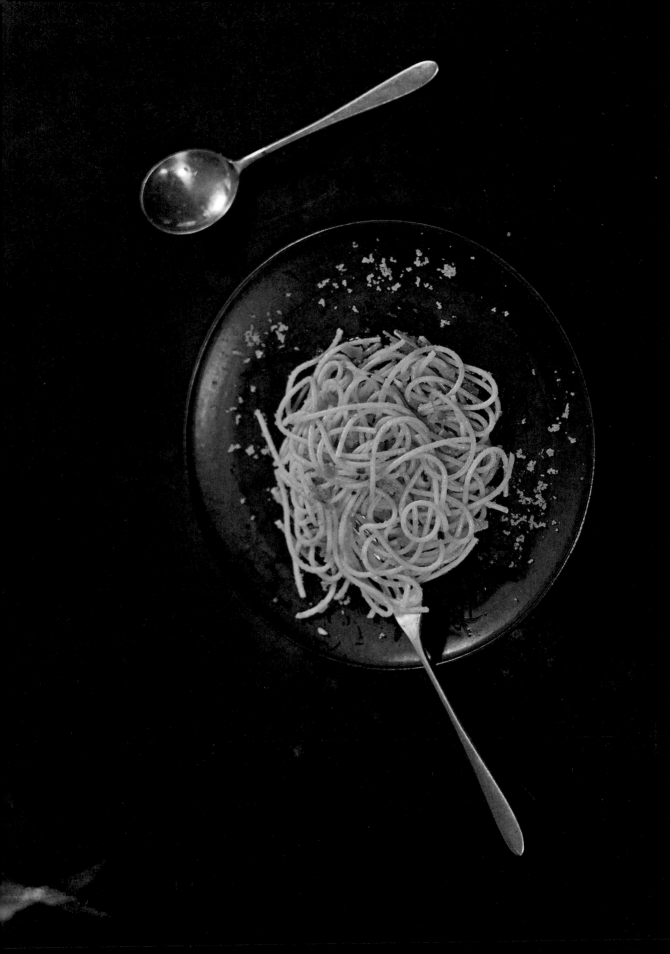

Spaghetti alla Bottarga

After I fell in love with this dish on the Sardinian coast, I asked my father-in-law to show me how it's done.

In many ways, it encapsulates the Italian philosophy of cooking, its essential idea: Get a very few excellent ingredients, then proceed to *not* fuck them up.

In a large, heavy-bottom pot, bring salted water to a boil and cook the spaghetti according to the package instructions until just al dente.

Meanwhile, in a large, high-sided skillet or sauté pan, warm the oil over medium-low heat. Add the garlic and pepper flakes and let them steep in the oil until they become fragrant, 2 to 3 minutes. Remove from the heat, let sit for 2 minutes, then add half the grated bottarga and gently swirl the skillet.

Drain the cooked pasta in a colander and transfer it to the skillet with the warm oil. Toss well to combine, then top the pasta with the remaining bottarga. Taste and season if necessary with salt (bearing in mind that bottarga is quite salty), then serve immediately in bowls.

1 pound dry spaghetti

½ cup extra-virgin olive oil

1 garlic clove, peeled and finely sliced

1 teaspoon red pepper flakes

4 ounces bottarga, grated, or more to taste

Salt to taste

Serves 4 to 6

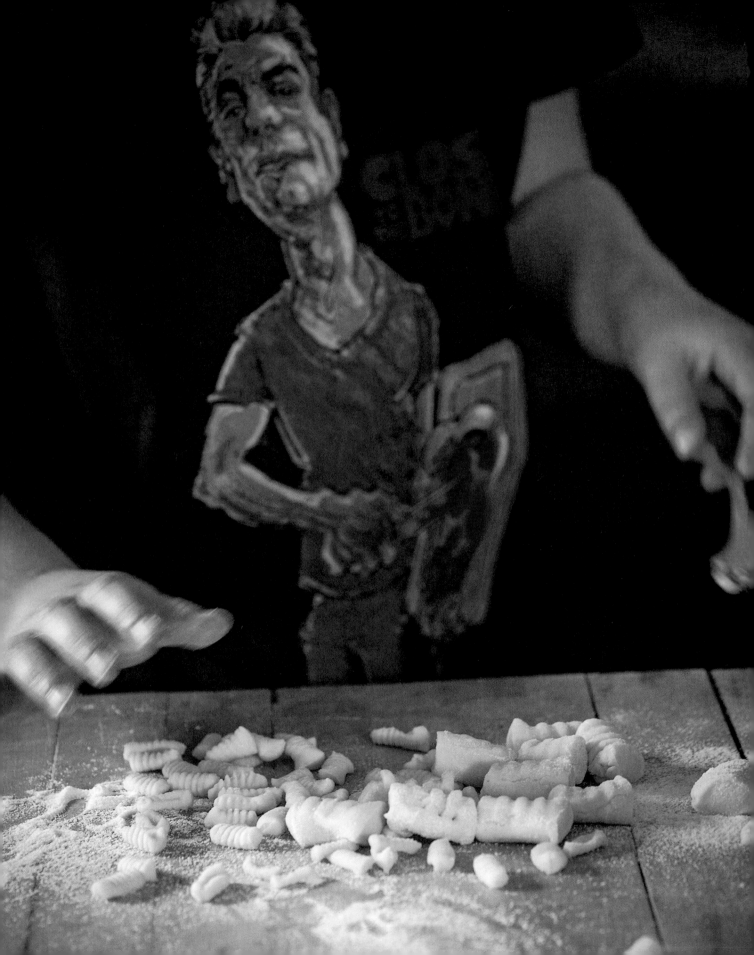

MALLOREDDUS WITH WILD BOAR SUGO

As much as I'm enjoying having married into a large Italian family, I'm even more delighted about the Sardinian wing of the family on my father-in-law's side. They live in a compound in the mountains, and they all carry knives—pretty much the picture of the perfect family to me.

When I met them for the first time, the whole bunch set to work killing me slowly with hospitality and glorious, glorious food. The greatest hits of Sardinian classics.

This dish is as traditional as it gets—and was a highlight of that first visit.

Note that the *sugo* recipe as written below is designed to leave you with extra sauce, to stash in the freezer or to send home with a particularly favored guest.

In a Dutch oven, heat the oil over medium heat until it shimmers. Add the meat, working in batches if necessary to avoid overcrowding the pan—there should be no more than a single layer of meat in the Dutch oven at one time, with a margin of space between the pieces. Brown the meat on all sides and remove to a plate as it is done.

Return all the meat to the Dutch oven and add the onion, garlic, and rosemary. Season with salt. Stir to incorporate the ingredients and gently scrape the bottom of the pan with a wooden spoon to dislodge some browned bits. After a few minutes, add the wine, stirring and scraping again; the liquid will help fully dissolve and dislodge the browned bits at the bottom. Cook over high heat until the wine has evaporated, then add just enough water to cover the mixture. As soon as the water boils, reduce the heat to a simmer, cover, and cook slowly for about 3 hours, stirring occasionally, until the meat is very tender and falling apart. Remove and discard the rosemary stems. Keep warm if serving with pasta on the same day, or refrigerate and gently rewarm on

$\longrightarrow$

FOR THE WILD BOAR SUGO

¼ cup extra-virgin olive oil

2 pounds boneless wild boar, cut into ½-inch chunks

1 white or yellow onion, peeled and finely chopped

1 garlic clove, peeled

4 sprigs fresh rosemary

Salt to taste

1 cup Vernaccia di Oristano (Sardinian white wine)

FOR THE PASTA AND TO SERVE

1 cup warm water

1 teaspoon salt, plus more for the pasta water

2 cups semolina flour, plus more for dusting

Freshly grated Sardinian pecorino or Parmigiano-Reggiano cheese, to taste

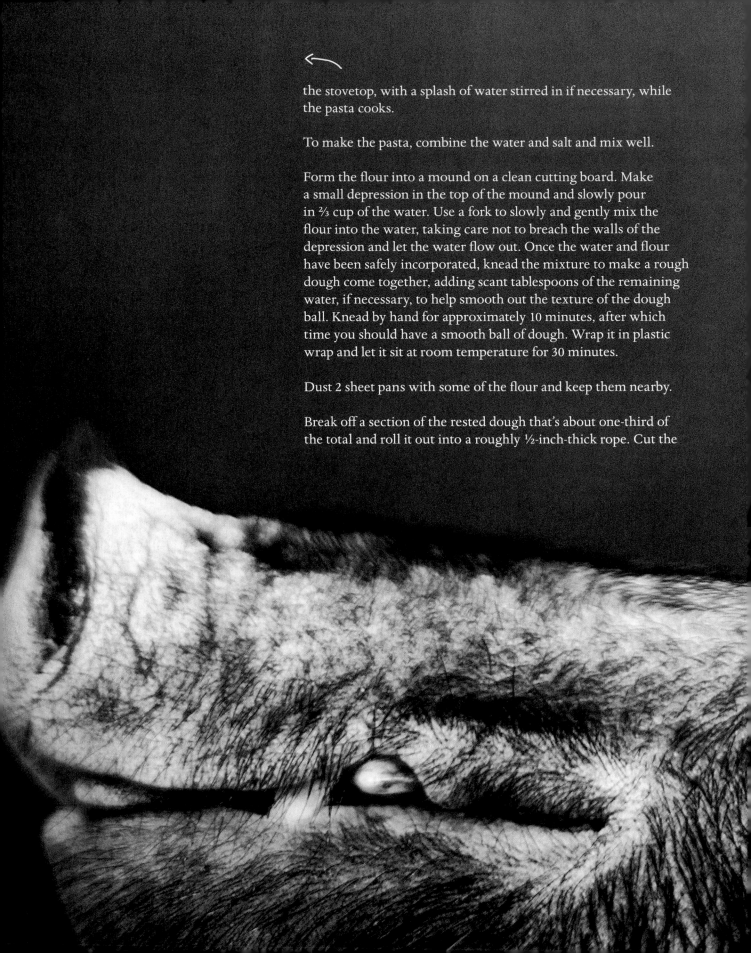

the stovetop, with a splash of water stirred in if necessary, while the pasta cooks.

To make the pasta, combine the water and salt and mix well.

Form the flour into a mound on a clean cutting board. Make a small depression in the top of the mound and slowly pour in ⅔ cup of the water. Use a fork to slowly and gently mix the flour into the water, taking care not to breach the walls of the depression and let the water flow out. Once the water and flour have been safely incorporated, knead the mixture to make a rough dough come together, adding scant tablespoons of the remaining water, if necessary, to help smooth out the texture of the dough ball. Knead by hand for approximately 10 minutes, after which time you should have a smooth ball of dough. Wrap it in plastic wrap and let it sit at room temperature for 30 minutes.

Dust 2 sheet pans with some of the flour and keep them nearby.

Break off a section of the rested dough that's about one-third of the total and roll it out into a roughly ½-inch-thick rope. Cut the rope into ½-inch pieces. Use your thumb to lightly press and roll each piece across a fork (or, if you have one, the grooved Sardinian pasta tool called a *ciurili*); gently form it into an elongated shell shape. As you finish each piece, transfer it to the prepared sheet trays to dry at room temperature for 1 hour.

Begin to gently reheat the sauce, and in a large, heavy-bottom pot, bring salted water to a boil. Gently transfer the pasta to the boiling water and cook until tender, 6 to 8 minutes. (Fresh pasta cooks more quickly than dried, packaged pasta, but fresh pasta made from semolina flour cooks more slowly than that made from all-purpose or Tipo "00" flour.)

Drain the pasta in a colander and discard the cooking water. Return the pasta to the hot pot and add the hot *sugo*. Using tongs or a wooden spoon, gently toss to coat the pasta with the *sugo*, and serve immediately, garnished with grated cheese.

Serves 6 to 8

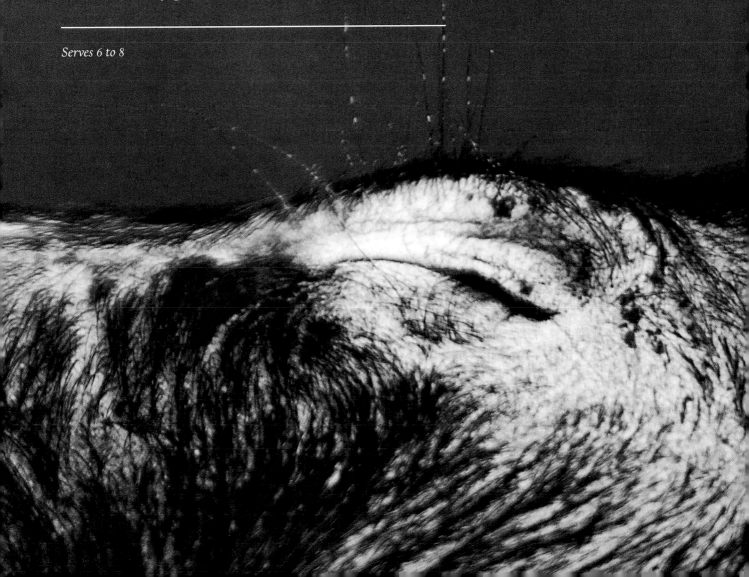

LASAGNE BOLOGNESE

It's a myth that you need to boil fresh or dried lasagne noodles before baking the whole thing, but what *is* true is that lasagne is better the second day when it has settled, so if you have the time, I recommend making this a day before you plan to serve it.

3 tablespoons olive oil

1 large white or yellow onion, peeled and finely chopped

2 large or 3 medium carrots, peeled and finely chopped

3 ribs celery, finely chopped

4 garlic cloves, peeled and finely chopped

½ teaspoon fresh thyme leaves

Salt and freshly ground black pepper to taste

½ pound chicken livers, trimmed of connective tissue and fat and finely chopped

¾ pound ground beef chuck

¾ pound ground veal

¾ pound ground pork

¾ cup tomato paste (about 6 ounces)

1 cup Vermentino, Trebbiano, or other Tuscan white wine

1½ cups whole milk

2 bay leaves

4 cups Béchamel Sauce (page 273)

¾ cup finely grated Parmigiano-Reggiano cheese

1 pound dry flat lasagne noodles

6 ounces fresh mozzarella cheese, very thinly sliced

To make the Bolognese sauce, heat 2 tablespoons of the olive oil in a medium, heavy-bottom pot over medium-high heat. Add the onion, carrots, celery, garlic, and thyme and season with salt and pepper. Cook, stirring regularly with a wooden spoon, until the vegetables are tender and have released their juices, 7 to 9 minutes. Stir in the livers and cook over high heat for 2 minutes, then add the beef, veal, and pork, stirring and breaking up over high heat. Season again with salt and pepper. Continue to cook over high heat until the meat is brown, stirring regularly and scraping the bottom of the pot as necessary to keep the meat and vegetables from scorching.

Once the meat is browned, stir in the tomato paste over medium heat. Let cook for about 20 minutes, stirring regularly. Add the wine, bring to a boil, and let cook until reduced by half, then add the milk and bay leaves and bring to a boil. Reduce the heat to a simmer and cook for 1½ to 2 hours, stirring occasionally. You may need to add a bit of water (or chicken or veal stock, if you have it) if the sauce seems to require it.

Taste the sauce and season with salt and pepper if necessary. Remove from the heat and stir to release steam and allow it to cool slightly. Skim the fat off the top with a ladle and discard.

Preheat the oven to 350°F.

Coat the inside of a 9 x 13-inch (or similar size) baking dish with the remaining 1 tablespoon oil. Cover the bottom of the dish with a layer of béchamel. Sprinkle some Parmigiano-Reggiano cheese atop the béchamel. Top it with a layer of noodles. Top the noodles with a layer of Bolognese sauce, and repeat with the béchamel, grated cheese, noodles, and Bolognese until the pan is full to the top. The top layer should be Bolognese, dotted with béchamel, with thin slices of mozzarella laid across the top. ⟶

Place the baking dish on a sheet pan and bake in the oven for about 50 minutes, until the lasagne is browned on top and beginning to bubble. Remove from the oven and let cool. If you must serve it the day you've made it, let it rest for 15 minutes before slicing. For best results, let cool completely overnight. The next day, reheat at 350°F, covered loosely with foil, until bubbling. Remove from the oven, let rest 20 minutes, then serve.

Serves 8 to 10

SPAGHETTI WITH GARLIC, ANCHOVIES, AND PARSLEY

This is a super-easy pasta that, with a well-stocked pantry and fridge, you should be able to start and finish inside of 15 minutes.

In a large, heavy-bottom pot, bring salted water to a boil.

In a medium or large sauté pan, warm the oil over medium-low heat. Add the garlic, pepper flakes, and anchovies, make sure they are well distributed so that everything is in the oil, and cook slowly, stirring occasionally with a wooden spoon, until the garlic is fragrant and the anchovies are melting into the oil. Monitor the heat carefully; you don't want burned or even browned garlic here.

Once the water is boiling, add the spaghetti and cook according to the package instructions until just al dente. Just before taking the pasta from the water, add the parsley to the sauté pan and toss gently. Remove the pasta from the water with tongs and add it directly to the pan—the water that clings to it will help form the sauce. Toss the pasta well with the pan ingredients, increasing the heat to medium. Add a small splash each of oil and pasta cooking water to keep everything slick. Taste a strand of pasta and season with salt as necessary. Transfer the pasta to individual serving bowls and top each with grated Parmigiano-Reggiano or serve it alongside.

¼ cup best-quality extra-virgin olive oil, plus more to taste

6 garlic cloves, peeled and thinly sliced

½ teaspoon red pepper flakes

8 oil-packed anchovy fillets, rinsed, drained, and patted dry

1 pound dry spaghetti

1 cup fresh Italian parsley leaves

Salt to taste

½ cup freshly grated Parmigiano-Reggiano cheese, plus more to taste

Serves 4 to 6

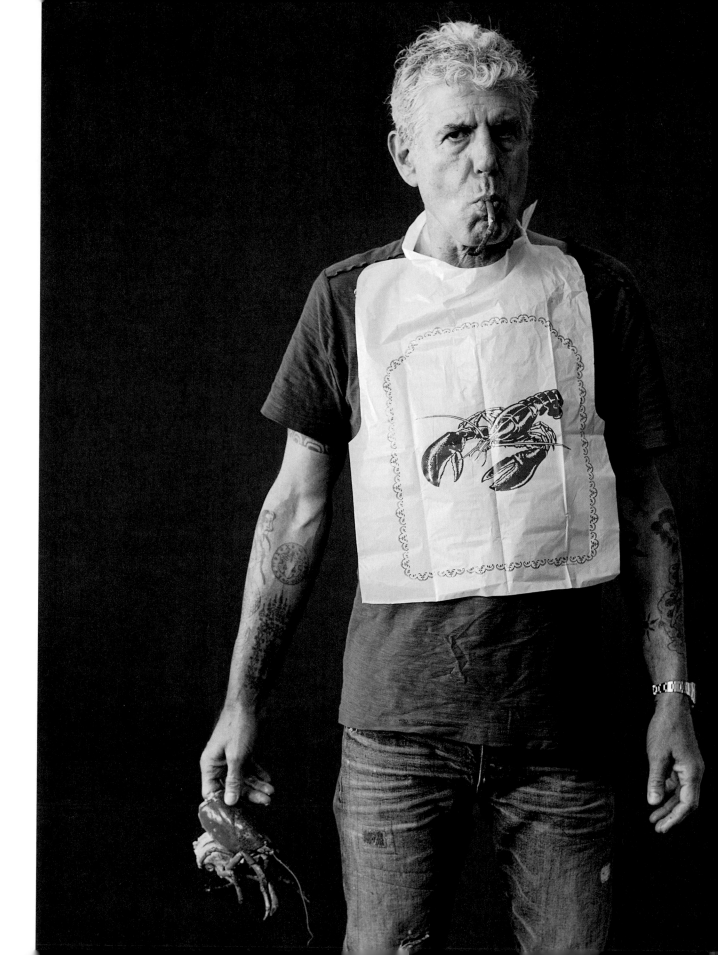

RAVIOLI OF SALT COD WITH LOBSTER SAUCE

I got a lot of mileage out of this dish back when I worked at Coco Pazzo Teatro (my first and last job as the chef of a high-quality Italian restaurant). It was a riff on something Scott Bryan was doing for a while back in the day at his restaurant Indigo. The original inspiration is lost in the fog of the eighties, but this? This shall live forever.

Place the cod in a large mixing bowl and cover by at least an inch with cold water. Soak the cod for 24 hours, to rehydrate and to reduce the intense saltiness that has preserved it to this point. You must change the water once an hour for the first few hours, and then, ideally, every few hours after that. In a perfect world, you'll start the dish in the morning or afternoon, and finish it the following morning or afternoon. And no, you won't have to interrupt your sleep to continue changing out the water, as long as you've taken care with it in the beginning.

Remove the fish from the water, pat it dry, and set aside.

In a large, heavy-bottom stockpot, combine 1 cup of the cream, the thyme, parsley sprigs, bay leaf, and garlic and bring to a boil. Add the cod and reduce the heat to a simmer. Cook for 5 to 8 minutes, then remove the fish with a slotted spoon and transfer it to a clean bowl. Once it's cool enough to handle, shred it finely, using very clean hands. Fold in the lobster knuckles and any odd bits, holding back the claws and tails for the main event.

Return the cream mixture to a boil, then reduce the heat to a high simmer to cook for 10 to 15 minutes, which should thicken up the mixture nicely. Strain it through a sieve into a clean bowl, stir in the oil, and set aside until it has cooled to room temperature, then slowly introduce the cream mixture to the shredded cod, mixing it in with the wooden spoon. This will be your ravioli filling, which should be moist enough to be appealing but not so moist that it will soak through a thin sheet of pasta. Taste the mixture, season with salt and pepper, then fold in the chopped parsley. $\longrightarrow$

1 pound salt cod

1¼ cups heavy cream

2 sprigs fresh thyme

2 sprigs fresh parsley

1 bay leaf

8 garlic cloves, crushed

1 lobster (about 2 pounds), steamed, shelled, and separated into its parts (see page 81)

¾ cup extra-virgin olive oil

Salt and freshly ground black pepper to taste

2 tablespoons finely chopped parsley leaves

¼ cup all-purpose flour, or more as needed

1 pound Fresh Pasta Dough, rolled into sheets (recipe follows)

½ cup semolina flour, or more as needed

2 tablespoons (¼ stick) unsalted butter

2 shallots, peeled and finely chopped

½ cup dry white wine

1½ cups Shellfish Stock (page 264)

Finely chopped fresh chives, for garnish

Lightly dust a clean, dry wooden cutting board or other work surface with all-purpose flour and set out one sheet of pasta on it. Dust a sheet pan with the semolina flour and keep it close at hand. Place about 1 tablespoon of the filling at even intervals, about 2 inches apart, across the sheet of pasta, then top this with a second sheet of pasta, pressing gently down around the filling lumps to form your ravioli. Cut around them, using a pasta cutter or chef's knife, and stash each raviolo on the sheet pan.

Fill the large pot, which you have washed, of course, with heavily salted water and bring it to a boil.

Cut the lobster tail and claws into large chunks.

While you wait for the water to come to a boil, heat 1 tablespoon of the butter in a large, heavy-bottom sauté pan over medium-high heat until it foams and subsides. Add the shallots and cook until just translucent, about 2 minutes. Stir in the wine and reduce by half, then add the stock and reduce until the mixture just barely coats the back of the wooden spoon. Stir in the remaining ¼ cup cream, taste, and adjust the seasoning. Add the chunks of lobster and remove the sauce from the heat a minute while you turn your attention to the ravioli.

Your water should be boiling by this point. Gently add the ravioli to the boiling water, separating them if they stick together, and cook until they float to the top, 3 to 5 minutes. Return your sauce to medium heat, and as they surface, use a slotted spoon to transfer the ravioli and the remaining 1 tablespoon butter to the sauce, agitating frequently to get them coated in the sauce. Taste and readjust seasoning if necessary. Serve at once, garnished with chives.

Serves 4 to 6

Fresh Pasta Dough

Mound the flour on a clean wooden, marble or plastic cutting board or other work surface and make a well in the center. Add the eggs, yolks, oil, and salt to the well. Use a wooden spoon or a fork to slowly incorporate the flour into the egg mixture to form a dough, taking care not to let the wet ingredients leak out of the well.

Once the dough is a single cohesive mass, knead it for at least 10 and up to 15 minutes, adding small amounts of flour to the work surface or hands as needed. (You may also choose to outsource this process to a stand mixer fitted with the dough hook attachment.)

Wrap the dough in plastic wrap and refrigerate for at least 30 minutes.

When you're ready to roll out the dough, remove it from the refrigerator, unwrap it, and let it come back to nearly room temperature. Cut it into four pieces. Run each piece through the pasta rolling machine, starting with the widest setting and folding the dough into thirds after each pass; dust it lightly with flour as necessary to keep it smooth and not sticky. Roll each piece through increasingly narrow openings in the pasta roller until you have reached the desired thickness (which should be quite thin for lasagne or ravioli). Set each rolled out piece on a sheet pan, between layers of parchment paper, to keep it from drying out. Cut into desired shapes.

Makes about 1 pound dough

2 cups all-purpose flour (about 10 ounces), plus more as needed for dusting work surface and rolled pasta

2 large eggs
3 large egg yolks
2 teaspoons olive oil
1 teaspoon salt

SPECIAL EQUIPMENT

Stand mixer with dough hook attachment (optional, if you choose not to knead by hand)

Pasta rolling machine or stand mixer with pasta-rolling attachment

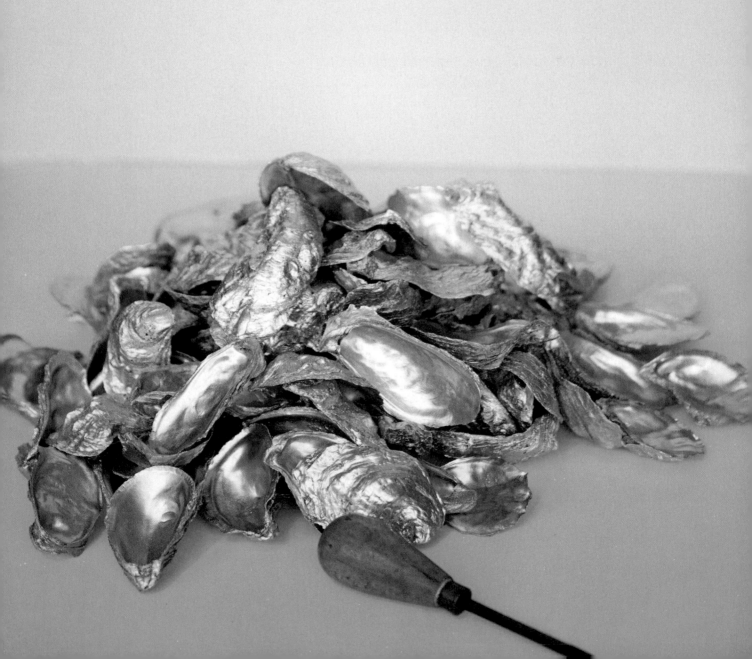

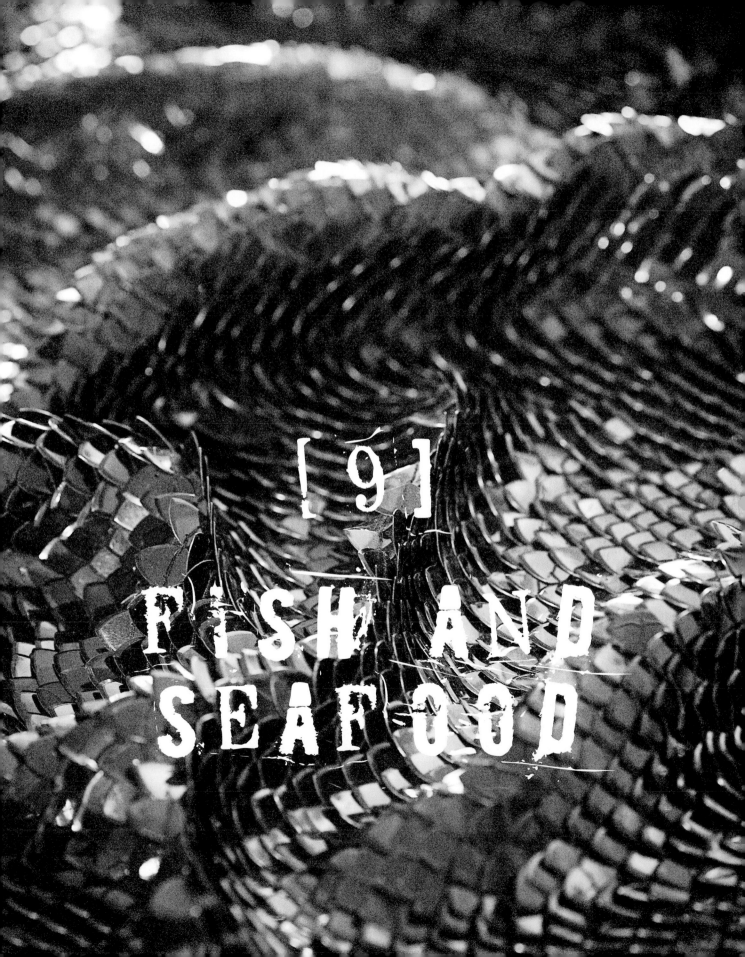

[9]

FISH AND
SEAFOOD

BLUEFISH IN TOMATO VINAIGRETTE

Juice of 1 lemon (about
   2 tablespoons)

3 tablespoons best-quality extra-
   virgin olive oil

1½ to 2 pounds bluefish fillets, cut
   into 4 portions

Salt and freshly ground black
   pepper to taste

2 shallots, peeled and thinly sliced

3 large ripe red tomatoes, any
   variety, cored and seeded

2 tablespoons sherry vinegar

1 teaspoon fresh thyme leaves

Oh, much maligned bluefish!

Perennially ignored by both restaurants and home cooks alike.

The ugly girl at the prom.

Rise up!

Bluefish is fun to catch but largely shunned by diners. I was introduced to it in Provincetown, where it was all over the menu at places favored by locals. We had it at my restaurant, but it never sold. I'd eat it steak cut, across the bone, at Tips for Tops'n restaurant, an affordable family joint around the corner from our summer rental.

I've been hoping for decades that bluefish catches on as "the next big thing." And I've been disappointed. Considered too perishable, it requires decisive yet delicate handling immediately after being caught to remove the blood line and dark red muscle running along its spine. But if bought fresh—and cooked very soon after—it's really one of the great fish experiences.

Preheat the broiler and set the oven rack so that the fish will be 4 to 6 inches from the broiler element.

In a small mixing bowl, whisk together the lemon juice and 1 tablespoon of the olive oil. Season the fish with salt and pepper and place it in a glass or ceramic casserole dish, skin side down, and pour this mixture over the fish, making sure that it's evenly distributed over the surface. Scatter the shallots over the fish and let sit for 20 minutes.

Meanwhile, grate the flesh of the tomatoes on the large-holed side of a box grater and transfer to a medium mixing bowl. Add the vinegar, the remaining 2 tablespoons oil, and the thyme. Season with salt and pepper, whisk together, taste, and adjust seasoning as desired.

Transfer the fish to a broiler pan, leaving the shallots intact, and broil for about 10 minutes, until the center of the thickest part is just barely translucent. Remove from the oven, transfer to a serving platter, drizzle with the tomato vinaigrette, and serve immediately.

Serves 4

CLAMS with CHORIZO LEEKS, TOMATO, AND WHITE WINE

2 tablespoons olive oil

6 ounces best-quality fresh chorizo, thinly sliced

1 large or 2 medium leeks (white parts only), trimmed and sliced (about 2½ cups)

4 garlic cloves, peeled and finely chopped, plus 2 garlic cloves, peeled and cut in half

Salt and freshly ground black pepper to taste

1 cup dry white wine

1 (28-ounce) can crushed tomatoes

4 dozen littleneck clams, scrubbed

4 thick slices crusty sourdough bread

You need the fresh, soft, fiery red version of chorizo for this dish, the kind that bleeds out bright red-orange grease into the pot when you heat it.

In a large sauté pan, heat 1 tablespoon of the oil over medium-high heat, then add the chorizo and cook, stirring with a wooden spoon, until the chorizo has rendered its fat and is crisp and browned at the edges, 5 to 7 minutes. Add the remaining 1 tablespoon oil, the leeks, and chopped garlic and stir to coat the vegetables with the oil. Season with salt and pepper and continue to cook until the vegetables are tender, about 5 minutes. Stir in the wine, increase the heat to high, and cook until the wine is reduced by half. Add the tomatoes and let the mixture come to a high boil. Add the clams, working in batches if necessary to ensure that they're in a single layer. Cover the pan and cook until the clams have opened. Discard any unopened clams.

While the clams cook, toast the bread, then rub the surface of each piece of bread with the cut sides of one of the remaining two garlic cloves.

Serve the hot clam mixture in a shallow serving bowl with the garlic toast alongside.

_____

Serves 4

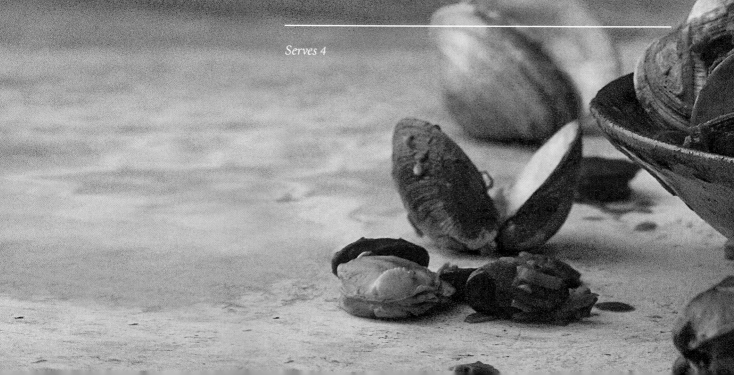

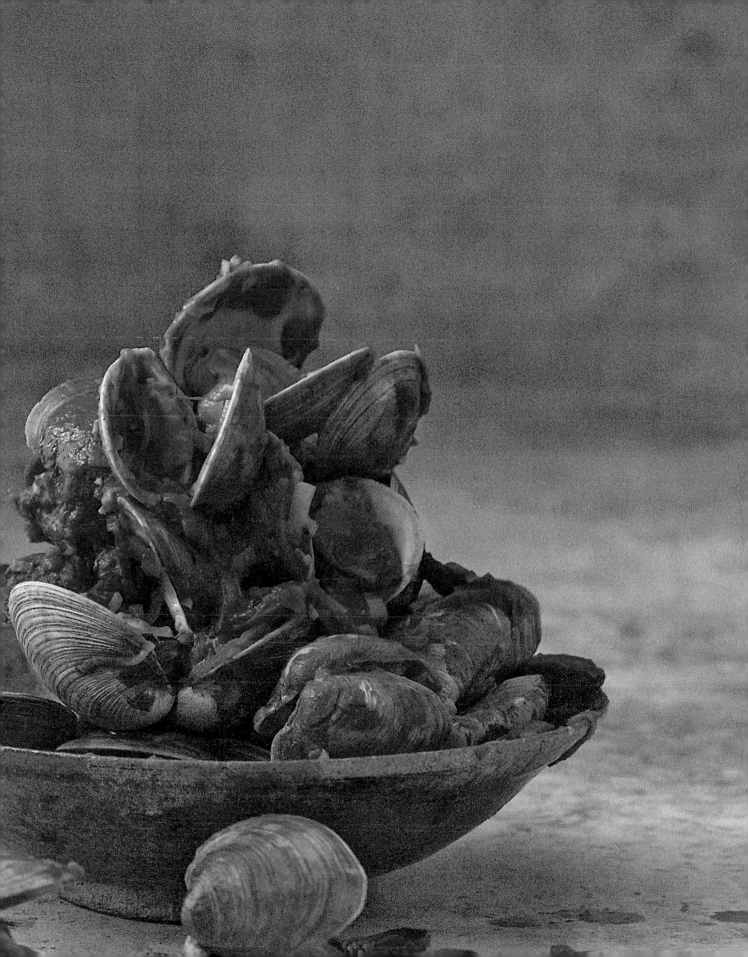

HALIBUT POACHED IN DUCK FAT

1 lemon

1 tablespoon canola or other neutral oil

1 tablespoon fennel seeds

Seeds from 2 cardamom pods

1 bay leaf

4 garlic cloves, peeled and sliced

2 halibut fillets (about 12 ounces each; ask your fishmonger to remove the white belly skin but to leave the dark dorsal skin attached)

Salt and freshly ground black pepper to taste

1 quart rendered duck fat (available at various gourmet retailers and some butcher shops)

Mashed potatoes (page 196)

SPECIAL EQUIPMENT

Microplane grater

Instant-read thermometer

This is a dead-easy recipe; the hardest part is the shopping.

Using the microplane grater, finely grate the lemon zest into a small mixing bowl and add the oil, fennel and cardamom seeds, bay leaf, and garlic, mixing well. Rub the fish on all sides with the mixture and refrigerate in a casserole or zip-sealed plastic bag for at least 2 hours and up to 24.

Remove the fish from the refrigerator about 15 minutes before you're ready to poach it. Brush off the excess garlic and seeds. Season it on all sides with salt and pepper. In a large, heavy-bottom pot, heat the duck fat over medium heat until it reaches 150°F, monitoring the temperature with the instant-read thermometer. Slip the fish into the pot and ladle the fat over so it is submerged. Let cook for 5 minutes, then remove from the heat, cover, and let sit for 10 to 15 minutes, until the fish has an internal temperature of 150°F.

Carefully remove the fish from the pot with a slotted spoon or fish spatula, adjust seasoning if necessary, and serve with mashed potatoes.

Serves 4

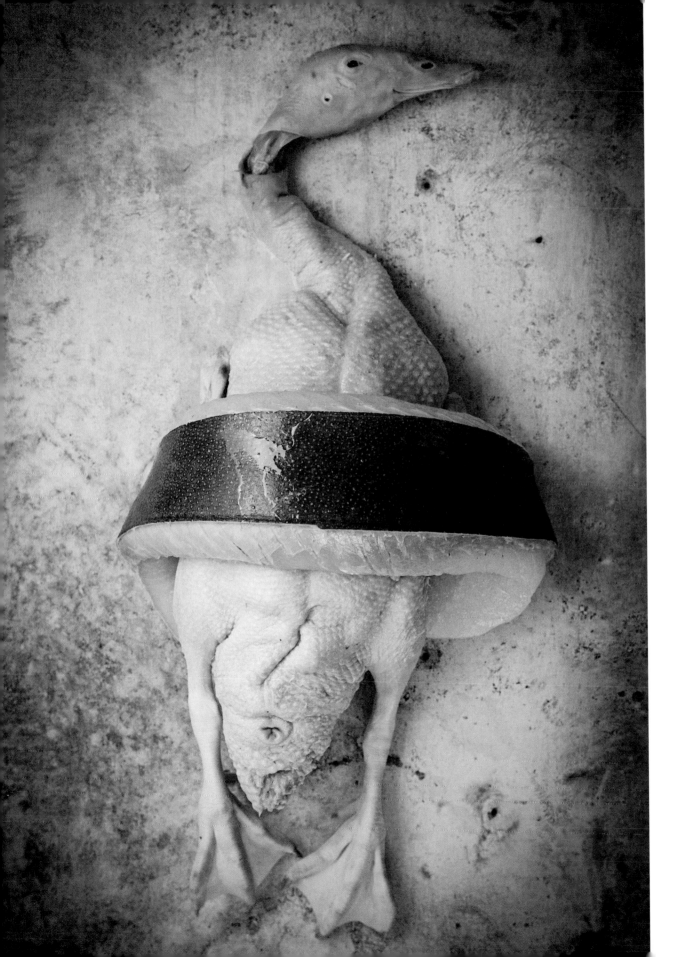

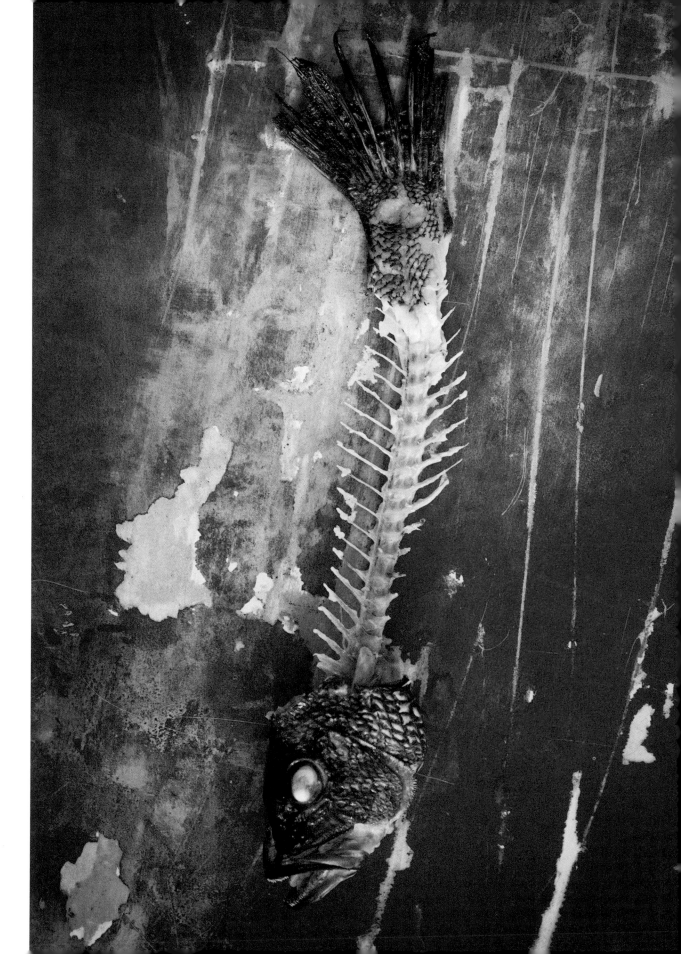

WHOLE ROASTED WILD BLACK SEABASS

If you suffer from even a modicum of performance anxiety, present this glorious thing whole to impress your guests, then take it back to the kitchen to fillet it in private.

Preheat the oven to 500°F.

Using kitchen shears, snip off and discard all of the seabass fins. Rinse the fish well under cold water and pat dry. Rub each fish inside and out with 1 tablespoon of the oil and season inside and out with salt and pepper. Place one or more sprigs of oregano and thyme, and a lemon slice or two, inside the cavity of each fish. Arrange the onion slices in a single layer on the bottom of a roasting pan so that they act like a rack for the fish. Arrange a layer of herbs and lemon slices atop the onions, then place the fish on top of this. Top the fish with a final layer of herbs and lemon slices, drizzle with the remaining 2 tablespoons oil, and cover tightly with foil.

Roast in the oven for 20 to 24 minutes. Look inside the cavity of one of the fish to make sure it's cooked through—the instant-read thermometer, inserted at the thickest part, should read 130°F. If it's slightly under, return the fish to the oven for 5 minutes, but turn it off, so that it continues to cook slowly and doesn't get dried out.

Remove from the oven and present the fish on a serving platter with all its herb and lemon garnish. In the dining room or, preferably, in the kitchen, fillet the fish: First, pull off and discard any visible remaining fin bones. Then, working on the fish one side at a time, slice through the skin and flesh, down to the bone, right behind the head and just above the tail. Starting from the head, work your knife down and under the fillet, then run your knife along the length of the spine, beneath the cooked flesh, before gently lifting the fillet off and onto the serving platter. Turn the fish and repeat on the other side. Season each fillet with additional salt, pepper, oil, and/or lemon juice. Serve with steamed new potatoes and rosé.

2 whole wild black seabass (1 to 1½ pounds each), gutted and scaled

4 tablespoons extra-virgin olive oil

Salt and freshly ground black pepper to taste

1 bunch of fresh oregano

½ bunch of fresh thyme

1 lemon, thinly sliced

1 white onion, peeled and cut into ¼-inch-thick slices

1 pound new potatoes, steamed

SPECIAL EQUIPMENT

Instant-read thermometer

Serves 2 to 4

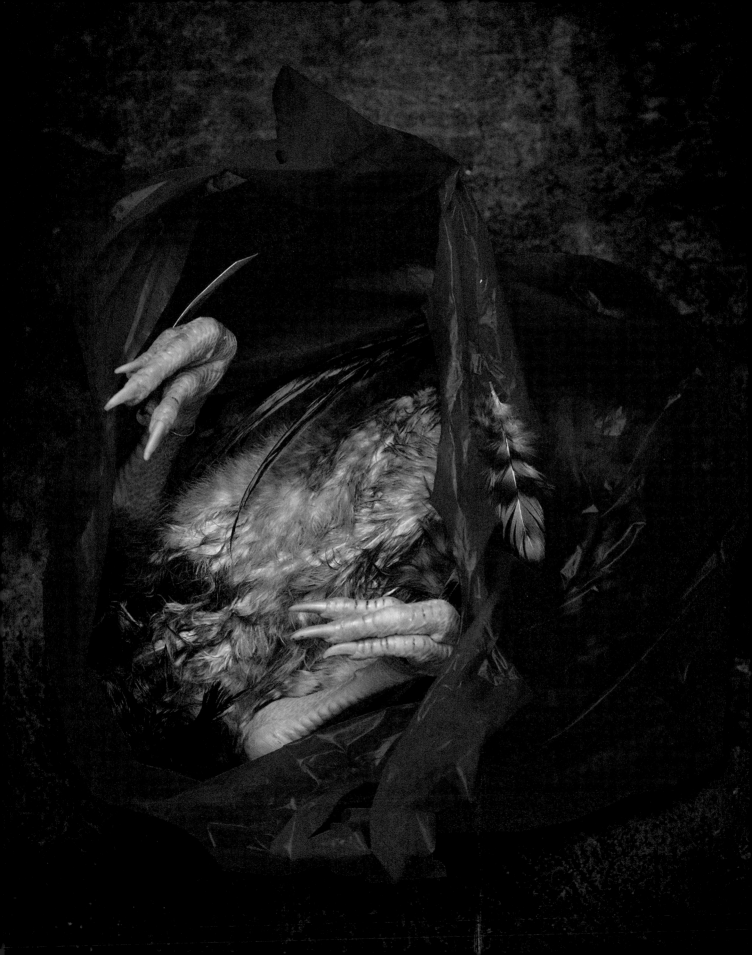

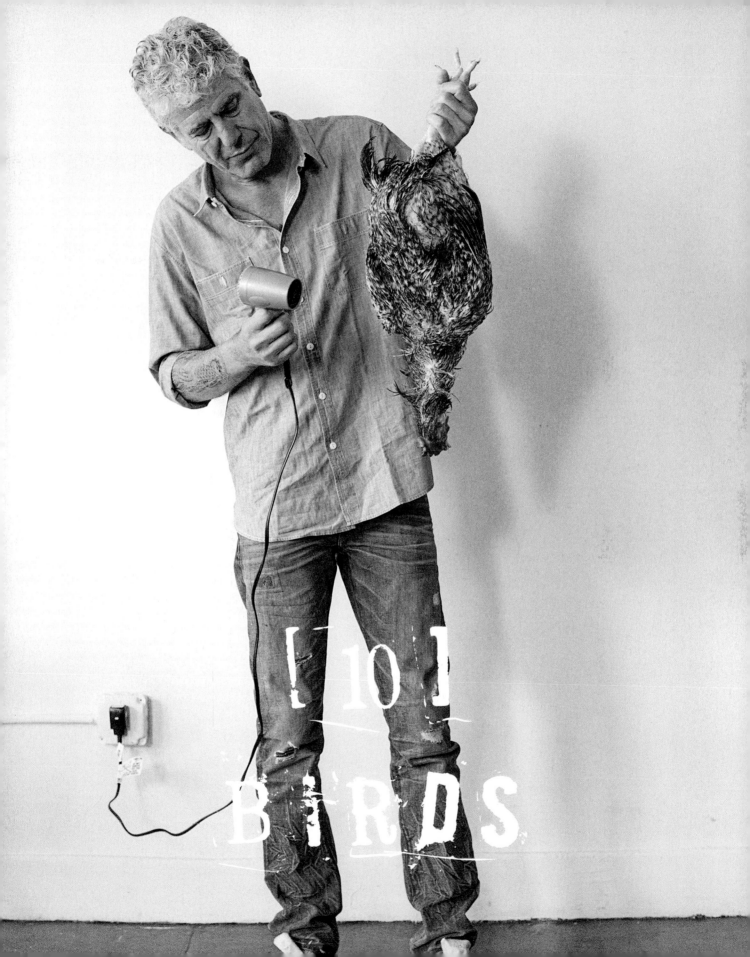

[10]

BIRDS

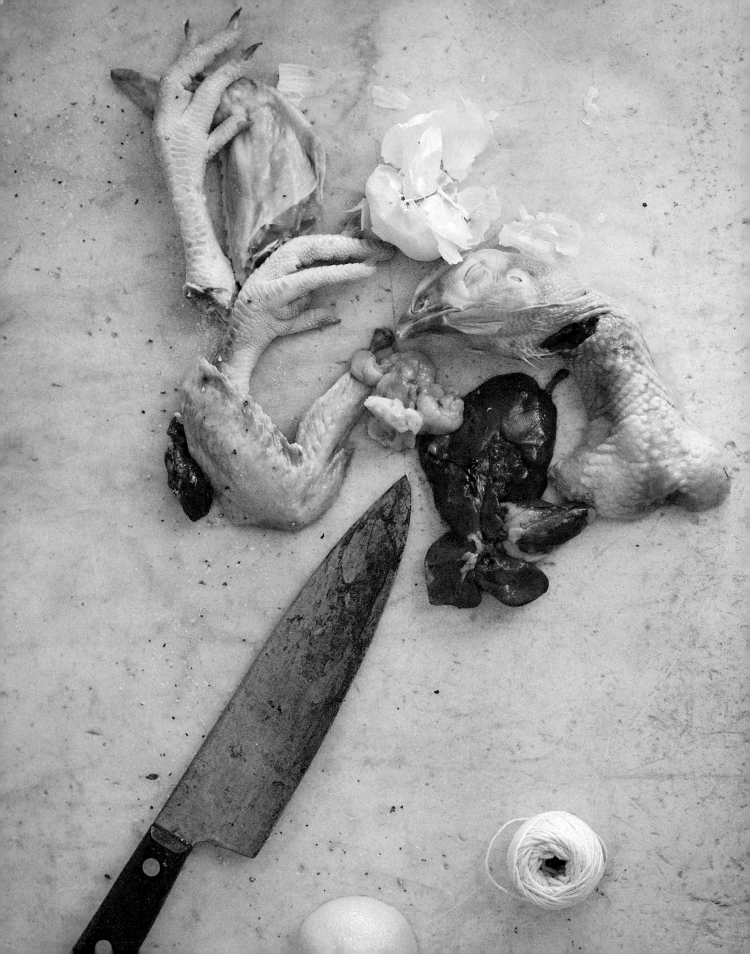

ROAST CHICKEN WITH LEMON AND BUTTER

Everyone should know how to roast a chicken. It's a life skill that should be taught to small children at school. The ability to properly prepare a moist yet thoroughly cooked bird, with nicely crisp skin, should be a hallmark of good citizenry—an obligation to your fellow man. Everyone walking down the street should be reasonably confident that the random person next to them is prepared, if called upon, to roast a chicken.

It seems like a simple thing. Yet there's a reason this task was a traditional test of a new cook's basic skills when auditioning for the great kitchens of Europe. It's as easy, if not easier, to fuck it up as to do it right.

Respect the chicken!

Preheat the oven to 450°F.

Rub the bird inside and out with salt and crushed peppercorns. Stuff two ½-tablespoon knobs of butter under the skin of each side of the breast. Stuff the thyme, bay leaf, and lemon wedges into the chicken's cavity.

Use the tip of a paring knife to poke a small hole in the skin just below each of the chicken's legs, and tuck each leg carefully into that hole. (You may also truss the chicken with butcher's twine if you know how, but this is much simpler.)

Place the chicken in a flame-proof roasting pan and roast for 30 to 40 minutes, rotating the pan, moving it to different parts of the oven to account for hot spots, and basting the bird two or three times with a bulb-top baster or long-handled metal spoon. Reduce the oven's heat to 300°F and continue to roast, basting frequently, for another 30 to 40 minutes or until the bird is done: When you poke the fat part of the thigh with the paring knife, the juices should run clear. ⟶

1 best-quality chicken (about 2½ pounds), preferably organic

Sea salt to taste

Crushed black peppercorns to taste

4 tablespoons (½ stick) unsalted butter

10 sprigs fresh thyme

1 fresh bay leaf

½ lemon, cut into 4 wedges

1 cup dry white wine

Juice of 1 lemon (about 2 tablespoons)

1½ cups chicken stock

¼ cup finely chopped fresh parsley

Freshly ground black pepper to taste

Pommes Anna (page 249)

SPECIAL EQUIPMENT

Butcher's twine (optional)

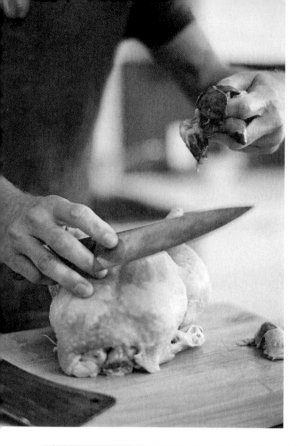

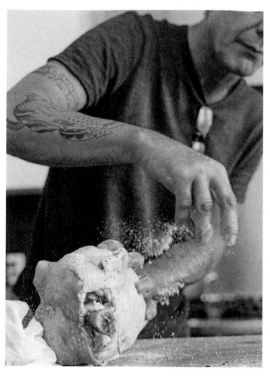

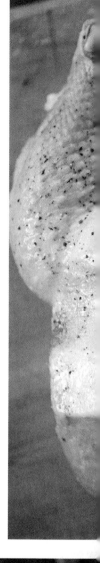

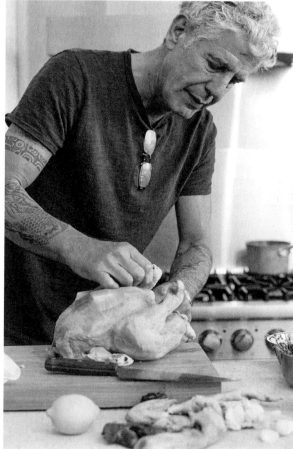

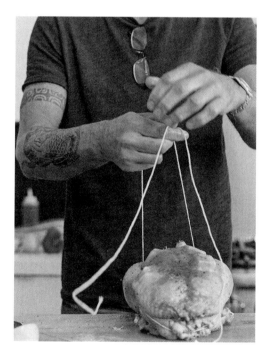

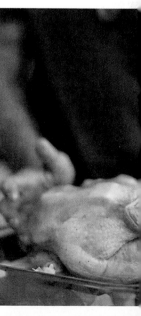

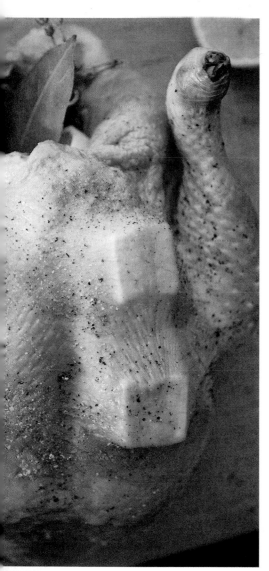

←

Remove the bird from the oven, let it rest 15 minutes, then remove the breasts and legs from the carcass, reserving everything. Use a ladle to skim off and discard as much surface fat from the pan juices as possible. Place the roasting pan on the stovetop over high heat and stir in the wine and lemon juice, scraping the bottom of the pan with a wooden spoon to dislodge and dissolve the browned bits. Bring this mixture to a boil and cook until it is reduced by half. Stir in the stock with the wooden spoon, bring to a boil, and reduce again by half. Remove from the heat and strain this sauce through a sieve into a medium, heavy-bottom saucepan over medium heat. Whisk in the remaining 2 tablespoons butter, a tablespoon at a time, until the sauce is thick and glossy. Fold in the parsley and adjust the seasoning with salt and pepper as necessary.

Serve the chicken—half of the breast plus a drumstick or a thigh per person—with the sauce ladled over, pommes Anna alongside, and any remaining sauce in a sauceboat on the table.

Serves 4

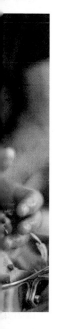

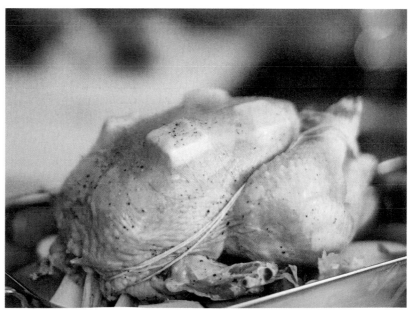

CHICKEN POT PIE

3 cups Dark Universal Stock (page 260) or chicken stock

3 pounds chicken thighs, with skin and bones, visible fat trimmed and discarded

Salt and freshly ground black pepper to taste

1 pound russet potatoes (about 3 large potatoes), peeled and diced

6 tablespoons (¾ stick) unsalted butter

8 pearl onions, peeled, trimmed, and quartered lengthwise

2 medium carrots, peeled and diced

2 ribs celery, diced

Leaves from 5 to 7 sprigs fresh thyme

4 to 8 fresh sage leaves, finely chopped

½ teaspoon celery salt

¼ cup all-purpose flour, plus more for dusting

1 cup whole milk

½ cup frozen sweet peas

1 batch Savory Pastry Dough (recipe follows), rolled to ¼-inch thickness

1 egg, beaten

The model, the Platonic ideal for this recipe, is the Horn & Hardart version. My dad worked two jobs in those days—managing Willoughby's camera store in Manhattan by day and being a floor manager at the nearby Sam Goody in the evenings. Sometimes my mom, my brother, and I would pick him up after work, and we'd go for late dinner at Horn & Hardart in the Garden State Plaza in Paramus, New Jersey. The chicken pot pie was delicious, though it never had enough chicken. This one addresses that problem.

In a medium, heavy-bottom saucepot, bring the stock to a boil, then reduce to a simmer and add the chicken. Poach the chicken in the stock for about 10 minutes, then remove from the heat, cover, and let sit for 25 to 30 minutes, until the chicken is cooked through. Remove the chicken from the stock with tongs; do not discard the stock. Once the chicken is cool enough to handle, remove and discard the skin and bones, and shred or coarsely chop the chicken, keeping large chunks mostly intact. Season the chicken with salt and pepper and set aside.

Preheat the oven to 400°F.

Add the potatoes to the warm stock and bring it back to a high simmer. Cook the potatoes in the stock for 5 to 8 minutes, until they are somewhat tender but not cooked through, as they will continue to cook in the oven. Remove from the stock with a slotted spoon and set aside with the chicken.

In a medium, heavy-bottom sauté pan, heat 2 tablespoons of the butter over medium-high heat until it foams and subsides. Add the onions, carrots, celery, thyme, sage, and celery salt and cook over medium heat until the vegetables are somewhat tender but not completely cooked through. Remove from the heat, season the vegetables with salt and pepper, and set aside with the chicken and potatoes.

Make sure you have both a whisk and a wooden spoon nearby, and something to rest them on. You will be switching back ⟶

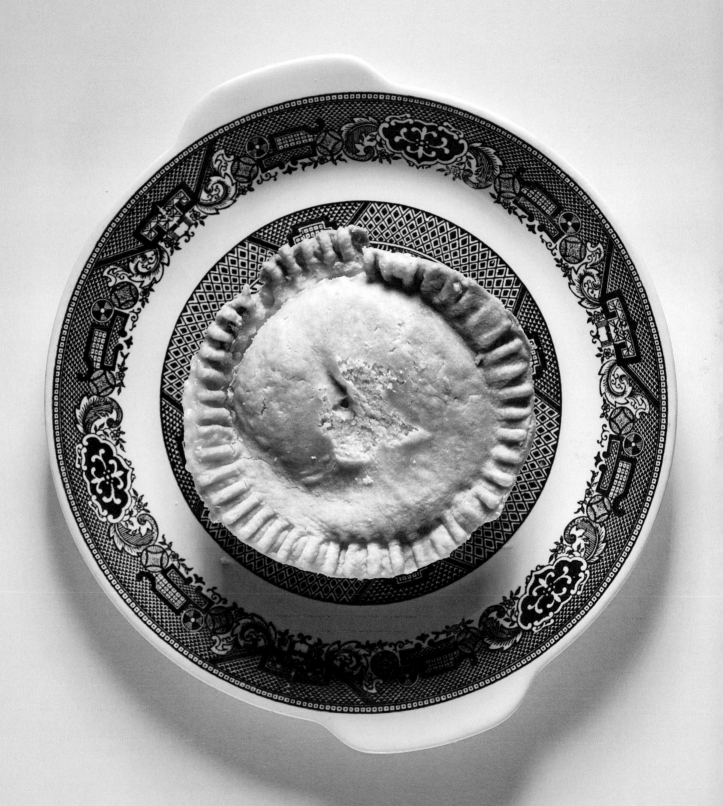

and forth between the two utensils as you first make a roux and then build on that to make a béchamel.

In a clean saucepot, heat the remaining 4 tablespoons butter until it foams and subsides, then stir in the flour with the wooden spoon and continue to cook and stir for 1 to 2 minutes, until the flour is slightly fragrant and just beginning to brown. Whisk in the milk and 1 cup of the reserved stock, whisking constantly to break up the flour and butter paste and quickly incorporate it into the milk. Switch to the wooden spoon and continue to stir, reaching all corners of the bottom of the pot to keep any flour from sticking and scorching, until the mixture is thick enough to coat the back of the spoon. Remove from the heat, season with salt and pepper, and stir in the reserved chicken, potatoes, cooked vegetables, and peas. Add a splash of the reserved stock if necessary to keep the matrix loose and liquid.

Transfer the mixture to a 9 x 13 (or similar size) baking dish and use a rolling pin to roll out the dough to roughly 10 × 14 inches, dusting liberally with flour. Roll the dough onto the rolling pin and carefully roll it out over the chicken mixture in the baking dish, folding over the edges and fluting with a fork. Cut four 1-inch slits in the top of the dough with a paring knife. Place the baking dish on a sheet pan and bake in the oven for 20 minutes, then remove from the oven and brush the dough with the beaten egg. Bake another 10 to 15 minutes, until the dough is golden brown and the liquid has begun to bubble and steam through the slits. Serve hot from the oven.

Serves 4 to 6

Savory Pastry Dough

Place the flour, salt, and butter in the bowl of the food processor and turn the machine on, processing until the ingredients form a cohesive whole. With the machine still running, add the water all at once; turn off the machine as soon as the dough binds and comes away from the sides of the bowl. Roll it all into a ball, wrap it in plastic wrap, and refrigerate for at least 1 hour, then roll out and bake as directed.

Makes one 10 × 14 crust

12 ounces (approximately 2⅓ cups) all-purpose flour

Pinch of salt

½ pound (2 sticks) cold unsalted butter, cut into small cubes

½ cup ice water

SPECIAL EQUIPMENT

Food processor

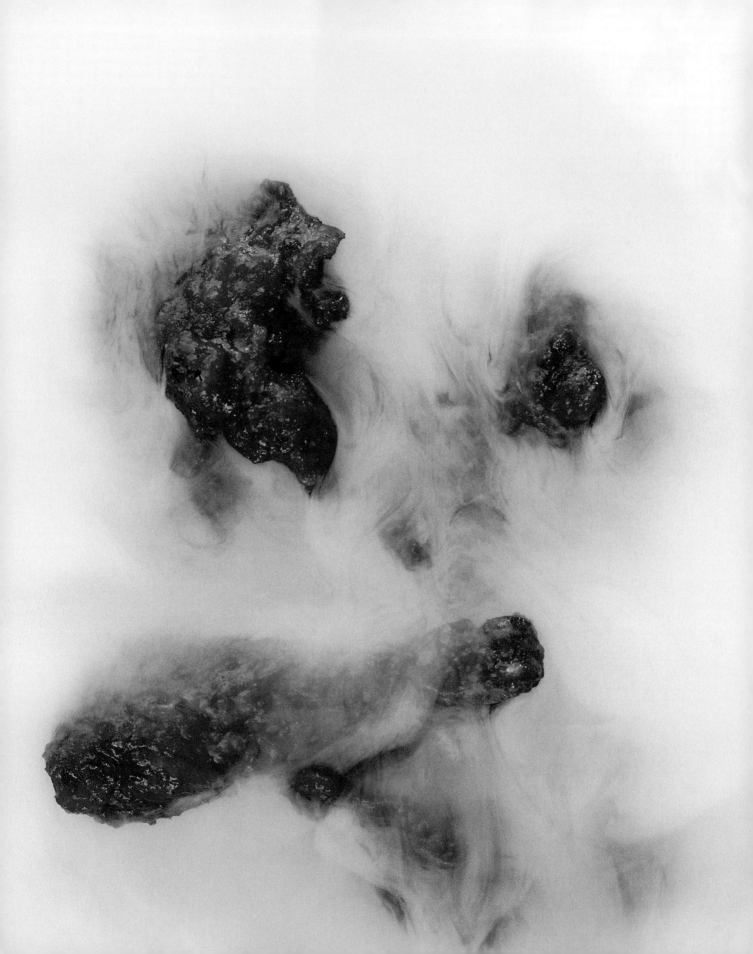

KOREAN FRIED CHICKEN

There are many ways to make tasty fried chicken, and I like them all, but I'm particularly enamored of the Korean way, which requires some planning ahead but is extremely satisfying. The blanching and freezing technique was lifted from Danny Bowien at Mission Chinese, who does this with his chicken wings. The freezing step makes this dish into a two-day affair, and you'll need to clear some room in your freezer, but it's essential for extra-crisp results.

In a large mixing bowl, whisk together the chili oil, salt, and *gochugaru*. Add the chicken and toss to coat with the marinade. Cover and refrigerate for at least 30 minutes and up to an hour.

Add frying oil to a large, deep, straight-sided frying pan (or other vessel suited to frying chicken) so that it is no more than half full. Bring to 300°F over medium heat, monitoring the temperature with a deep-fry thermometer.

Place the potato starch in a shallow bowl. Working in batches, remove the chicken from the marinade, letting the excess drip off, then toss into the potato starch to coat.

Set the cooling racks over each lined sheet pan.

Working in batches, carefully transfer the chicken to the hot oil. Blanch in the oil for 6 to 8 minutes per side, turning the chicken as necessary. The chicken should be opaque looking, and about 75 percent cooked through. (If you're unsure, cut into a piece of chicken to inspect the doneness from the inside.) Use tongs or a slotted spoon to remove the chicken to the cooling rack, and continue until all of the chicken has been blanched.

Once it is completely cool, transfer the chicken to a clean sheet pan (or remove the rack and discard the newspaper from one pan), wrap it tightly with plastic wrap, and freeze for 8 hours or overnight.

The next day, combine the *gochujang,* garlic, maple syrup, soy sauce, fish sauce, *cheongju,* hot sauce, and, if using, the MSG $\longrightarrow$

FOR THE MARINADE

1 cup roasted chili oil

¼ cup kosher salt

1 tablespoon medium/fine gochugaru (ground Korean red pepper)

FOR THE CHICKEN

4 pounds chicken legs, separated into thighs and drumsticks

About 4 quarts peanut or soy oil, for frying

1 cup potato starch or tapioca starch

FOR THE SAUCE

1 cup gochujang (fermented Korean pepper paste)

8 garlic cloves

½ cup pure maple syrup

1 tablespoon soy sauce

2 teaspoons fish sauce

¼ cup cheongju (Korean rice wine)

¼ cup Frank's RedHot sauce

2 teaspoons MSG (optional but recommended)

TO SERVE

Korean-Style Radish Pickles (page 251)

SPECIAL EQUIPMENT

Deep-fry or candy thermometer

2 sheet pans lined with newspaper

2 cooling racks, each
approximately the same size as
the sheet pans

Food processor or immersion
blender

in the food processor and blend well. This is the sauce that you
will brush the chicken with as it comes out of its finishing fry.

Pull the chicken from the freezer and unwrap it about 1 hour
before cooking.

Add frying oil to your pan or pot so that it is no more than half
full. Bring it to 350°F over medium heat, again monitoring the
temperature with the thermometer. Set up your lined sheet pans
with the cooling racks. Working in small batches, fry the chicken
for 10 to 12 minutes, rotating in the oil as needed, until golden
brown. Let drain and cool slightly on the cooling rack, then use
a pastry brush to coat each piece with the sauce. Serve with the
radish pickles and cold beer.

Serves 6 to 8

CAST-IRON GRILLED CHICKEN

Outdoor grills, and the space to operate them safely, are tough to come by in New York City, but anyone can use a cast-iron grill pan to get real char on their food. Chicken thighs are tender and forgiving, and don't necessarily require a marinade, so you could simply season them and throw them on a hot cast-iron grill with great results. However, the yogurt marinade here lets you add to the flavor with spices and herbs that would otherwise get scorched in cooking, and the texture of cooked chicken that's been marinated in yogurt reminds me of street meat, without the explosive diarrhea.

In a medium mixing bowl, whisk together the yogurt, olive oil, cumin, cardamom, oregano, and pepper. Place the chicken in a plastic zip-seal bag or nonreactive container with lid, and pour the yogurt mixture over, making sure each piece of chicken is evenly coated on all sides. Seal or cover and refrigerate for at least 2 hours and up to 24 hours.

Preheat the oven to 400°F (or if using an actual outdoor grill, light it).

Remove the chicken from the refrigerator and let it sit at room temperature for about 15 minutes. Rub a grill pan with 1 to 2 tablespoons canola oil, depending on its size. Begin to heat the grill pan over high heat; you'll know it's ready to go when you can see waves of heat shimmering off it. This would be a good time to turn on your kitchen vent and turn any other fans on.

Remove the chicken from the marinade, letting any excess drip off. Pat the chicken dry with paper towels and season it liberally with salt. Place on the hot grill pan and let cook, undisturbed, for 6 to 7 minutes, so that it is distinctly grill marked. Using tongs, turn the chicken to cook on the other side for about 5 minutes, then transfer the chicken, still on the grill pan, to the hot oven to finish cooking for about 10 minutes. The internal temperature should be 150°F at the thickest part. Remove from the oven, let rest for a few minutes, then serve, sliced or whole, with hot sauce if desired.

1½ cups plain whole milk yogurt

¼ cup olive oil

1 tablespoon ground cumin

15 cardamom pods, crushed

1 tablespoon dried oregano

1 teaspoon freshly ground black pepper

2 to 2½ pounds boneless, skinless chicken thighs

1 to 2 tablespoons canola or grapeseed oil, for brushing the grill

Salt to taste

Frank's RedHot sauce (optional)

SPECIAL EQUIPMENT

Cast-iron grill pan or grill

Instant-read thermometer

Serves 4 to 6

POULET "EN VESSIE": HOMMAGE À LA MÈRE BRAZIER

This is a riff on a French classic, perfected by the legendary Mère Brazier in Lyon. The original calls for a heavily truffled chicken to be painstakingly steamed inside an inflated pig bladder. As pig bladders are increasingly difficult to come by, I give you this alternate version.

It's a perfect combination of extravagant and austere. It's basically a steamed chicken, after all. But what a chicken!

If you don't fuck this up, it will impress the *shit* out of your guests.

1 small leek, white and light green parts only

1 medium carrot, peeled and cut into 3 pieces

1 rib celery, cut into 3 pieces

3 garlic cloves, peeled

1 cup dry white wine

1 sprig thyme

1 teaspoon salt, plus more to taste

1 teaspoon white peppercorns

4 black summer truffles

1 Bresse or other high-quality chicken (about 3½ pounds), preferably with feet intact, wing tips removed at the first joint

4 tablespoons (½ stick) unsalted butter

Freshly ground black pepper to taste

1 cup heavy cream

4 ounces foie gras

Freshly ground white peppercorns to taste

SPECIAL EQUIPMENT

Dutch oven or similar vessel with lid and steaming basket large enough to hold the chicken

2 yards cheesecloth

Butcher's twine

Blender

In a large, heavy-bottom stockpot, combine the leek, carrot, celery, garlic, wine, thyme, 1 teaspoon salt, and peppercorns with 2 quarts cold water. This is your court bouillon. Bring to a boil, and cook at a boil for 15 minutes. Strain through a sieve into the Dutch oven.

Cut 1 truffle into thick slices—you'll need enough slices to cover the chicken breast. Slip the truffle slices under the breast skin, and place 1 tablespoon butter under the skin of each side of the breast. Season the cavity with salt and black pepper and truss the chicken. Wrap it in the cheesecloth and secure it with the twine.

Bring the court bouillon to a boil, then reduce to a high simmer. Steam the chicken in the basket until cooked through, 45 to 50 minutes. Let it rest for 10 minutes before carving.

While the chicken rests, make the sauce. In the blender, combine ½ cup hot court bouillon, the remaining 2 tablespoons butter, heavy cream, foie gras, and 1½ to 2 remaining truffles (leaving enough to garnish the finished dish), cut into chunks. Season with salt and white pepper and puree until smooth. Transfer to a small, heavy-bottom saucepan. Thin the sauce with additional court bouillon as needed. Warm gently for service.

Portion the chicken and serve with the sauce and sliced truffles for garnish.

Serves 4 to 6

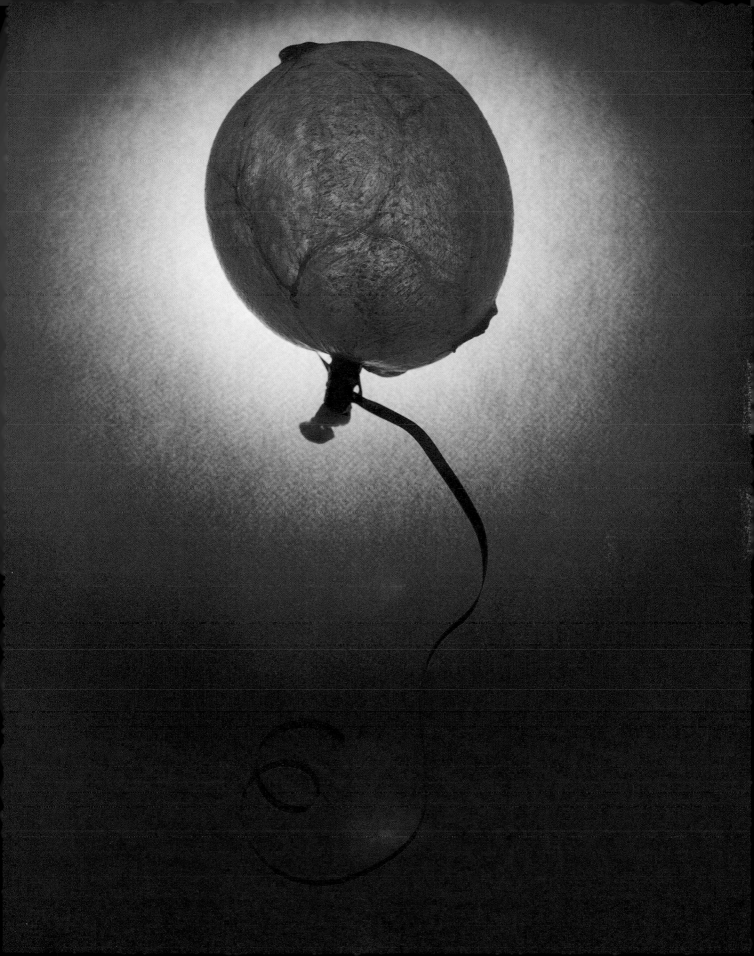

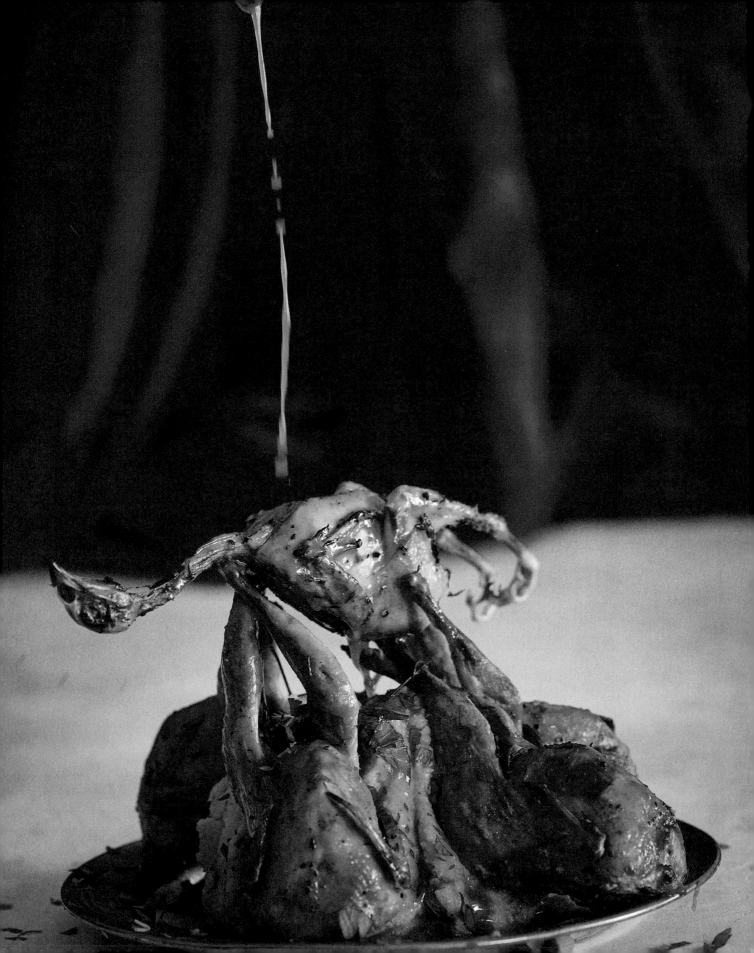

ROASTED QUAIL WITH POLENTA

Just after I first met Ottavia, I asked her about the place in Italy where she grew up. "So . . . what are the specialties of the area? Like for food?"

She looked at me like I was simple-minded, and said, "What do you mean? In the summer, we eat the feesh from the lake. In the winter, we eat the birds from the mountains!"

Later, on my first visit to the Lago di Garda area, my new father-in-law took the family to an *agriturismo* popular with the locals. They served game birds, roasted on spits over coals, nestled into mounds of polenta. Atop each mound was a depression, a carefully shaped crater, containing a pool of the birds' rendered fat and juices.

In a large bowl, combine 5 cups of the stock and the polenta, stir a bit, cover, and refrigerate at least 4 hours and up to 12. (You may skip this step, which will just mean a longer cooking time—closer to 60 rather than 30 minutes. Your call.)

Preheat the oven to 500°F. While the oven heats up—this may take 20 to 30 minutes—melt 4 tablespoons of the butter in a small saucepan. Season the inside of each quail with salt and pepper and stuff them with 1 sprig each of the rosemary and thyme. Use a pastry brush to coat each quail with the melted butter, then season the outside with salt and pepper and transfer to a stovetop-safe roasting pan. Set aside—the quails will cook quickly, and you'll need to start cooking the cornmeal first so that everything is done and hot at the same time.

Take the polenta and stock out of the fridge and transfer it to a large, heavy-bottom saucepot. Give it a quick stir and bring it to a boil, then reduce to a simmer and cook, stirring regularly but not necessarily constantly, for about 15 minutes. Slide the quails into the hot oven. Cook and stir the polenta for another 5 minutes, then turn the quail roasting pan and rotate the quails within it to keep them cooking more or less evenly. Let the quails roast ⟶

6 cups Dark Universal Stock (page 260)

1 cup medium-coarse polenta (also known as "corn grits")

6 tablespoons (¾ stick) unsalted butter

8 whole quails (about ¼ pound each)

Salt and freshly ground black pepper to taste

8 sprigs fresh rosemary

8 sprigs fresh thyme

1 cup finely grated Parmigiano-Reggiano cheese

2 tablespoons extra-virgin olive oil

1 cup coarsely chopped fresh parsley leaves

SPECIAL EQUIPMENT

Stovetop-safe roasting pan, preferably cast iron

for another 5 minutes, while you tend to the polenta, then remove them from the oven and let rest for another 5 to 10 minutes, while you finish the polenta.

Once the polenta is tender, creamy, and has absorbed all of the liquid, stir in the remaining 2 tablespoons butter and the cheese, whip well with a wooden spoon, taste and season with salt, then remove from the heat and transfer to the center of a serving platter. Use a ladle to fashion a volcano-style depression in the center of the polenta, then arrange the quails around the edge of the platter, in the polenta.

Transfer the roasting pan to the stovetop over medium-low heat. Whisk in the remaining stock and the oil and reduce slightly, until the sauce lightly coats the back of a wooden spoon. Season with salt and pepper to taste, then fill the volcano depression with the hot sauce. Cover the whole platter with parsley and serve immediately, with napkins.

Serves 4 to 8

PAN-ROASTED DUCK WITH RED CABBAGE

Do *not* overcook the duck breast. And you can make the cabbage the day before. It only gets better overnight.

With a heavy chef's knife or boning knife, remove the breasts, with wing joint intact, from each side of the duck. Remove and save the wings tips for the duck stock and save the tenderloins for the sauce. Lightly score the skin on the duck breasts in a cross-hatch pattern, taking care not to cut into the meat.

Remove the whole leg (including the thigh) from each side of the duck carcass. Set aside the carcass with the wing tips for stock.

In a small bowl, combine the 1½ tablespoons salt, 1 teaspoon black pepper, the sliced garlic, the rosemary, sage, and bay leaves. Rub this mixture on the surface of all of the duck pieces. Cover and refrigerate for at least 2 hours and up to 24 hours.

Preheat the oven to 300°F. Remove the duck legs from the refrigerator, rinse off the salt and herb mixture, and pat dry. Heat an ovenproof sauté pan over medium-high heat and add the legs, skin side down. Sear the legs for 5 to 7 minutes per side. Turn the legs so that the skin side is facing up. Cover the pan with foil and transfer to the oven. Roast for 1½ to 2 hours, then remove the cover, turn the legs, and roast for another 30 minutes, until the skin is crisp and the meat is very tender.

While the legs are in their last hour or so of roasting time, begin the cabbage. Heat another sauté pan over medium heat and add the bacon. Cook over medium heat until the bacon has rendered much of its fat and is golden brown. Add the onion and cook over medium heat in the bacon fat until it is translucent and soft but not yet browning. Add the cabbage, season with salt and pepper, and cook over medium-high heat until the cabbage begins to wilt and soften, about 5 minutes. Increase the heat to high and stir in the wine and vinegar. Bring to a boil and continue to cook until the liquid is reduced by half. Add the caraway seeds, allspice, and sugar. Make a sachet out of the cheesecloth and secure the cinnamon stick, bay leaf, rosemary, and sage inside it with the twine; add it to the pan. Stir well, reduce the heat to a simmer,

FOR THE DUCK

1 whole Muscovy duck (about 4 pounds)

1½ tablespoons kosher salt, plus more to taste

1 teaspoon freshly ground black pepper, plus more to taste

6 garlic cloves, peeled and sliced, plus 2 garlic cloves, peeled and finely chopped

2 sprigs fresh rosemary

6 to 8 fresh sage leaves, coarsely chopped

2 bay leaves, crumbled

1 tablespoon unsalted butter

2 shallots, peeled and finely chopped

8 to 10 cremini mushrooms, diced (about 2 cups)

1 tablespoon all-purpose flour

⅓ cup dry red wine

2 cups veal or duck stock or Dark Universal Stock (page 260)

FOR THE CABBAGE

½ pound slab bacon, cut into lardons

1 large yellow onion, peeled and finely sliced

½ small head of red cabbage, cored and cut into chiffonade (about 5 cups)

Salt and freshly ground black pepper to taste

1½ cups dry red wine

¼ cup red wine vinegar

1 teaspoon caraway seeds

½ teaspoon ground allspice

2 teaspoons sugar

2 cinnamon sticks

1 bay leaf

1 sprig fresh rosemary

1 sprig fresh sage

SPECIAL EQUIPMENT

5-inch square of cheesecloth

Butcher's twine

Instant-read thermometer

and let cook until the cabbage is very tender and fragrant, about 30 minutes, adding a splash of water as necessary if the mixture begins to seem too dry.

While the cabbage simmers, remove the duck breasts from the refrigerator. Rinse off the salt and herb mixture and pat dry.

Remove the duck legs from the oven and set aside on a plate, covered with foil to keep warm. Increase the oven's heat to 450°F.

Heat an ovenproof sauté pan over medium-high heat, then add the duck breasts, skin side down, and sear well, for about 5 minutes. Add the duck tenderloins to the pan and cook through, 2 to 3 minutes, then remove them and set them aside. Transfer the pan to the oven to finish cooking to medium-rare, when an instant-read thermometer reads 135°F at the thickest part of the breast, 5 to 7 minutes. Remove from the oven and set the duck aside on a cutting board to rest while you make the sauce—the breasts should rest at least 5 minutes.

In a medium, heavy-bottom saucepot, heat the butter over medium-high heat until it foams and subsides. Add the shallots, chopped garlic, and mushrooms and season with salt and pepper. Cook over medium heat, stirring regularly, until the mushrooms have released their juices and the vegetables have been nicely browned, 8 to 10 minutes. Sprinkle the flour over the vegetables and mix well to coat, scraping the bottom of the pot with a wooden spoon. Add the wine, continuing to scrape and stir until the liquid has largely evaporated, which won't take long. Stir in the stock, bring to a boil, and reduce by half. Strain the sauce through a sieve and into a clean small bowl. Chop the reserved tenderloins and add them to the sauce. Taste and adjust seasoning as desired.

Slice the duck breasts on an angle. Separate the duck thighs and drumsticks at the joint. Divide the meat evenly among four dinner plates, add a portion of cabbage, and ladle the sauce over the meat.

Serves 4

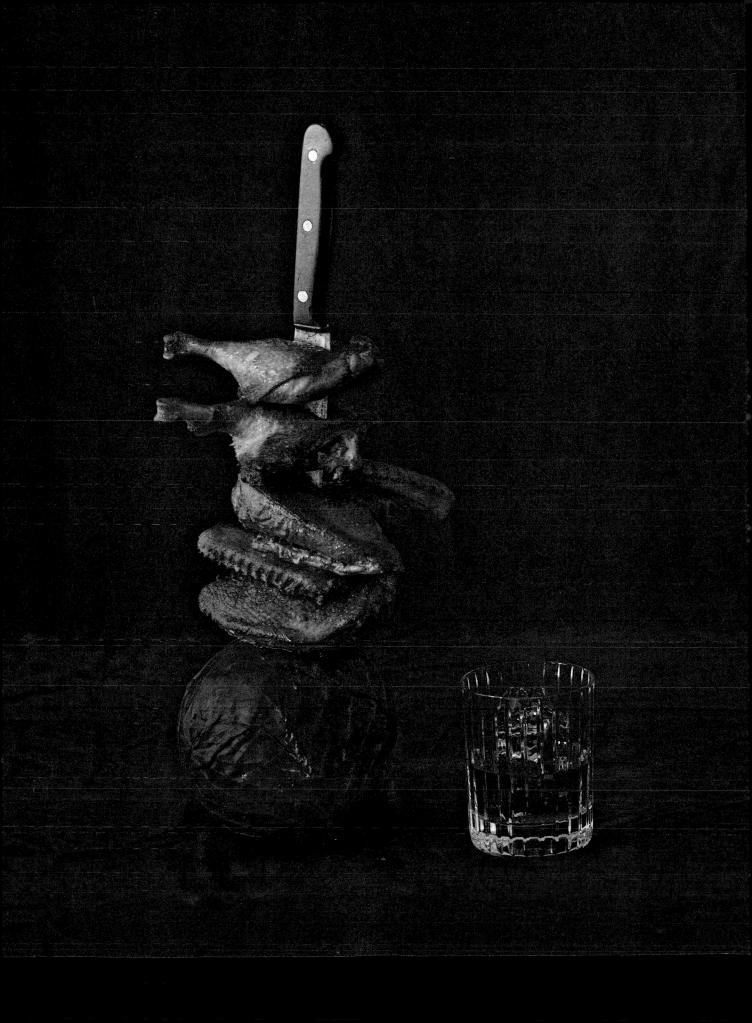

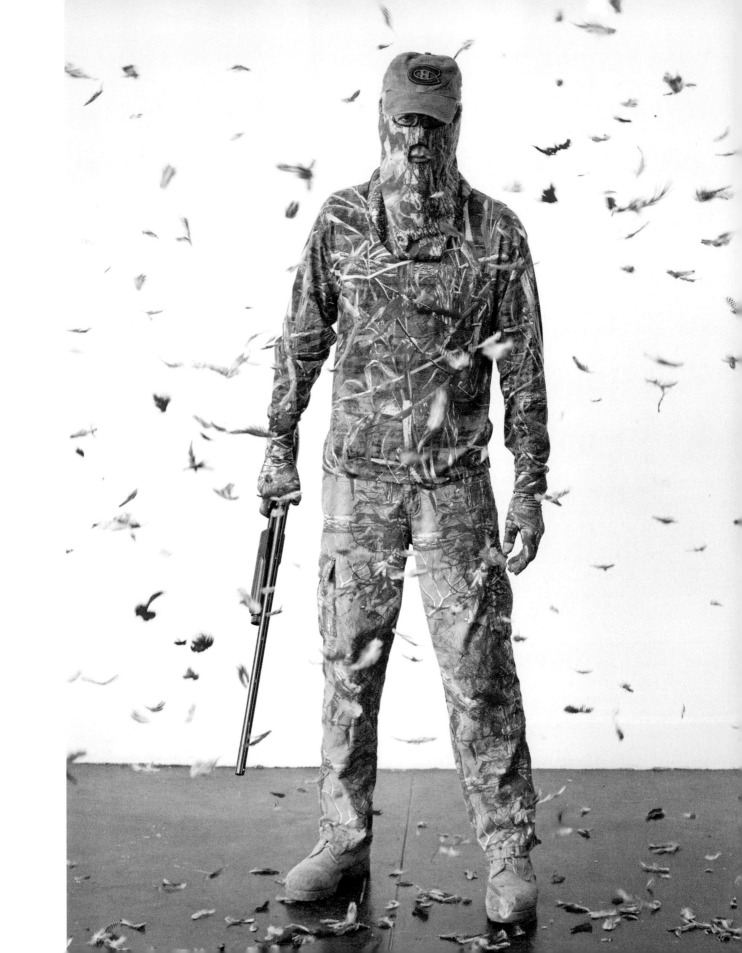

British-Style Pheasant with Bread Sauce

The British do old-school game cookery really, really well. Shoot a bird in the brain, hang it until funky—then cook it and serve it like this. Doesn't get any better.

Press 6 of the cloves into the cut surface of each onion half and place them in a large, heavy-bottom saucepot. Add the milk, bay leaf, peppercorns, and nutmeg to taste, bring nearly to a boil—keep a close eye on this, because milk boils over quickly—then remove from the heat, cover, and let sit for 30 minutes, to infuse the milk with the flavors of the aromatics.

While the milk infuses, fill a medium, heavy-bottom stockpot about halfway full with salted water and bring to a boil. Add the beets and parsnips to the pot and cook until penetrable with a paring knife, 10 to 15 minutes for the parsnips and 15 to 20 minutes for the beets. Transfer the vegetables to the ice-water bath to stop cooking. Once they have cooled, remove from the ice-water bath, cut the parsnips into smaller lengths, and set aside.

Preheat the oven to 350°F. Season the pheasants inside and out with salt and pepper and stuff each bird's cavity with 5 sprigs of the thyme.

In a large, heavy-bottom sauté pan, heat 2 tablespoons of the butter over medium-high heat until it foams and subsides. Place the birds in the pan and sear in the butter on all sides, basting them with the butter in the pan as they cook, and adding an extra tablespoon of butter if necessary. When they have been browned on both sides, transfer the birds to a roasting pan, ideally one that has a rack, and lay 3 slices of the pancetta over each bird, covering as much surface as possible and tucking the ends in as best you can to keep the birds covered. This is called barding the birds. Transfer to the hot oven and cook for 45 to 60 minutes, until the thickest part of the thigh registers 155°F on the instant-read thermometer. Let the birds rest 15 minutes before carving.

While the birds roast, pour off all but about 1 tablespoon of the butter in the pan you used to sear the birds, then return the pan to the stovetop over high heat and deglaze it with the wine, scraping and stirring to dislodge the browned bits. Once the wine has been reduced by half, pour in the stock, bring to $\longrightarrow$

12 whole cloves

1 white onion, peeled and sliced in half

1 quart whole milk

1 bay leaf

1 teaspoon black peppercorns

Several gratings of fresh nutmeg

4 medium beets, peeled and cut into quarters or sixths, depending on size

8 medium parsnips, peeled

Salt and freshly ground black pepper to taste

2 whole pheasants (2 to 3 pounds each), wing tips trimmed and reserved

10 sprigs fresh thyme

6 to 8 tablespoons (¾ to 1 stick) unsalted butter

6 thin slices pancetta

½ cup dry red wine

1½ cups game stock or Dark Universal Stock (page 260)

1 slightly stale loaf white Pullman bread, crusts removed, cut into cubes

1 teaspoon fresh thyme leaves

1 bunch of watercress, washed, for garnish

SPECIAL EQUIPMENT

Ice-water bath (large bowl filled with ice and cold water)

Instant-read thermometer

a boil, and reduce by half. Whisk in ½ to 1 tablespoon of the butter, taste, and season with salt and pepper as desired and set aside, keeping warm.

To make the bread sauce, strain the infused milk through a sieve into a mixing bowl and discard the solids. Return the milk to the saucepot and bring it to a simmer, then add the bread cubes in batches and stir frequently to help the bread break down and thicken the sauce. Add 1 tablespoon of the butter and mix it in, then taste and season with salt and pepper and top with more grated nutmeg if desired. Set aside, keeping warm.

Remove the birds from the oven and rest for at least 15 minutes. The final step is to finish the vegetables. In a clean sauté pan, heat 1 tablespoon of the butter over medium-high heat until it foams and subsides, then add your reserved parsnips and beets and the thyme leaves and toss over high heat for a few minutes, until the vegetables begin to caramelize and the thyme is fragrant. Season with salt and pepper and remove from the heat.

Divide pheasant breast and leg meat among four dinner plates and ladle some of the pan sauce over it. Add some bread sauce and root vegetables to each plate, garnish with watercress, and serve.

Serves 4

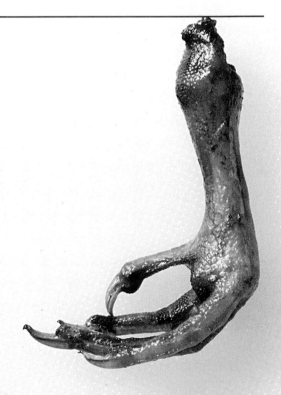

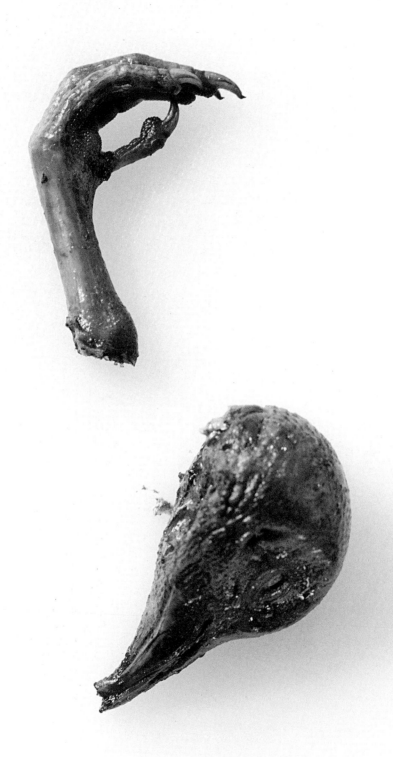

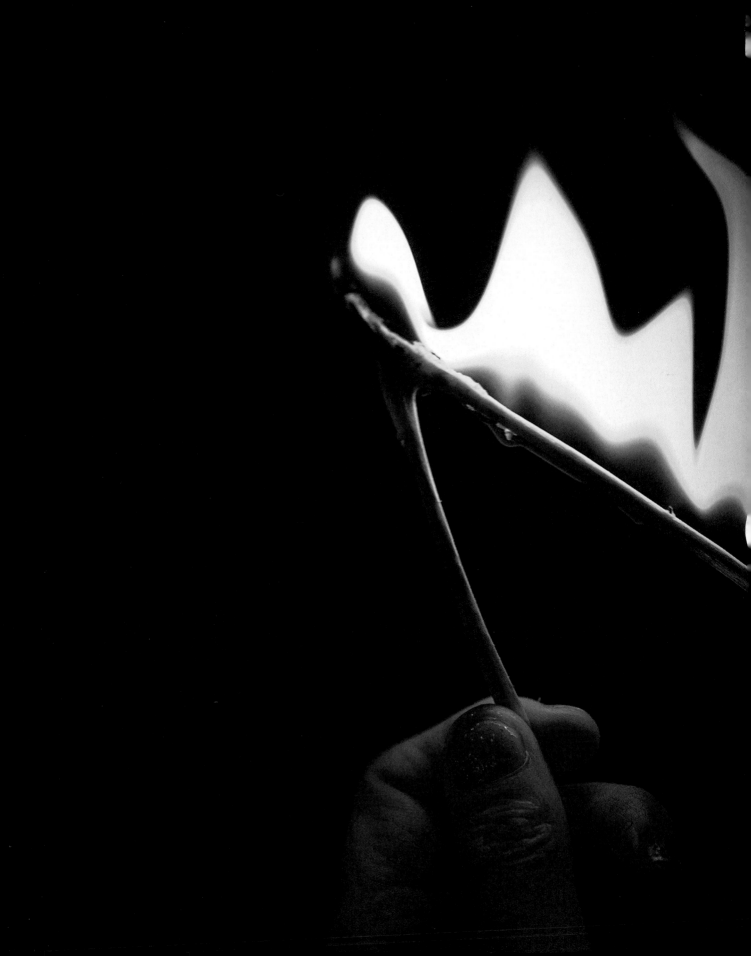

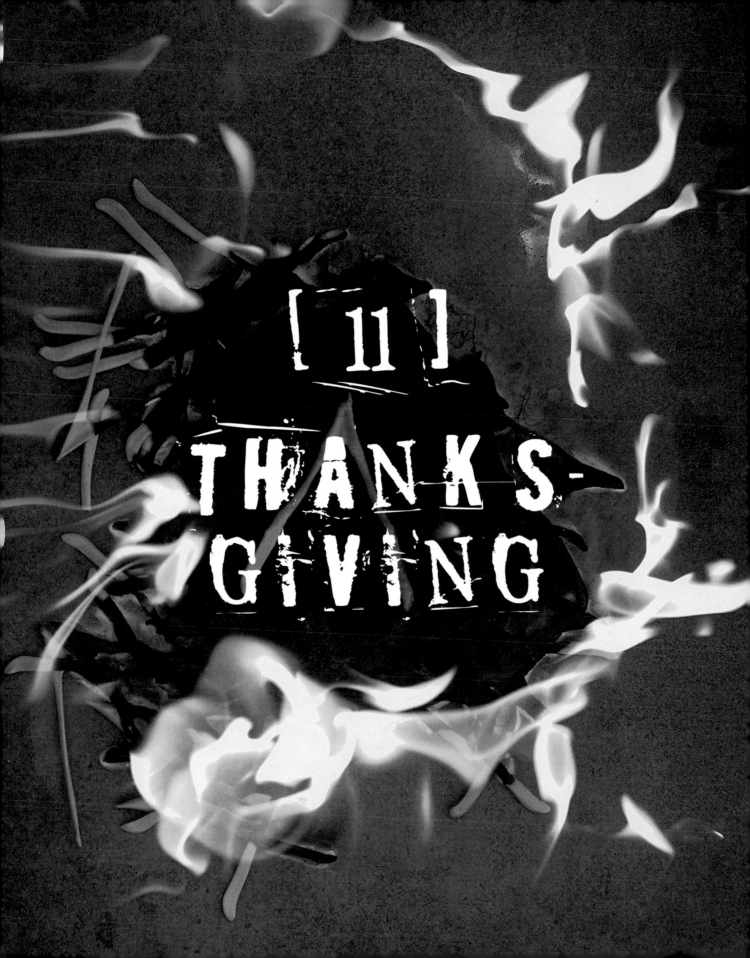

[11]

THANKS-
GIVING

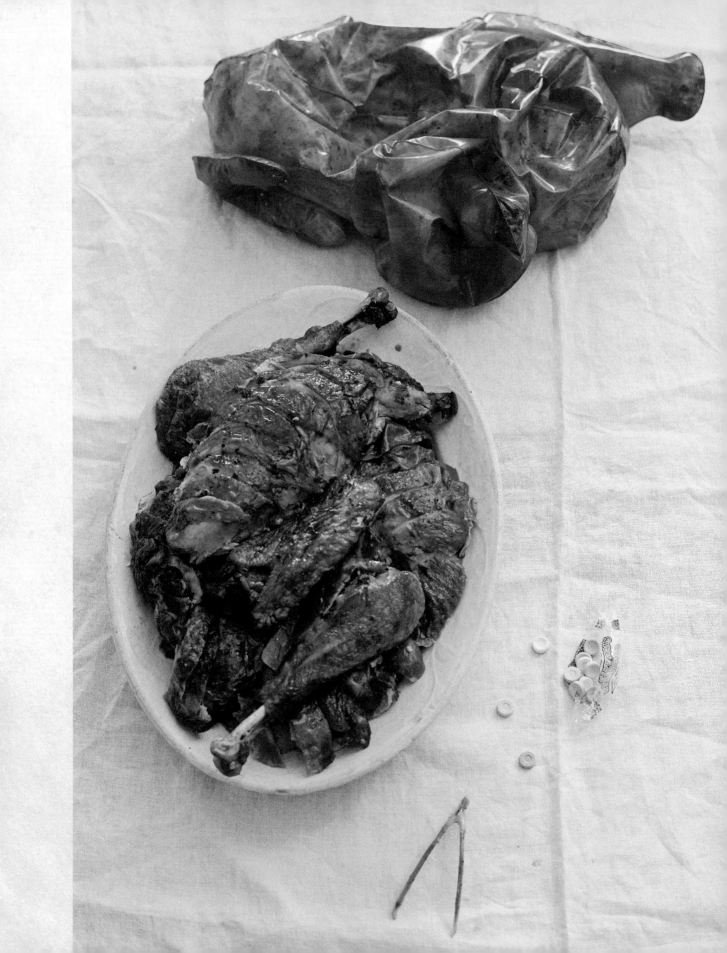

Thanksgiving
A Tactical Primer

Preparing a holiday meal can be a stressful affair. It's no mystery why murder rates spike between mid-November and late December, what with all those relatives convened awkwardly around a table, many of whom see each other only rarely, some with long-simmering resentments and grudges that festered all year. It takes only one ill-considered remark or unfairly apportioned drumstick to turn what should have been a festive gathering into a slaughterfest of senseless butchery. And when you look at the list of "must-have" dishes expected, the prep work seems daunting, a logistical nightmare.

No need.

The following recipes may *look* long and complicated, but they're really not if you remember that the key to a relatively easy, smooth-running, violence-free Thanksgiving is to adopt the following three-day strategy, which calls for a stunt turkey, a business turkey, and an understanding, at all times, that the real point of Thanksgiving is the leftovers. That at the end of the whole ordeal, when all the guests have gone home and you are alone in the house, you can smoke a little weed, sit there in front of the TV in your underwear, and enjoy a nice roast turkey sandwich with some reheated stuffing and gravy.

Thanksgiving shopping, prep, and cooking should be broken down as follows:

DAY 1

✻ **In the morning (or the weekend before Thanksgiving), buy all the shit you'll need, store it in organized fashion, and cross-check it against your recipes to make sure there isn't anything you've forgotten.** If there is, you've still got plenty of time.

   In addition to extra turkey parts (see next page), various aromatic vegetables, herbs, butter, oil, wine, bread, fruit, nuts, and seasonings, there's the matter of the bird—

or actually, birds. You'll need both a small "stunt turkey" and a large "business turkey," which, if frozen, you should start defrosting immediately.

☙ **Make your stock.** This is where the extra turkey parts come in. By all means, reserve the necks and wing tips from your stunt and business turkeys, and make the most of the pan drippings and the "fond," or scrapings, from the bottom of the roasting pan. But you'll need a solid turkey stock before you start fucking around with any actual turkeys. This means buying a separate bag of wings and necks, about 5 to 7 pounds total, to make the stock that will give the stuffing its essential turkey flavor and provide the base for what you might call "gravy" but what is, in fact, a sauce.

☙ **Leave the bread out to get stale for stuffing.**

DAY 2

☙ **Turn your turkey stock into turkey sauce** or, if you must, "gravy." Don't worry, you can still enhance it with pan drippings at the last minute.

☙ **Assemble and bake the stuffing,** *covered,* **so that it doesn't yet brown at all.** Tomorrow you can jack it with turkey grease and brown it a bit on top when you roast the birds.

☙ **Make your cranberry relish and store it in the fridge.** It'll be even better tomorrow.

☙ **Knock out your side-dish prep.** Trim and halve your Brussels sprouts, trim your baby onions if you're doing creamed onions, dice your slab bacon, and scrub your sweet potatoes. Label, group, and refrigerate everything, so that you can quickly finish side dishes tomorrow, while the birds roast.

DAY 3

☙ **Roast the (small) "stunt turkey."** This is the pretty one that you'll display for your guests. Keep it moist and shiny—moist towels and a light brush of oil—as it cools out of the way of the action. Ready your garnishes and feel free to dress it up like a showgirl: such embellishments as chop frills, elaborate fruit garnishes, a bed of old-school curly parsley or kale, and a bit of stuffing to obscure the bony cavity entrance are all totally appropriate visual fireworks to be employed liberally here.

⚹ **While the turkeys roast, finish your side dishes.** Brussels sprouts and creamed onions have already been prepped, potatoes just need to be peeled, and the sweet potatoes can go straight into the water unpeeled. You can get everything done on the stovetop while the birds are cooking, and hold it for quick reheating just before dinner.

⚹ **Roast (and dismantle) the business turkey.** By the time your guests arrive, the business turkey should be ready, which is to say, just completely cooked, breasts removed from the bone and ready to slice, legs removed, drumsticks and thighs separated, wings good to go, moist towels on top.

⚹ **Jack your stuffing with turkey grease and brown it,** *uncovered,* **in a hot oven.**

⚹ **Display the intact, artfully garnished stunt turkey in all its glory, which should elicit much oohing and ahhing from your amazed guests.** Then, whisk it into the kitchen, presumably to be carved.

⚹ **In the relative privacy of your kitchen, pull out your business turkey, which is ready to slice, and get busy.** The whole process should take only a couple of minutes. Use a good serrated knife to ensure that each slice of breast comes with a strip of golden skin. To build the platter, I like to put a heap of stuffing in the center, cross the drumsticks decoratively, then slice and shingle first the dark thigh meat, then the breast meat, like a deck of cards around the stuffing. Throw on some parsley or watercress, if you like, and the effect is complete. No embarrassing and inept hacking at a whole turkey while your family looks on with horror: This bird is ready to serve.

Just be *sure* that you've stashed away some choice turkey bits. Later, after you've packed up thoughtful leftover kits for your guests to take home, you want to be certain that after all your hard work, you've got plenty of the good stuff for yourself.

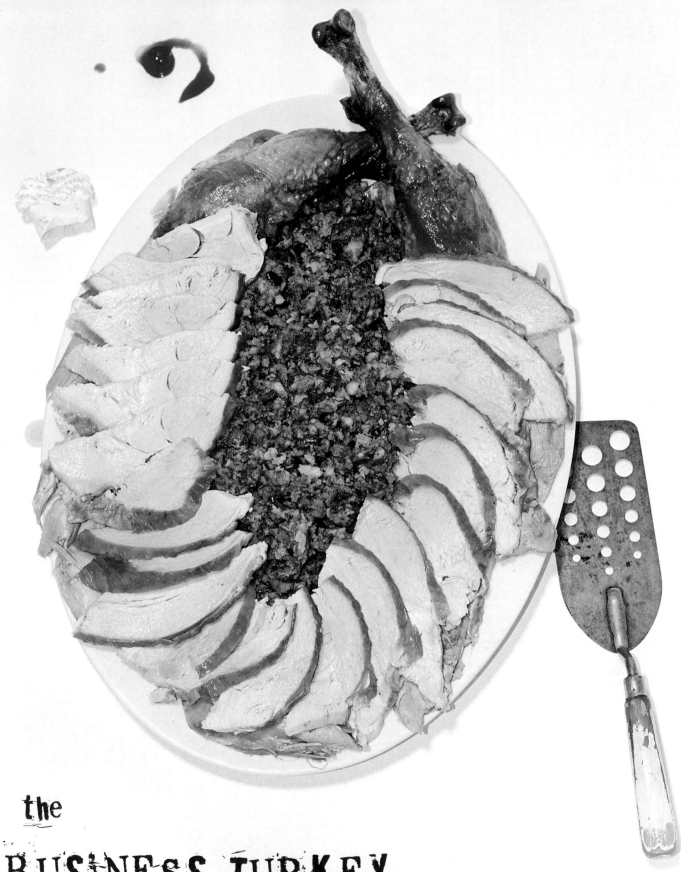

the
BUSINESS TURKEY

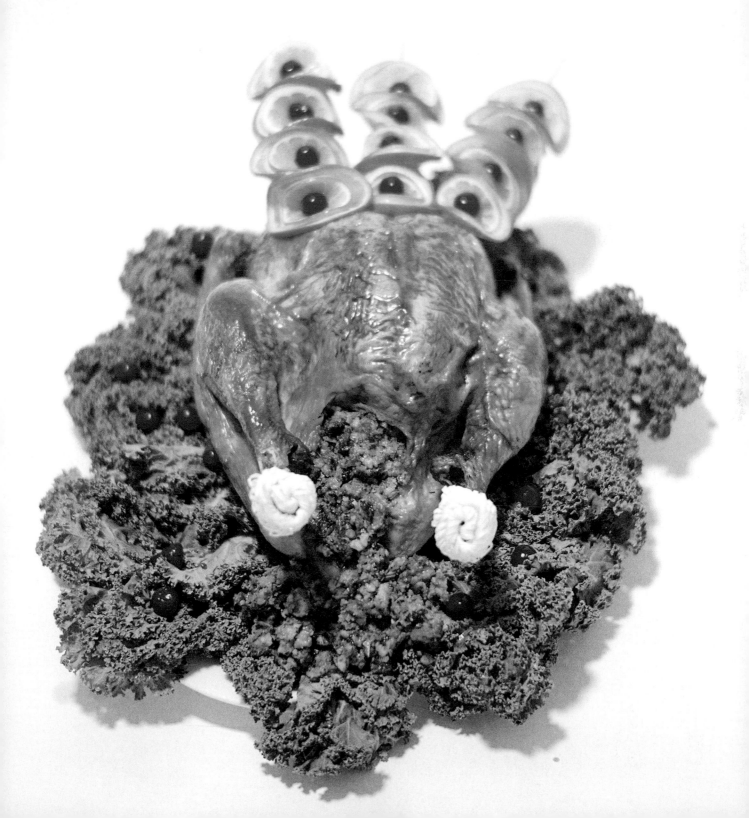

THANKSGIVING GRAVY, STUFFING, AND TURKEY

1 small (8- to 10-pound) turkey
(aka "the stunt turkey")

1 large (18-pound) turkey (aka "the
business turkey")

5 pounds total turkey wings and
necks, cut into 3 to 6 pieces
each

Salt and freshly ground black
pepper to taste

1 cup dry white wine

2 large yellow onions, peeled and
finely diced

4 ribs celery, finely diced

2 large carrots, peeled and finely
diced

6 to 8 sprigs fresh thyme, plus
2 teaspoons fresh thyme leaves

1 large loaf of white bread

2 cups dry red wine

2 shallots, peeled and coarsely
chopped, plus 4 shallots, peeled
and finely chopped

⅔ cup all-purpose flour, or as
needed

A few splashes of Thai fish sauce
(optional)

Worcestershire sauce (optional)

1½ cups peeled chestnuts

½ pound (2 sticks) unsalted butter,
plus more as needed

¼ cup finely chopped fresh sage,
plus 2 additional sprigs

1 pound mixed wild mushrooms,
finely chopped

⅓ cup finely chopped fresh parsley

2 large eggs, beaten

Soy sauce or Kitchen Bouquet
(a flavor and color enhancer;
optional)

DAY 1: DEFROSTING

If they're frozen, start your turkeys defrosting in the fridge as
soon as you get them home. If they're fresh, use a heavy chef's
knife or poultry shears to remove the wing tips and wishbones
from both turkeys, and remove the necks and giblets from the
inside of the birds. Refrigerate the giblets, which will go into the
gravy, and the turkeys themselves. (If the birds are frozen, you'll
deal with all of this later.)

Make the turkey stock. Preheat the oven to 425°F. Assemble
the wings and necks, and anything you have harvested from
your fresh turkeys, if applicable, on one or more stovetop-ready
roasting pans and season them with salt and pepper. Roast in
the oven until nicely browned and fragrant, about 45 minutes,
rotating the pans (and possibly the wings and parts themselves, if
they're looking very browned on one side) about 20 minutes in,
for even roasting. Remove from the oven.

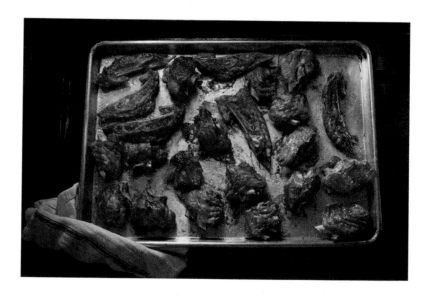

Transfer the roasted wings and bones to a large, heavy-bottom
stockpot. Pour the excess grease and juices from the pan into a
small bowl or jar, and cover and refrigerate it. (You will use it

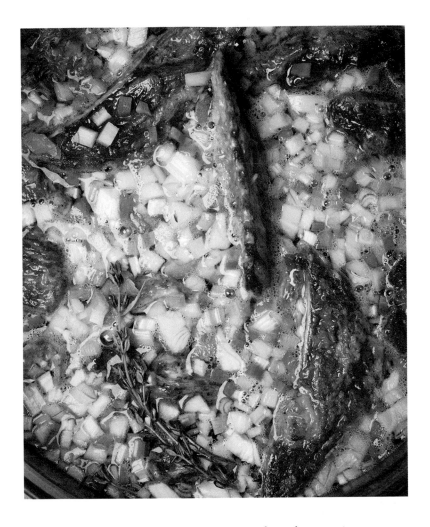

Heavy chef's knife

Poultry shears (optional)

2 (or more) roasting pans, at least
  1 of which should be stovetop-
  ready, and at least 1 of which
  should have a rack

Serrated knife (or better yet, an
  offset serrated knife)

Bulb-top turkey baster

Instant-read thermometer

Large carving board, ideally with
  trenches to catch juice

later, to build the roux for your gravy.) Place the roasting pan
over medium-high heat and stir in ½ cup of the white wine,
scraping the bottom of the pan with a wooden spoon to dislodge
the fond, or browned bits. Cook until the alcohol smell no longer
remains. Transfer this liquid to the stockpot along with the
bones, and add half of the onions and celery, the carrots, and
4 to 6 thyme sprigs. Cover with cold water and bring to a high
simmer (*not a boil*). Use a ladle to skim off and discard any scum
that floats to the top. Reduce to a medium simmer and cook for
about 5 hours.

Pour the stock into a wide bowl to cool down at room
temperature for about 20 to 30 minutes, stirring occasionally
to release steam and speed cooling. Transfer it into quart-sized
plastic or glass containers or sturdy zip-sealed plastic bags and
refrigerate. If you've done it right, the stock should be dark golden
brown and have a definitively gelatinous quality. With 5 to ⟶

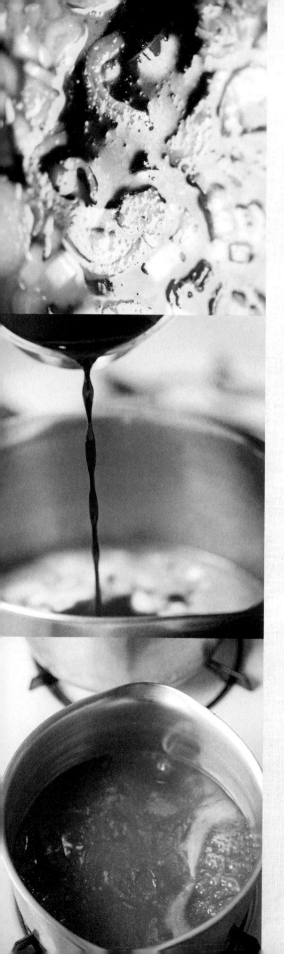

7 pounds of bones in a full 4-gallon stockpot, you can expect to get around 4 quarts of good-quality stock.

Prep your bread for stuffing. While the stock simmers, use a serrated knife to dice the bread for stuffing. You're looking to yield about 10 to 12 cups of diced bread. Scatter the bread cubes in a single layer on sheet trays and leave them out to dry.

DAY 2: TURN YOUR STOCK INTO GRAVY

Pull 3 quarts of turkey stock from the fridge and pour it into a medium, heavy-bottom pot. Add the red wine and coarsely chopped shallots, and bring to a high simmer. Cook, stirring occasionally, for about 30 to 45 minutes, until reduced by half. Strain the mixture into a bowl, discard the shallots, and return it to the pot.

Retrieve the container of reserved turkey fat and drippings from yesterday and scrape off enough fat—it will self-separate from the drippings in the refrigerator—to equal ⅔ cup. (You may supplement, if necessary, with butter.) Place the fat in a medium, heavy-bottom pot. Measure out ⅔ cup flour and, with your whisk and wooden spoon handy, heat the fat over medium heat until hot. Sprinkle the flour into the fat, whisking the mixture together to make a roux. Swap your whisk for the wooden spoon and continue to cook over medium heat for 1 to 2 minutes, stirring until the flour is lightly toasted and fragrant. Whisk in the stock and red wine mixture. Switch back to the wooden spoon and continue to stir and scrape to ensure that you pull up all the roux. Once the mixture comes to a boil, reduce to a high simmer, continuing to stir regularly until the gravy is thick enough to coat the back of the wooden spoon.

Taste and season as desired with salt and pepper. Some people use a hit of fish sauce, which I endorse. If the emotional needs of your guests require a darker gravy, you can brown it up with some Worcestershire sauce, soy sauce, or Kitchen Bouquet. Tomorrow, you can further enhance the flavor with drippings from the turkey roasting pans.

Make stuffing. Preheat the oven to 375°F. Remove the remaining quart of stock from the fridge and bring it to a high simmer in a medium saucepot. Turn off the heat and cover the pan to keep the stock warm.

Arrange the chestnuts in a single layer on a sheet pan and roast in the oven until browned and fragrant, about 10 minutes. Remove from the oven, let cool for about 5 minutes, then chop them to a medium-coarse consistency, as you would for chopped walnuts. Place the chestnuts in a large mixing bowl along with the bread cubes.

In a large sauté pan, heat 4 tablespoons butter over medium-high heat until it foams and subsides. Add the finely chopped shallots and the remaining onions and celery and sauté until translucent and fragrant, 3 to 5 minutes. Season with salt and pepper and stir in the thyme leaves and chopped sage. Continue to cook for another minute or two, until the herbs are fragrant, then transfer the mixture to the mixing bowl with the chestnuts and bread cubes.

In the same pan, heat another 4 tablespoons butter until it foams and subsides. Add the mushrooms and sauté, seasoning with salt and pepper and stirring regularly until they release their juice and it sizzles away. Deglaze the pan with the remaining ½ cup white wine, scraping the bottom to gather browned bits of mushroom. Add the mushrooms and reduced wine to the mixing bowl.

Grease another roasting pan with 2 tablespoons butter.

Add the parsley, eggs, and warm stock to the mixing bowl and mix with a light touch to get everything incorporated without compressing it too much. Transfer this mixture to the greased roasting pan, cover with foil, and cook in the oven for about 45 minutes. Remove from the oven and let cool for about 15 minutes without the foil, then re-cover it tightly and refrigerate until tomorrow, when you'll jack it with drippings and brown the top.

Make your cranberry relish (page 195) while the stuffing bakes, and do the prep for Brussels sprouts (page 201) and creamed onions (page 197).

$\longrightarrow$

DAY 3

Roast the business turkey. Preheat the oven to 425°F. If you haven't already, trim off the wing tips and remove the neck and the wishbone from the business turkey; these things can be saved, from both the business and stunt turkeys, in the freezer for your next round of stock-making. Set those giblets, and the ones from the stunt turkey, in a medium saucepot and fill it about halfway with cold water. Bring to a boil.

Rub the turkey all over with 2 to 3 tablespoons butter, and season inside and out with salt and pepper. Place it in a roasting pan with a rack, pour 2 cups of water into the pan, and transfer to the oven to roast. Periodically rotate the pan and use the bulb-top baster to baste the turkey with the grease and juices from the pan. An 18-pound bird should take just under 4 hours to cook through; the thickest part of the thigh should register 165°F on the instant-read thermometer.

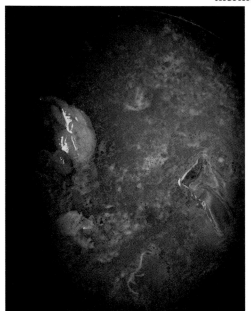

Are your giblets boiling yet? Good. Let them cook for about 5 minutes, then drain and discard the water. Wash out the pot, and return the giblets to it. Add the remaining thyme and sage sprigs, cover with cold water, then let cook at a low simmer as the roasting continues.

About 15 minutes before you take the business turkey from the oven, remove the giblets from the pot, strain them, and discard the cooking liquid. In a medium sauté pan, heat 2 tablespoons of the butter over high heat. Season the giblets with salt and pepper and sear them to golden brown in the butter. Remove from the pan, cut them into fine dice, and set aside.

Once your business turkey is done, take it out of the oven, transfer it to the carving board, and let it rest for at least 15 to 20 minutes. Reserve the juices and turkey grease from the pan in a bowl or jar.

Finish the creamed onions (page 197) and Brussels sprouts (page 201) while the business turkey roasts. Make the sweet potatoes (page 200) and, if you have time, mashed potatoes (page 196).

Roast the (small) "stunt turkey." Rub the outside of the stunt turkey with 2 tablespoons of the butter and season it inside and out with salt and pepper. Place it in a roasting pan with a rack, pour about 2 cups of water into the pan, and roast in the oven. As it roasts, periodically rotate the pan and use the bulb-top baster to baste the turkey with the grease and juices from the pan. A 10-pound bird should take about 2½ hours; the thickest part of the thigh should register 165°F on an instant-read thermometer. Remove from the oven and let it rest for 15 minutes, then carefully transfer the turkey to your serving platter to be garnished at will. Add the turkey grease and juices from the roasting pan to those you collected from the business turkey.

Finish those side dishes that you haven't yet finished. Pull the stuffing out of the fridge and let it come to room temperature.

Dismantle the business turkey. Remove each leg, at the thigh joint, from the carcass. Separate the thigh from the drumstick, and pull or cut the meat from the thigh bones. Run your knife down the center of the breast, just to the left and right of the bone that divides them, and continue to guide your knife to the ribs, gently cutting the intact breast muscle away on either side. Place all the meat on a sheet tray, cover with damp, clean towels, and stash it out of sight of nosy guests.

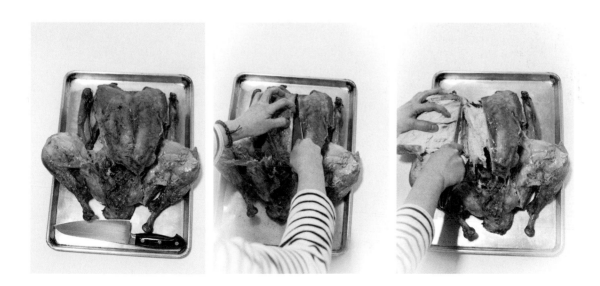

Jack the stuffing with grease, drippings, and giblets. Fold the reserved cooked giblets into the stuffing, and add enough reserved grease and juices so that it glistens. Slide the stuffing, uncovered, into the oven for about 15 to 20 minutes, until it's sizzling at the edges and browned on top. $\longrightarrow$

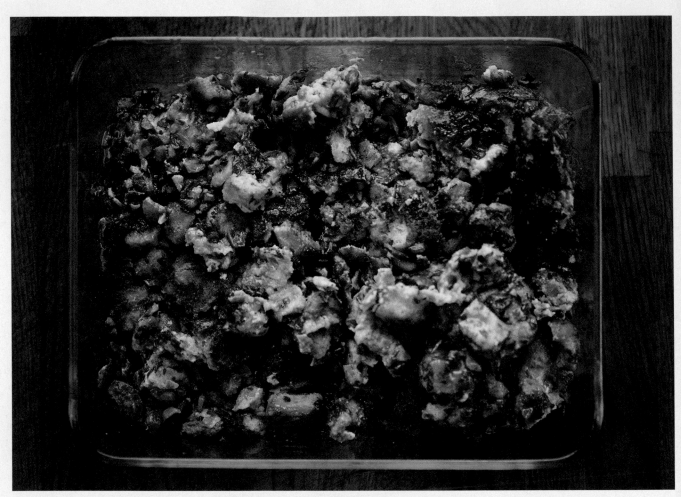

←

After you have received big praise and glory from your guests for the presented stunt turkey, return to the kitchen to finish the job. You may wish to enlist a trusted accomplice for this. Get all your side dishes and your gravy gently warmed in the oven or on the stovetop. Whisk some reserved turkey grease and drippings into the gravy as it simmers, if desired. Carefully slice the breast meat, making sure to leave a strip of skin intact on each piece. Mound the stuffing in the center of the serving platter. Arrange the thigh meat around the stuffing, then top the thigh meat with shingles of breast meat, attractively arranged. Serve the platter, with gravy and all side dishes.

Serves 10 to 12, with leftovers

CRANBERRY RELISH

This is delicious, and truly one of the easiest recipes in the world, as long as you use a food processor. It contains a shocking amount of sugar, which you should not balk at. It's a holiday.

Wash the outside of the orange well under warm water, then dry well and coarsely chop it—skin, pith, flesh, and all. Place the orange pieces in the food processor along with the cranberries. Pulse the fruits until the mixture appears grainy, then transfer to a medium mixing bowl. Fold in the sugar with the spatula, taste, and add even more if necessary to keep your ears from ringing with the sour intensity of the cranberries. Cover and refrigerate overnight to let the flavors marry and the color intensify. Serve chilled or at room temperature.

1 large orange
12 ounces (3 cups) fresh cranberries
1 cup sugar

SPECIAL EQUIPMENT

Food processor

Serves 8 to 12 as a side dish

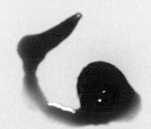

MASHED POTATOES, KIND OF ROBUCHON STYLE

This is not how the great chef Joël Robuchon makes his mashed potatoes. I *have* heard how from cooks who've worked for him, but they swore me to secrecy. If I told you, I'd have to kill you. I'm not sure they were telling me the whole truth in any case, so terrifying is the man's reputation. What I do know for sure is there's a *lot* of butter in them—and that the way that Robuchon actually makes them is too hard and too complicated for you (or me) to do sensibly at home.

But this will approximate—roughly—the kind of buttery, ethereal suspension that dreams (and Joël Robuchon's mashed potatoes) are made of.

2¼ pounds Yukon Gold potatoes (about 6 to 8 large potatoes), peeled and cut in half

2 tablespoons salt, plus more to taste

1 pound (4 sticks) unsalted butter, cut into cubes

⅓ cup heavy cream

SPECIAL EQUIPMENT

Ricer or food mill

Place the peeled potatoes in a medium pot and cover them with cold water. Stir in the salt and bring the water to a boil. Continue to cook until the potatoes are easily penetrated with a paring knife, 15 to 20 minutes. Be vigilant; a waterlogged potato is a disaster.

Drain the potatoes in a colander and let cool for about 3 minutes. Pass the potatoes through the ricer, back into the hot pot. Place the pot over medium heat and stir the potatoes with a wooden spoon until you see steam being released. Add a quarter of the butter cubes at a time, stirring until most of the butter has been absorbed before adding the next batch.

Once the butter has been incorporated, add the cream, season with salt as necessary, then whisk the mixture vigorously to fluff it up. Serve immediately.

Serves 4 to 8 as a side dish

CREAMED PEARL ONIONS

This is a classic part of my Thanksgiving table. Yes, pearl onions are a pain in the ass to peel. Blanching them makes the job infinitely easier.

Preheat the oven to 375°F.

Place the salt, peppercorns, and bay leaf in a large saucepot, cover with cold water, and bring to a boil. Add the onions, let boil for 1 to 2 minutes, remove the onions from the hot water using a slotted spoon or tongs (but do not dump the water, as you're going to use it again), and transfer them to the ice-water bath so that they're easy to handle. Slip off and discard the skins, and return the onions to the hot water. Cook at a simmer for about 8 to 10 minutes, until easily pierced with the tip of a paring knife. Remove them from the cooking liquid (which you may now discard, along with the aromatics) and transfer to a baking dish.

Make sure you have both a whisk and a wooden spoon nearby, and something to rest them on. You will be switching back and forth between the two utensils as you first make a roux and then build on that to make a béchamel.

In a medium heavy-bottomed saucepot, heat the butter over medium-low heat until it foams and subsides, then stir in the flour with a wooden spoon, making sure it is completely incorporated. Cook and stir regularly for about 3 minutes, then whisk in the milk, switching back to the wooden spoon to dislodge and break up any lumps of flour that might form and stick to the pan. Season with salt and pepper, add the thyme and sage, and continue to cook and stir until the mixture coats the back of the wooden spoon, 3 to 5 minutes. Pour this over the onions and transfer to the oven to cook until bubbling and browning at the edges, 15 to 20 minutes.

1 tablespoon salt, plus more to taste

1 teaspoon black peppercorns

1 bay leaf

1 pound pearl onions

2 tablespoons (¼ stick) unsalted butter

2 tablespoons all-purpose flour

1⅓ cups whole milk

Freshly ground black pepper to taste

¼ teaspoon chopped fresh thyme leaves

3 fresh sage leaves, finely chopped

SPECIAL EQUIPMENT

Ice-water bath (large bowl filled with ice and cold water)

Serves 6 to 8 as a Thanksgiving side

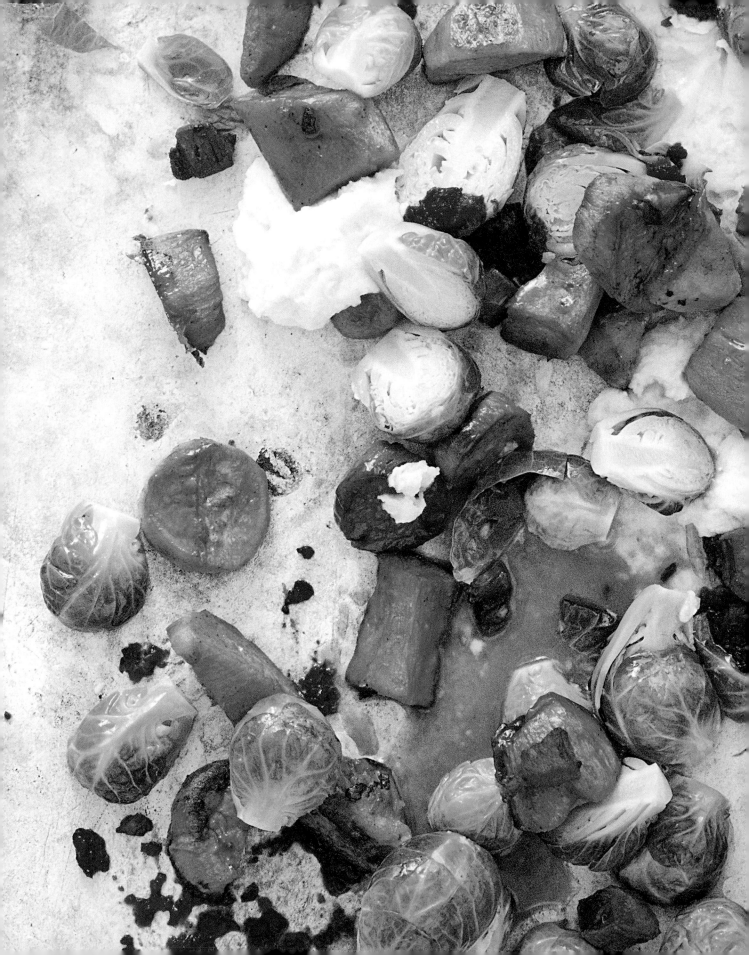

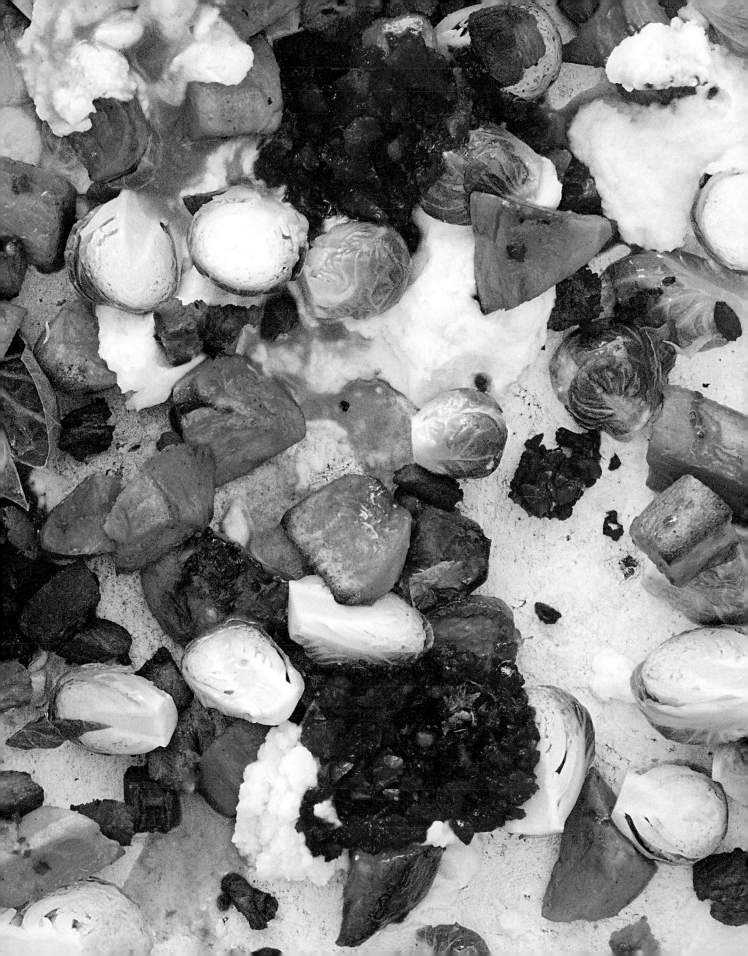

CANDIED SWEET POTATOES

Put those goddamn marshmallows away.

3 pounds sweet potatoes (about 6 to 8 large potatoes), more or less equally sized, cut into quarters

6 tablespoons (¾ stick) unsalted butter

1 cup dark brown sugar, packed

⅓ cup apple cider

Pinch of salt

¼ cup bourbon

Preheat the oven to 375°F.

Place the sweet potatoes in a medium pot and cover with cold water. Bring to a boil, reduce the heat to a high simmer, and cook for 15 to 20 minutes, at which point the sweet potatoes should be cooked through but still offering a bit of resistance to a fork. Drain and, once they are cool enough to handle, peel the potatoes and cut them into 1-inch chunks.

Use 1 tablespoon of the butter to grease a roasting pan that's large enough to hold the chunks in a single layer, and place the sweet potatoes in it.

In a small skillet, melt the remaining 5 tablespoons butter and the sugar together, then whisk in the cider, salt, and bourbon. Let bubble on the stovetop for 1 minute, then remove and drizzle the mixture over the sweet potatoes, tossing gently to coat. Roast in the oven, stirring the sweet potatoes with a wooden spoon and rotating the pan every 10 minutes, for about 40 minutes, until the sweet potatoes are very tender and the liquid is syrupy.

Serves 8 as a side dish

BRUSSELS SPROUTS WITH BACON

Forget a salad on Thanksgiving; this is the only green thing you need on the table.

Place the bacon and ¼ cup water in a large, heavy-bottom sauté pan and bring the water to a boil. Reduce the heat to medium-high and continue to cook until the water evaporates completely and the bacon browns and renders its fat, stirring occasionally with a wooden spoon to make sure that the bacon cooks evenly. Once the bacon is good and brown, remove the pieces from the pan with tongs and let drain on the lined plate.

Assess how much bacon grease is in the pan; you'll need about 3 tablespoons to cook the Brussels sprouts. If there's a lot more than that in the pan, discard the excess.

Add the sprouts to the pan along with ⅓ cup water. Turn and toss the sprouts to coat them evenly with the fat and cook for 15 to 20 minutes, stirring regularly, until browned and tender. Add the butter and toss over the heat to coat the sprouts. Taste one and season with salt and pepper as needed. Add the reserved bacon and the lemon juice, toss once again over the heat, and serve.

Serves 8 as a side dish

¾ pound slab bacon, cut into 1-inch cubes

2 pounds Brussels sprouts, bottoms trimmed, cut in half lengthwise

1 tablespoon unsalted butter

Salt and freshly ground black pepper to taste

Juice of ½ lemon (about 1 tablespoon), or to taste

SPECIAL EQUIPMENT

Plate lined with newspaper

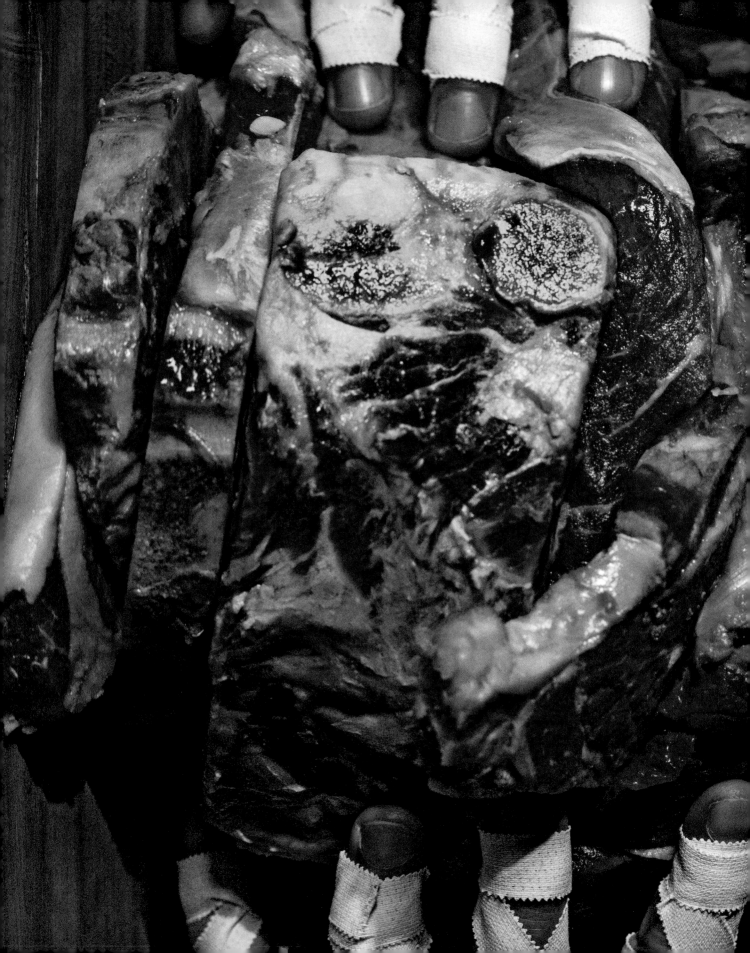

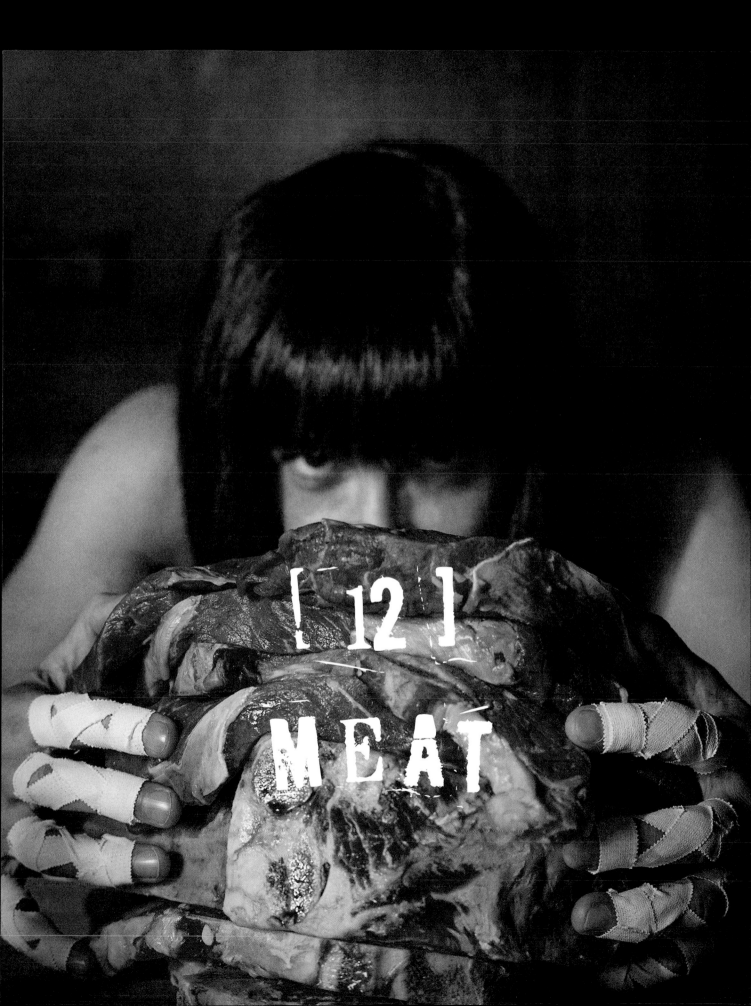

[12]
MEAT

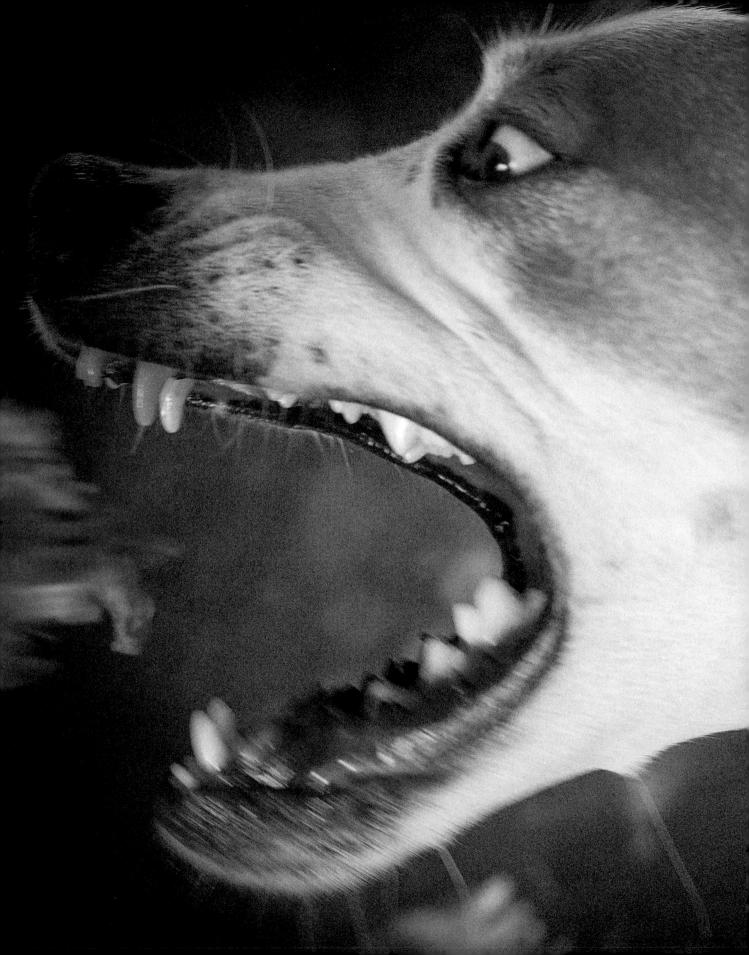

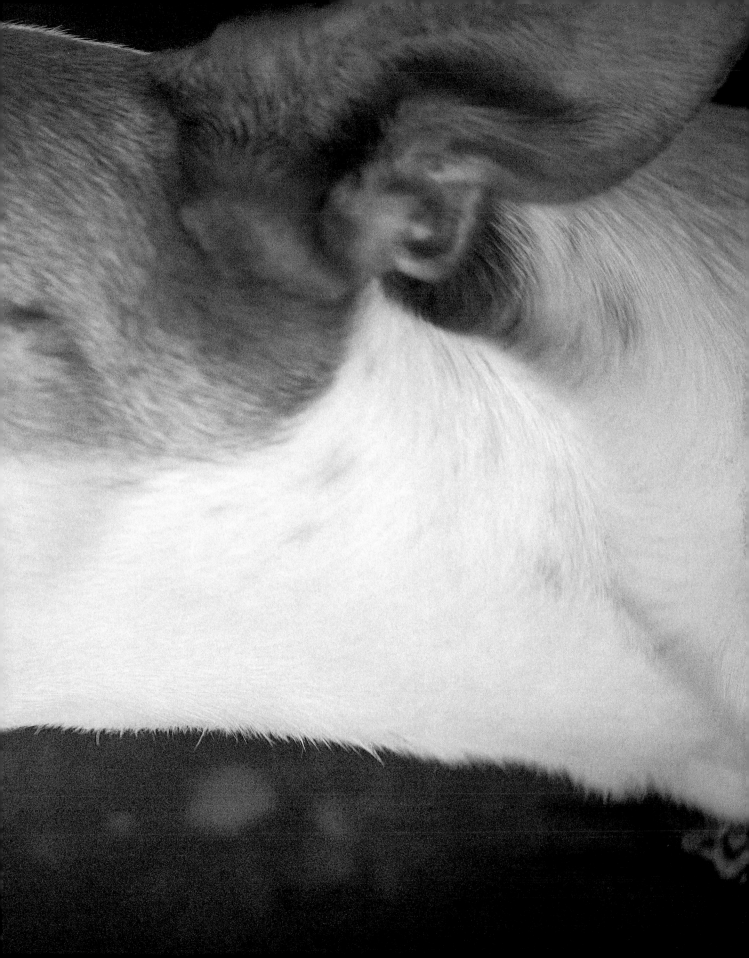

BIG FUCKING STEAK

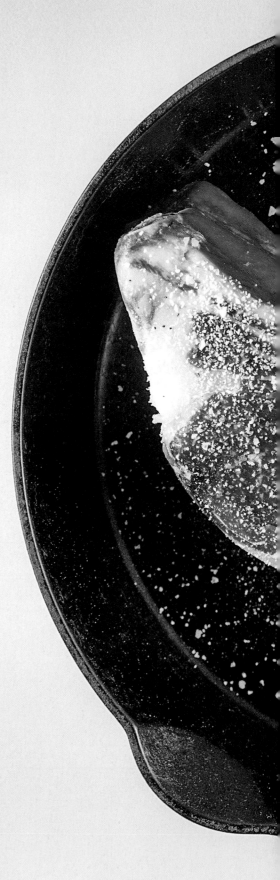

Choose your steak well. If buying a rib eye or a bone-in rib steak, for instance, insist on the loin end, which has less connective tissue. If buying sirloin, get the rib end, for the same reason. Look for marbling—the white fat should be rippling through the actual muscle tissue.

Be wary of the term *grass fed*. While it's surely a good thing in principle, an exclusively grass-fed animal will usually be decidedly less fatty and well marbled. Better to ask your butcher for something that's been grass fed and grain finished.

American wagyu and *Kobe* are also two terms you want to be cautious about, as they are often little more than marketing bullshit and douche bait.

Real Kobe beef, in fact, is *so* lush and *so* fatty that it's possibly *too* much as a main-course-size steak. A few ounces and you're done!

How you cook it is your choice: Either grill your steak or pan-sear it in a preheated cast-iron skillet, basting it with butter and finishing it in a 400°F oven.

But whatever you do, however you get there—when it's done—or just shy of being done, *rest your steak before poking, slicing, or otherwise interfering with it!*

Let it sit there on the board for a full 5 minutes. *Then* slice it—against the grain.

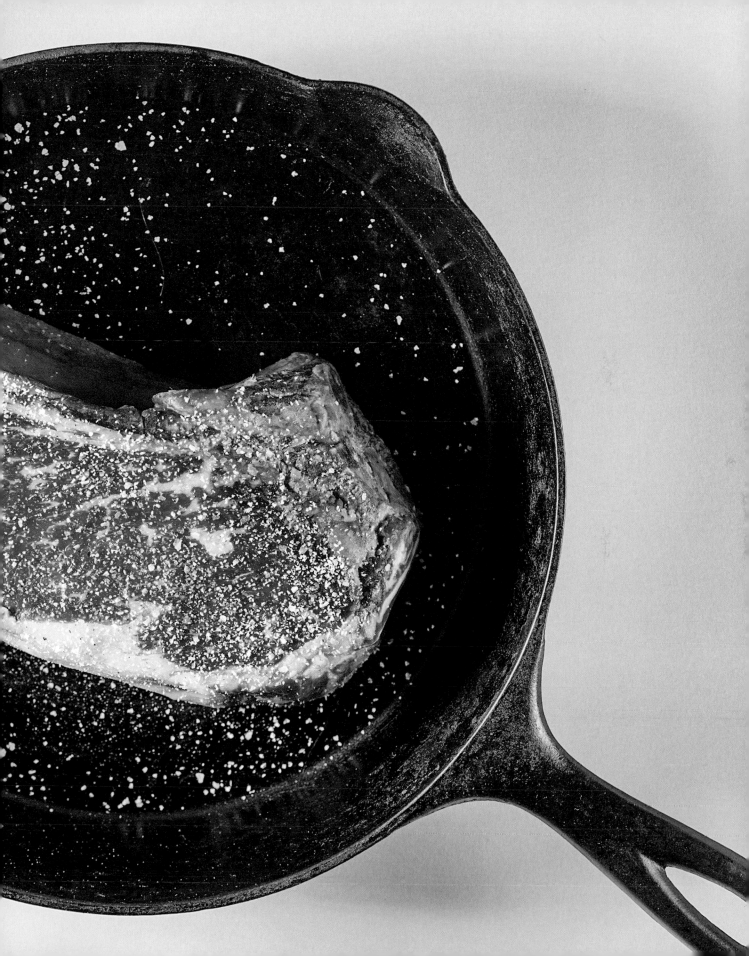

BRAISED PORK SHOULDER WITH FRIED SHALLOTS AND PICKLED VEGETABLES

1 whole or 2 half pork shoulders or Boston butts, bone in (8 to 9 pounds total)

2 tablespoons salt, plus more to taste

Freshly ground black pepper to taste

2¼ to 2½ cups peanut oil

1 large yellow or white onion, peeled and cut into chunks

20 garlic cloves, peeled

10 to 12 thin slices fresh ginger

½ cup rice vinegar

1 cup soy sauce

3 cups cola

¼ cup red miso

1 red onion, peeled and thinly sliced

4 medium cucumbers or 2 English cucumbers, peeled and sliced

1½ cups white vinegar

1½ cups water

¼ cup sugar

4 large shallots, peeled and thinly sliced

Cooked sticky rice

Hot sauce

SPECIAL EQUIPMENT

Plate or sheet pan lined with newspaper

I'll *drink* a Coke only in the service of fighting the effect of a hangover and in the company of superspicy Kung Pao chicken. It's a wholly unnecessary category of beverage for all other occasions. But: It possesses magical properties as a braising liquid, especially in combination with soy sauce, vinegar, garlic, and onions. Hold on to those free cans of Coke that are often thrown in with a large enough order of cheap Chinese delivery, and use them in this dish.

NOTE: *As with many braised meat dishes, this one is best if left to cool in its cooking liquid overnight, but you can always skip that step if you're pressed for time, or really hungry.*

Preheat the oven to 300°F.

Season the pork all over with salt and pepper. In a large oven-proof braising pan, heat ¼ cup of the peanut oil over high heat until it shimmers. Add the pork and sear until golden brown on all sides. If you're using two half shoulders, you may need to dump out and replace the oil halfway through if it starts to smoke or get browned.

Once the meat has been seared, remove it from the pan with tongs and set it aside. Dump out all but about a tablespoon of the fat in the pan, and add the yellow onion, garlic, and ginger to the pan, stirring to coat with the oil, and adding a bit more oil if necessary to keep the vegetables from scorching or sticking. Season the vegetables with salt to get their juices released. Scrape the bottom of the pan with a wooden spoon to dislodge browned bits. Once the vegetables are browned and beginning to soften, which should only take a few minutes, stir in the vinegar, soy sauce, cola, and miso, which you'll have to break up a bit with a spoon or spatula to help it melt quickly into the liquids. Bring to a boil and let reduce for about 5 minutes. Return the pork to the pan, cover, and transfer to the oven, where it should braise for at least 4 hours, or until extremely fork tender.

Remove the pork from the oven, uncover and let cool in the braising liquid. Using scrupulously clean hands, remove the meat from the bone-in chunks, placing it in a clean container large enough to hold all of the meat plus the strained liquid, and discard the bones and skin (reserve if you plan to make a roasted pork bone stock, cracklins, or the like). Strain the braising liquid through the sieve into the container with the meat, discarding the solids. Cover and refrigerate overnight.

At least an hour before you're ready to serve, place the red onion and cucumbers in a nonreactive mixing bowl. In a second bowl, combine the vinegar, water, sugar, and 2 tablespoons salt, and whisk to dissolve the sugar and salt. Pour this mixture over the cucumbers and onions, toss gently, cover, and refrigerate for at least 1 hour.

Remove and discard the hard cap of fat from the top of the braising liquid. Use 2 forks to shred the meat. Add as much of the braising liquid as necessary to flavor it and keep it nice and moist.

In a small, heavy-bottom saucepan, combine the remaining 2 cups oil and the shallots and cook together over medium-high heat until the shallots become brown and tender, 12 to 15 minutes. You may need to stir them occasionally to keep them from sticking together. Remove the shallots from the oil with the slotted spoon and let them drain on the lined plate or sheet pan. Season with salt.

To serve the dish, reheat the meat on a griddle or in a cast-iron pan until it is cooked through and crisp on the edges, adding a bit of the peanut oil if necessary. Serve the meat, topped with the fried shallots, with the pickled vegetables, sticky rice, and hot sauce.

Serves 8 to 12

PAN ROASTED VEAL CHOP WITH WILD MUSHROOMS

If you're going to do this one, go to the best butcher you can find. Don't waste your time and effort on those puny chops—often of questionable age and freshness—that are set out in your average grocery store meat bathtub. Veal is a subtle thing. Like sushi. And like sushi, the difference between decent and great is the difference between driving a Prius and a Ferrari. When buying veal, buy the best.

4 veal chops (each 12 to 14 ounces), trimmed

Salt and freshly ground black pepper to taste

2 tablespoons canola oil

2 tablespoons (¼ stick) unsalted butter

1 pound mixed wild mushrooms, thinly sliced

4 shallots, peeled and finely chopped

5 garlic cloves, peeled and finely chopped

Scant tablespoon fresh thyme leaves

¼ cup dry white wine

2 tablespoons Madeira or sherry

½ cup veal stock or Dark Universal Stock (page 260)

Preheat the oven to 450°F.

Take the chops out of the refrigerator about 20 minutes before you're ready to cook them. Season both sides with salt and pepper.

In a large, oven-proof sauté pan, heat the oil over high heat until it is smoking. Working in two batches if necessary, sear the chops in the hot oil for 3 minutes on one side. Turn the chops and sear on the second side for 1 minute. Transfer the chops to the hot oven and let cook for 6 minutes for medium-rare (which is what you want here). Remove the chops to a holding plate to rest while you cook the mushrooms.

Discard the accumulated oil and veal fat in the pan and add the butter. Cook over high heat, stirring gently with a wooden spoon to start to dislodge the browned bits and keep them from burning. Once the butter has foamed and subsided, add the mushrooms, stirring frequently. You should hear a squeak as they cross the pan. Once they start to get juicy, stir in the shallots, garlic, and thyme and season with salt and pepper. Continue to cook for another few minutes, scraping the bottom of the pan, until the mushrooms are browned and tender. Add the wine and Madeira and cook until the pan is dry and there is no smell of alcohol evident, which should take about 3 minutes. Add the stock, stir briefly, and remove from the heat. Taste and adjust the seasoning if necessary. Serve the chops with the mushrooms alongside.

Serves 4

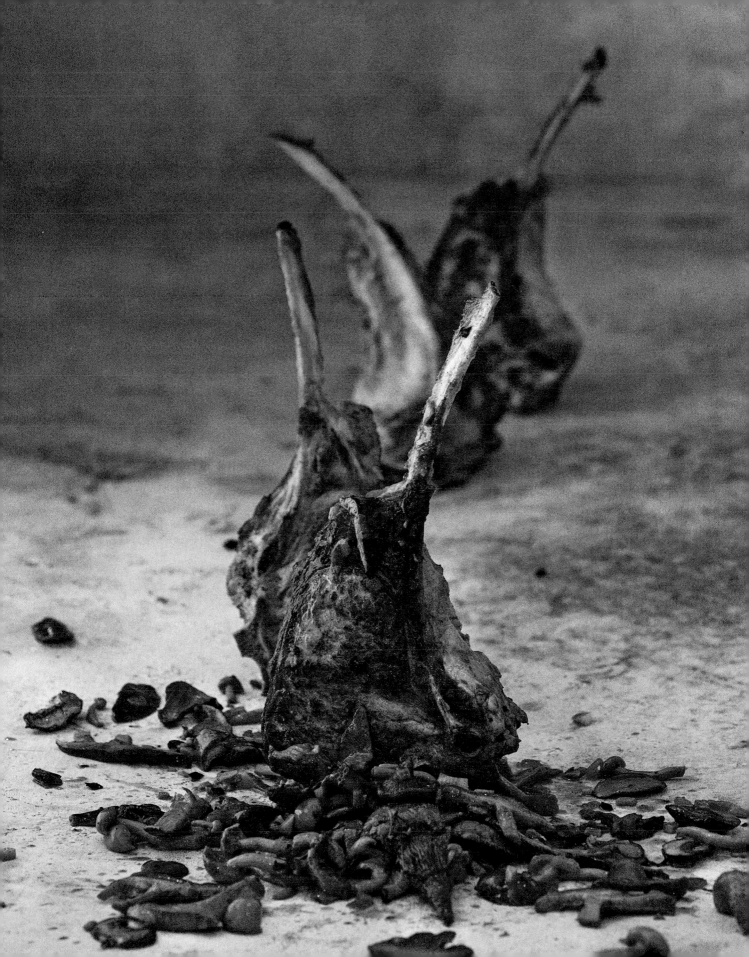

CALF'S LIVER WITH BACON, LEEKS, APPLES, AND CALVADOS

Liver . . . booze . . . fire!

½ pound slab bacon, cut into small lardons

1½ pounds calf's liver, cut crosswise into ¼- to ⅓-inch-thick slices

Salt and freshly ground black pepper to taste

½ cup all-purpose flour

1 to 2 tablespoons canola oil

2 leeks (white parts only), trimmed and diced

1 Granny Smith or similarly tart apple, cored and diced

½ cup Calvados

¾ cup veal stock or Dark Universal Stock (page 260)

1 tablespoon unsalted butter

Mashed potatoes (page 196)

SPECIAL EQUIPMENT

Plate lined with newspaper

Place the bacon in a sauté pan (one that has a lid that fits, which you'll need later) over medium heat, adding a splash of water if necessary, and cook, stirring regularly with a wooden spoon, until most of the fat has rendered and the bacon is lightly browned. Remove the bacon to the lined plate to drain; discard the fat and wipe out or wash the pan.

Season the liver on both sides with salt and pepper, and dredge it in the flour, patting off the excess. Heat 1 tablespoon of the oil in the pan until it is smoking, then add the liver, working in batches if necessary, and cook for about 1 minute per side, taking care not to overcook it—it should still have a pink tinge inside. If the flour smells like it is scorching or there's anything turning too dark in the pan, add the remaining 1 tablespoon oil. Using tongs, remove the liver to a serving platter. Add the leeks to the pan over high heat, stirring and scraping up any browned bits with the wooden spoon. Season the leeks with salt and pepper and add the apple and the bacon, continuing to cook over high heat until all are browned and the pan juices have sizzled away.

Working decisively, with sleeves and hair and kitchen towels safely secured, and your pan lid close at hand, add the Calvados, which, for safety's sake, you have poured into a second vessel, to the hot pan. If you do it right, you should experience a brief, dramatic flare-up of flame. Don't freak out—it'll disappear quickly. If it's burning too long or too high for your comfort level, put the lid on the pan, which will quickly extinguish the flames. Once the flames have disappeared, let the mixture cook for another 30 seconds, then add the stock and let reduce slightly. Add the butter and toss the pan over high heat. Taste and adjust seasoning as desired, then transfer the mixture to the serving platter alongside the liver. (You may wish to cut it into small portions for easy serving.) Serve immediately with mashed potatoes alongside.

Serves 4 to 6

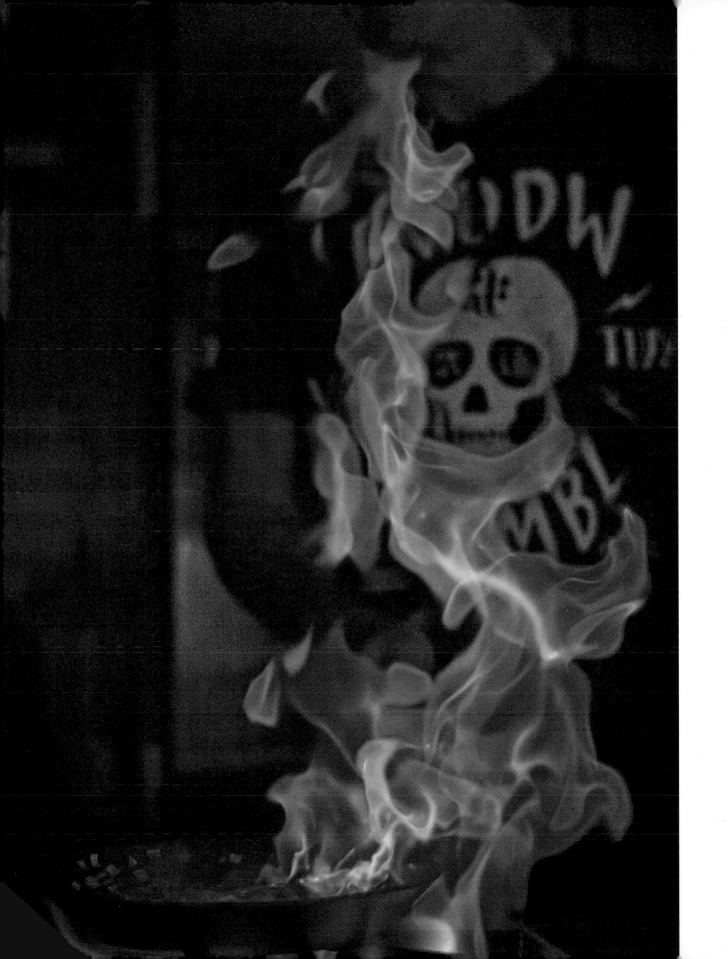

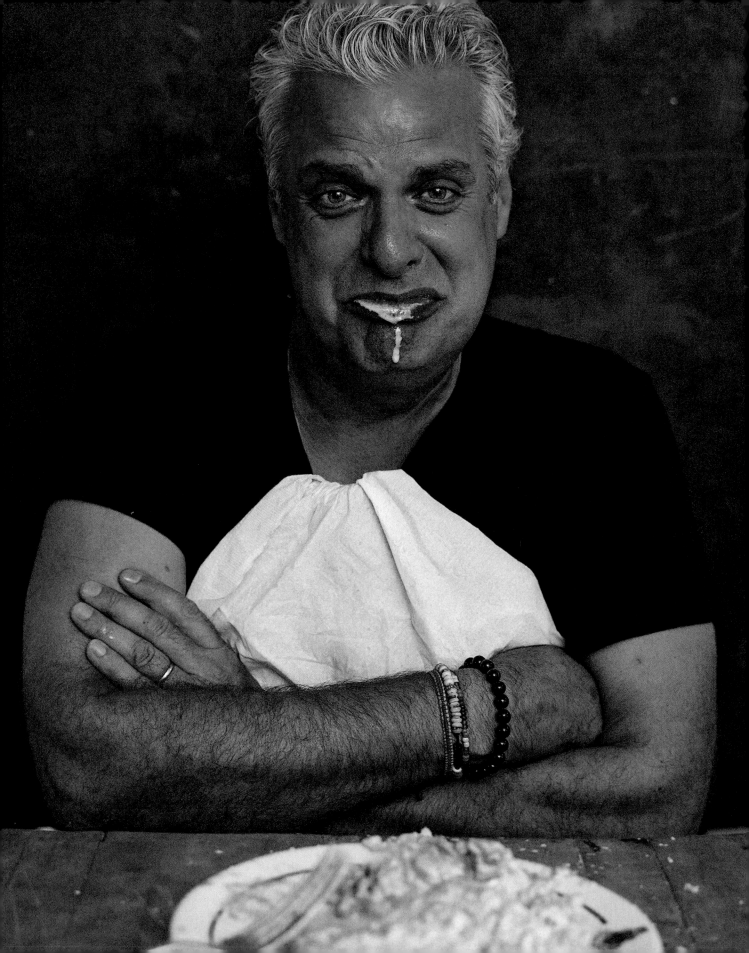

SAUSAGE GRAVY WITH BISCUITS

If you ever get the chance, introduce a Frenchman, preferably one with no cultural understanding of Southern foodways, to sausage gravy with biscuits. Comedy *will* ensue.

Ever feed a grape to a dog? The look of confusion on its face as it rolls the grape around in its mouths, unsure whether to bite the thing or spit it out? That was the look on Eric Ripert's face when he first tried sausage gravy and biscuits.

Toast the biscuits lightly, if desired. Spread each biscuit half generously with margarine and place two halves, margarine side up, on each of four plates.

Heat a large frying pan or skillet over medium-high heat and crumble the sausage into the pan. Let it render its fat and get brown and crisp as it cooks, then stir in the half-and-half, cooking and scraping up the browned bits in the pan with the wooden spoon. Season with the hot sauce and salt and pepper and ladle the gravy over each of the four biscuits. This is a slightly sloppy dish that may hit your digestive tract like a greasy bomb; I suggest Tums and Wet Wipes.

4 Buttermilk Biscuits (page 254), split

2 to 4 tablespoons margarine

2 pounds breakfast sausage

1 cup half-and-half (or equal parts heavy cream and whole milk)

Generous lashings of Frank's RedHot sauce or similar

Salt and freshly ground black pepper to taste

Serves 4

COUNTRY HAM WITH RED-EYE GRAVY AND BISCUITS

This is a good thing to make with the country ham you procured on that last road trip to the South and, indeed, a good reason to seek out high-quality country ham in the first place.

2 (¼-inch-thick) slices country ham

2 to 3 tablespoons unsalted butter

2 Buttermilk Biscuits (page 254), sliced in half

½ cup very strong black coffee

Salt and freshly ground black pepper to taste

Grape jam (optional)

Place the ham in a shallow bowl or casserole—you may need to cut each slice in half crosswise to make it fit—and cover with cold water, to reduce the saltiness. Let soak for about 20 minutes, then drain, rinse, and pat dry with paper towels.

Trim the ring of fat from around each slice of ham and place the fat in a cast-iron skillet. Cut 6 or so 1-inch slices around the perimeter of each slice of ham, which will keep it from curling in the pan. Render the ham fat in the pan over medium-low heat. Remove any remaining rind. If necessary, add a bit of butter (about a half tablespoon) so that there is enough fat in the pan to cook the ham. Add the ham to the pan and cook until browned on both sides, about 8 minutes total.

While the ham cooks, toast the biscuits lightly if desired. Spread each biscuit half generously with the remaining butter and set aside.

Once the ham is done, place 1 slice on each of 2 plates and add the coffee to the pan over high heat, stirring and scraping with a metal spatula to incorporate the browned bits and fat, though it will not actually emulsify in a meaningful way. Let the mixture bubble and reduce to about half its volume. Taste and season with salt and pepper if necessary. Serve the gravy splashed over the ham, along with hot coffee, the biscuits, and grape jam, if desired.

Serves 2

FEGATO ALLA VENEZIANA

The Venetians tend to slice the liver into small pieces—
and then proceed to cook it to shit.

I prefer to cut it into thin (but not too thin) slices, and
sauté to medium-rare. Make sure your onions are deeply
caramelized, which takes some time.

In a large, heavy-bottom sauté pan, heat 3 tablespoons of the oil
over medium-low heat, then add the onions and stir well to coat
completely. Season lightly with salt and cook, stirring frequently
with a wooden spoon, for 25 to 30 minutes, until the onions are
soft and caramelized. You can't rush this process with high heat.
Set the strainer over a medium bowl and place the onions in a
strainer to drain off the excess oil.

In a shallow bowl, whisk together the flour and enough salt and
pepper to well season all the liver.

In the same wiped-out pan used for the onions, or in a separate
large, heavy-bottom sauté pan, heat 1 tablespoon of the oil over
high heat until it is just smoking.

While the oil heats, dredge the liver pieces in the flour, patting
off the excess. Sauté the liver in the hot oil for 1 to 2 minutes per
side, and use tongs to remove the cooked pieces to a holding plate
as you add the next batch to the pan, adding the remaining oil
as necessary. Once all the liver has been cooked, reduce the heat
to medium and stir in the lemon juice, scraping the bottom with
the wooden spoon to dislodge browned bits. Return the liver and
onions to the pan and add the butter, gently tossing and agitating
the content of the pan to evenly distribute the butter. Add the
parsley and season with salt and pepper if desired. Serve at once
with the polenta crescents.

6 tablespoons olive oil

4 to 6 yellow onions, peeled and
thinly sliced (about 1 quart)

Salt to taste

1 cup all-purpose flour

Freshly ground black pepper to
taste

1½ pounds calf's liver, cut into
approximately 2-inch-wide
¼- to ⅓-inch-thick slices

Juice of 1 lemon (about
2 tablespoons)

2 tablespoons (¼ stick) unsalted
butter

½ cup freshly chopped Italian
parsley leaves

8 to 12 Fried Polenta Crescents
(page 248)

Serves 4

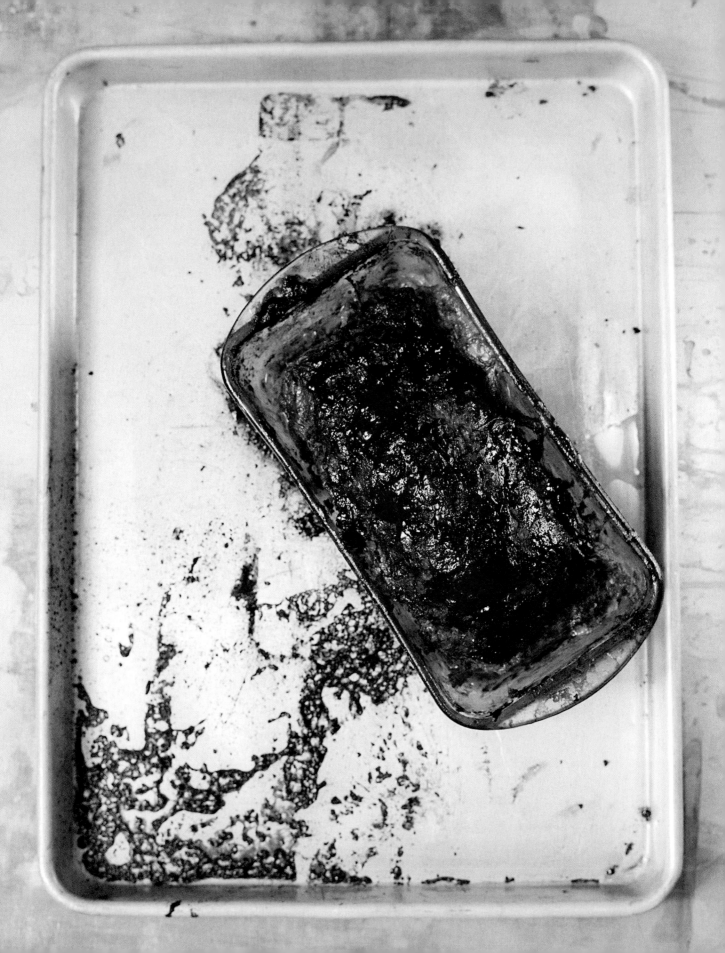

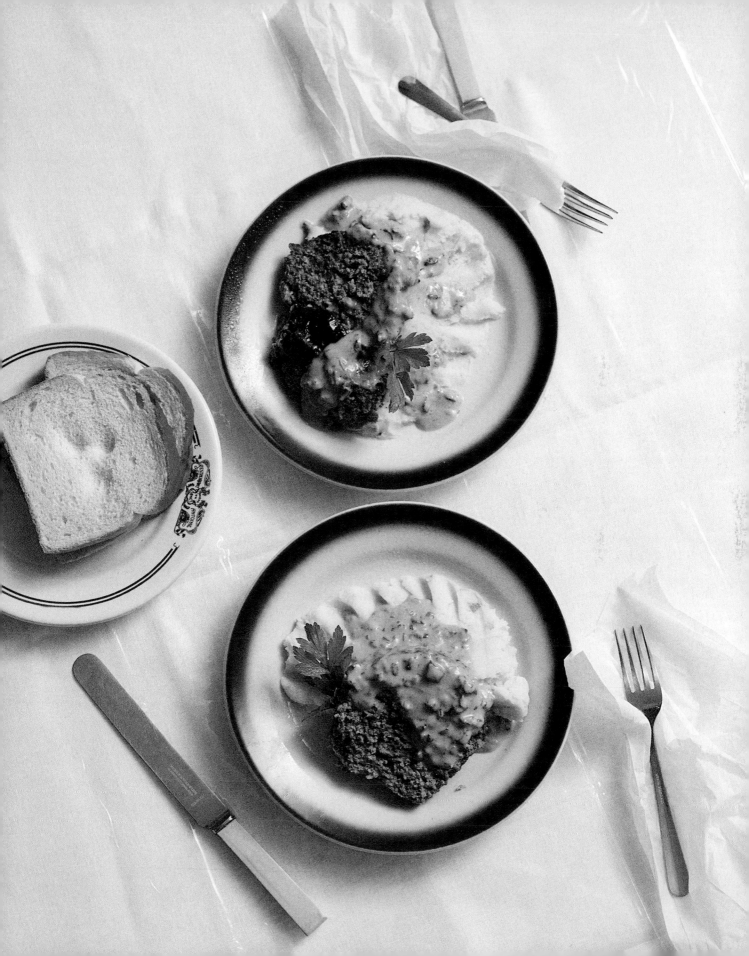

MEAT LOAF WITH MUSHROOM GRAVY

My mom's meat loaf is inarguably better than yours, but this is not my mom's meat loaf recipe. This one is an amalgam, intended to evoke all the important meat loaves in my life—and there have been many:

⁕ The meat loaf I'd get at the family table as a child.

⁕ The meat loaf I'd find (if I was lucky) in the steam table in the school cafeteria, usually festering in a pool of grayish commercial gravy. (God, I loved that stuff—especially when stoned.)

⁕ The meat loaf in the familiar foil tray of a Swanson TV dinner (which freed me from the oppression of a loving dinner table!).

⁕ The meat loaf my bosses insisted I keep on the menu at my first chef job. The restaurant failed, but the meat loaf was quite good.

This, then, is the sum of all those experiences.

2½ tablespoons canola oil

1 large yellow or white onion, peeled and very finely chopped

3 ribs celery, very finely chopped

2 sprigs fresh marjoram, leaves only, very finely chopped

3 sprigs fresh thyme, leaves only, very finely chopped

Salt and freshly ground black pepper to taste

2 pounds ground beef chuck

1⅓ pounds ground veal

3 eggs, lightly beaten

1 cup panko bread crumbs

¼ cup tomato paste

3 tablespoons unsalted butter

1 pound cremini mushrooms, diced

2 large or 3 to 4 small shallots, peeled and finely chopped (about ½ cup)

2 tablespoons all-purpose flour

1¼ cups veal stock

½ cup heavy cream

SPECIAL EQUIPMENT

Instant-read thermometer

In a large, heavy-bottom sauté pan, heat 2 tablespoons of the oil over medium heat and add the onion, celery, marjoram, and thyme. Season with salt and pepper and cook over medium-low heat, stirring regularly with a wooden spoon, until the vegetables are soft and translucent but not browned. Remove from the heat and transfer to a large mixing bowl to cool.

Preheat the oven to 350°F.

Once the vegetable mixture is cool, add the beef, veal, eggs, bread crumbs, and about 2 teaspoons salt and ½ teaspoon pepper and mix well with scrupulously clean or rubber-gloved hands. Use the remaining ½ tablespoon oil to grease a loaf pan and transfer the mixture to the pan, packing it down gently. Cover the loaf with foil and place the loaf pan on a sheet pan. Cook in the oven for 1 hour.

Remove the foil and spread the top of the meat loaf with the tomato paste. Continue to cook for another 30 to 45 minutes, until the instant-read thermometer inserted into the center reaches 150°F. Remove from the oven and let the meat loaf rest, in the loaf pan, on a wire rack.

While it rests, make the gravy. In a large, heavy-bottom sauté pan, heat the butter until it foams and subsides. Add the diced mushrooms and cook over high heat, stirring occasionally, until their released juices evaporate and the mushrooms begin to squeak against the surface of the pan when stirred. Add the shallots and salt and pepper to taste and continue to cook until the mushrooms get browned and the shallots are translucent or slightly golden, 3 to 5 minutes. Sprinkle the flour over the mushrooms and stir well to evenly coat. Cook over medium heat, stirring more or less constantly, for about 2 minutes, to cook off the raw flour taste, then stir in the stock. Whisk the mixture to pull the stuck flour up from the surface of the pan and into the gravy. Add a splash more stock or water if necessary if the mixture seems too thick, then reduce the heat to low and stir in the cream. Taste and season with salt and pepper as needed.

Serve the meat loaf in slices, with the gravy ladled over or alongside. Accompany with mashed potatoes (page 196) if you like.

Serves 6 to 12

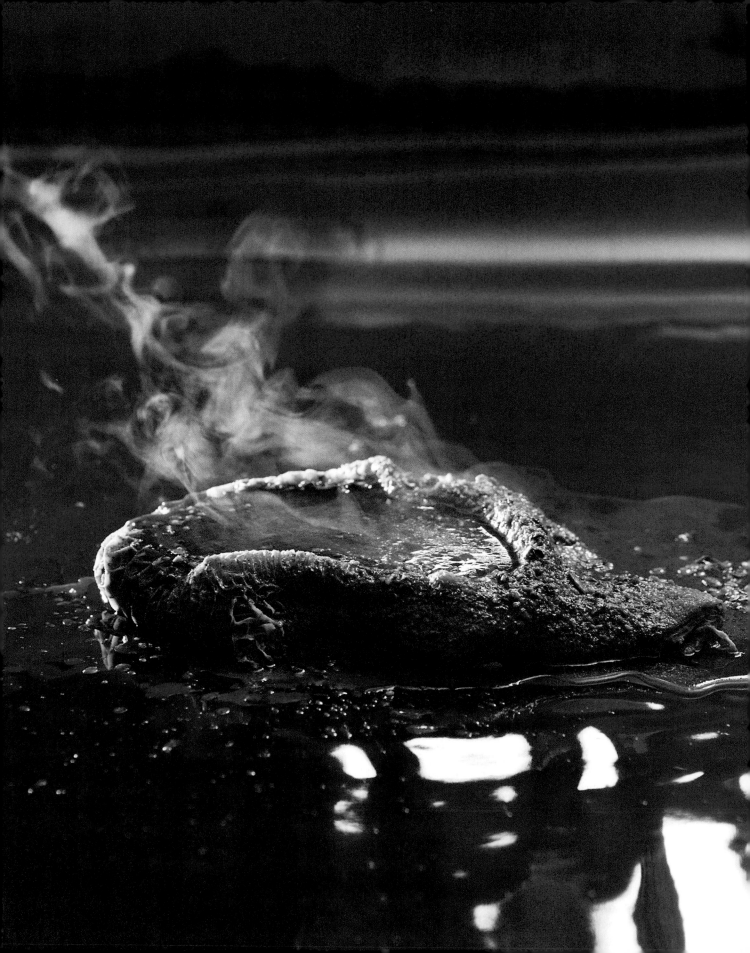

MA PO TRIPE AND PORK

Ma po tofu (*ma po* means "pockmarked grandma"), the classic Szechuan dish from which this recipe is adapted, taught me a lot of thing about myself. Dark things.

I had previously been aware of certain aspects of the "pain/pleasure" relationship, and I would err, always, on the "no pain" side. I didn't care if it was a supermodel holding the nipple clamps and the riding crop. Pain—or even mild discomfort—never sounded even remotely enticing to me.

Then I visited Chengdu in China, and among other spicy, burning, numbing, endorphin-activating, highly addictive delights, I found *ma po* tofu. And my life changed forever.

This riff, which owes a debt to Danny Bowien's constantly evolving *ma po* tofu at Mission Chinese, is intended as both an argument for tripe—and for pain.

It burns. It burns so good.

In a small cast-iron skillet or heavy-bottom sauté pan, heat 2 teaspoons of lard or fat over high heat until it is almost smoking, then add the chili peppers and reduce the heat to medium. Toast the peppers in the lard until dark red on both sides, about 4 minutes total. Use tongs to transfer the peppers to a small mixing bowl. If you want to dial back the heat, discard some of the seeds from inside the peppers once they are cool enough to handle, then transfer them to the spice grinder and grind into a fine, slightly pasty powder. Set aside.

Place the tripe in a large, heavy-bottom stockpot and add the vinegar. Cover with cold water, bring to a boil, and let boil for 10 minutes. Drain in a colander and shock in the ice-water bath. Clean out the stockpot and set aside. $\longrightarrow$

- 2 teaspoons plus 2 tablespoons rendered lard or duck fat
- 12 whole dried red chili peppers
- 1 piece tripe (3 to 4 pounds), cut into 1-inch squares
- 1 tablespoon white vinegar
- 1 ounce dried shiitake mushrooms, ground to a powder in a spice grinder
- 2 teaspoons kosher salt, plus more to taste
- 2 teaspoons freshly ground Szechuan peppercorns, plus more to taste
- 1 to 1½ pounds pork shoulder, cut into 1-inch chunks
- ¼ cup Szechuan peppercorn oil, plus more for finishing
- ⅓ cup fermented black beans
- 12 garlic cloves, peeled and finely chopped
- 8 ounces cremini mushrooms, finely chopped
- ½ cup doubanjiang (spicy fermented bean paste)
- ⅓ cup tomato paste
- 1 to 2 teaspoons powdered MSG (optional)
- 12 fluid ounces beer of no special distinction
- 2 to 3 cups Dark Universal Stock (page 260) or chicken stock
- 1 tablespoon fish sauce
- 2 tablespoons cornstarch
- Optional garnishes: pork floss, finely chopped fresh chives and/or chive blossoms, scallions, fresh cilantro leaves, steamed white rice

SPECIAL EQUIPMENT

Ice-water bath (large bowl filled
with ice and cold water)

Spice grinder

In a wide, shallow bowl, whisk together the mushroom powder and 2 teaspoons each salt and Szechuan pepper. Toss the pork cubes in this mixture to evenly coat and season.

In the stockpot, heat the remaining 2 tablespoons of lard over high heat. Working in batches to avoid overcrowding the pan, sear the pork on all sides in the hot lard, removing the meat with tongs to a nearby plate as it finishes.

Pour off any excess oil in the bottom of the pan, and over medium heat, add the Szechuan peppercorn oil, fermented black beans, garlic, mushrooms, and reserved ground chili peppers and stir, scraping the bottom of the pan with a wooden spoon to dislodge the browned bits of pork. Cook this mixture for about 5 minutes, or until the moisture from the mushrooms has largely sizzled away, then stir in the *doubanjiang,* tomato paste, and, if using, MSG and cook, stirring regularly, for 3 to 5 minutes, to let the mixture darken. Deglaze with the beer, continuing to scrape the bottom of the pan. Once the beer has reduced slightly and there is no whiff of alcohol, which should only take a few minutes, stir in 2 cups of the stock and the fish sauce and let the mixture come to a boil. Add the reserved tripe and pork and the accumulated pork juices, and add more stock if necessary to barely cover the meat. Bring to a boil, reduce the heat to a simmer, and cook, stirring occasionally, for 2 to 2½ hours, until the pork and tripe are very tender.

In a clean mixing bowl, whisk together the cornstarch and 2 tablespoons cold water to form a slurry, then add this mixture to the simmering sauce, whisking and stirring well to incorporate it into the sauce and thicken it slightly.

Taste the sauce and adjust the seasoning with additional ground peppercorns, salt, MSG, and peppercorn oil as desired. Serve in a bowl, garnished with pork floss, chives, scallions, and cilantro as desired, and possibly splashed with more peppercorn oil or with more ground peppercorns sprinkled on top, with steamed white rice alongside.

Serves 8

Roast Leg of Lamb with Flageolets

The question here is, do you want to use dry flageolet beans—which have to be soaked overnight, or at least double cooked? Or do you want to simply crack a can? There's a significant school of thought suggesting the canned might even be better. I cook my beans (canned or not) with plenty of lamb fat and seasoning. And my lamb is always roasted medium-rare—no more.

Place the beans in a medium, heavy-bottom saucepot and add 6 cups water. Bring to a boil, let cook for 5 minutes, then cover and let sit 1 hour. This method is for dried beans. If using canned beans, method can be followed as in the 3rd paragraph, but with a much shorter 15-20 minute simmering time.

Preheat the oven to 400°F. Trim and reserve the excess fat from the lamb.

Drain and rinse the beans, and return them to the pot, along with the lamb fat, 3 cloves' worth of chopped garlic, the tomatoes, oregano, bay leaves, and oil. Add water just to cover—the tomatoes will release a lot of liquid as they break down. Stir well, bring to a boil, reduce to a simmer, and cook for 45 to 60 minutes, stirring occasionally, until the beans are very tender. Season with salt and pepper once the beans are done cooking. Cover to keep warm.

While the beans simmer, in a small mixing bowl, combine the remaining garlic, the anchovies and about 2 tablespoons of the oil they were packed in, the thyme, and pepper flakes and mix well. Remove and discard the netting that the lamb has inevitably been wrapped in, and open it up to lay flat on a clean work surface. Spread it with about half of the anchovy mixture, then roll and tie it into a cylinder with the twine. Use the remaining mixture to coat the outside of the lamb. Season lightly with salt and pepper and place it in a roasting pan, ideally one with a rack.

Roast for about 1 hour and 10 minutes, rotating the pan and turning the meat after about 45 minutes, until the instant-read thermometer registers 135°F. (The temperature will rise to 140°F as it rests, for medium-rare meat.) Let the meat rest for at least 10 minutes before slicing thinly. Serve with the flageolets alongside.

2 cups dried or 3 cups canned flageolets

1 boneless lamb shoulder (or leg, about 3 pounds)

15 garlic cloves, peeled and finely chopped

2 large very ripe beefsteak or similar red tomatoes, peeled and coarsely chopped

1½ tablespoons finely chopped fresh oregano leaves

2 bay leaves

2 tablespoons extra-virgin olive oil

Salt and freshly ground black pepper to taste

20 oil-packed anchovies, drained with oil reserved and finely chopped

2 tablespoons finely chopped fresh thyme leaves

½ teaspoon red pepper flakes

Special Equipment

Butcher's twine

Instant-read thermometer

Serves 6 to 8

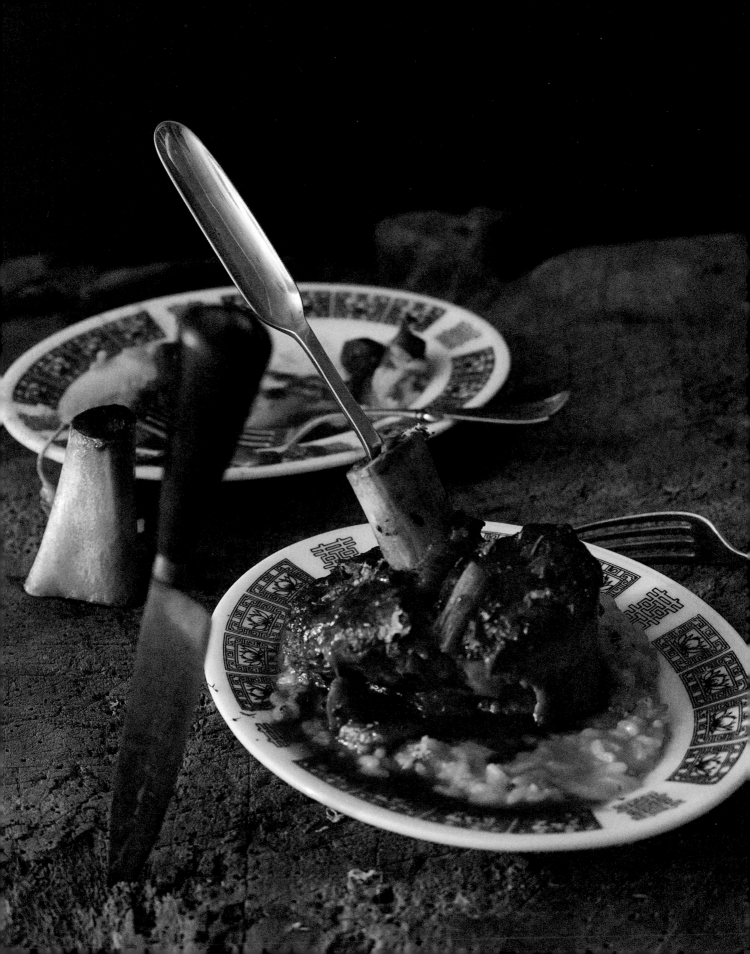

OSSO BUCCO

I learned how to make this dish at the restaurant Le Madri, which, like so many places on my résumé, is sadly no longer with us. It was, I can say without bragging (I was only the sous-chef), a very good restaurant. And this braised veal shank was a revelation. I made this for my wife (then girlfriend) on an early date. She hails from a town not far from Milan—where the dish originated—and when she saw what I'd cooked for her in my small apartment above Manganaro's Hero Boy on Ninth Avenue, she called her mom and mocked me (in Italian), incredulous that I'd do something so stupid and ambitious.

At the end of the meal, however, she said, "Not bad."

Which, coming from my wife, is high praise.

Season the veal shanks on all sides with salt and pepper, then dredge in the flour, patting off the excess.

In a large, heavy-bottom sauté pan, heat ¼ cup of the oil over medium-high heat until it shimmers. Add the veal shanks and sear until golden on both sides, working in batches if necessary. Once each shank is seared, use tongs to remove it to a sheet pan or large plate until they're all done.

In a Dutch oven, heat the remaining 3 tablespoons oil over medium heat and add the onion, carrots, celery, and garlic. Season with salt and pepper and cook, stirring regularly with a wooden spoon, until the vegetables are soft and beginning to brown, 8 to 10 minutes. Add the wine, bring to a boil, and let it reduce by half, stirring occasionally. This should take 15 to 20 minutes. Add the tomatoes and their juices and the stock, and bring to a rolling boil. Add the orange quarters, the bay leaf, rosemary, and the reserved veal shanks, return to a boil, then reduce the heat to a simmer.

Cook at a simmer, stirring very occasionally, for about 3 hours, until the veal is extremely tender and yielding to the touch. If serving immediately, place 1 shank in each of six shallow $\longrightarrow$

6 veal shanks, each about 2½ to 3 inches thick

Salt and freshly ground black pepper to taste

½ cup all-purpose flour

¼ cup plus 3 tablespoons extra-virgin olive oil

1 large yellow onion, peeled and cut into large dice

6 medium carrots, peeled and cut into large dice

2 ribs celery, cut into large dice

2 garlic cloves, peeled and thinly sliced

1 bottle dry white wine

1 (28-ounce) can whole peeled tomatoes and their juices, crushed by hand (let some chunks remain)

1½ quarts veal stock

½ orange, zested, peeled, and cut into quarters, with zest reserved for garnish

1 bay leaf

4 sprigs fresh rosemary

Whole parsley leaves (optional)

Saffron Risotto (page 238)

bowls. If serving later, remove the shanks and let cool separately from the sauce. (To reheat, return the shanks to the sauce and bring the whole thing, slowly, to a high simmer over medium heat.)

Remove and discard the rosemary sprigs, orange sections, and bay leaf from the sauce. Taste the sauce and adjust with salt and pepper as desired. Ladle some of the hot sauce over each shank and garnish with the reserved orange zest and, if using, the parsley. Serve with saffron risotto alongside or in the same bowl.

Serves 6

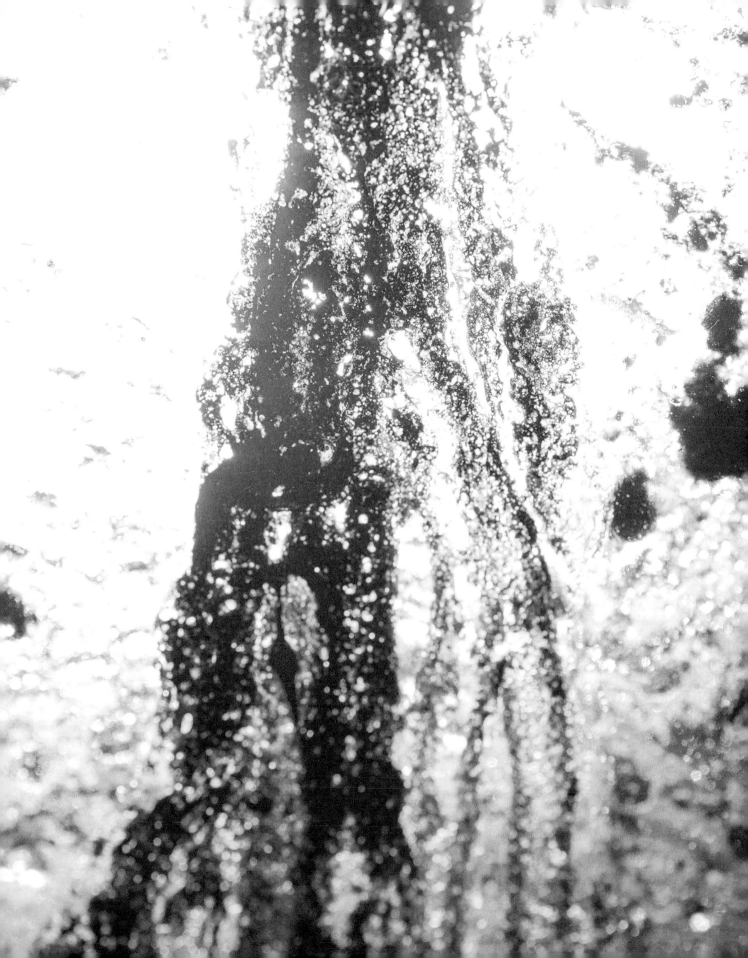

New Mexico-Style Beef Chili

4 poblano peppers

1 pound hatch chilis, fresh, frozen, or canned

½ cup all-purpose flour

Salt and freshly ground black pepper to taste

2 pounds beef chuck, cut into 1- to 2-inch chunks

2 to 3 tablespoons canola oil

1 large white or yellow onion, peeled and coarsely chopped

3 garlic cloves, peeled and coarsely chopped

1½ teaspoons ground cumin

1½ teaspoons ground coriander

1½ teaspoons dried oregano, preferably from Mexico

2 tablespoons tomato paste or harissa

1 cup beer

3 cups Dark Universal Stock (page 260) or chicken stock

Jalapeño peppers, thinly sliced, for garnish

Fresh cilantro leaves, for garnish

Toasted tortillas or freshly fried tortilla chips

Sour cream

SPECIAL EQUIPMENT

Broiler pan

No beans, no rice—chili should be about the meat and the peppers; in this case, New Mexico hatch chilis, which, outside of that fine state, can be found canned or frozen. They're piquant but mild, so you'll want to add heat with roasted poblanos at the beginning and jalapeños as a garnish. You can sub in harissa paste for tomato paste if you have it, which might be a geographic world away from the American Southwest but tastes fucking awesome.

Turn on your oven's broiler. On a broiler pan that you've lined with foil, arrange the poblano peppers, and position the oven rack so that the pan will be as close as possible to the broiler. Place the pan under the broiler and let cook until the peppers' skin is blackened, turning the peppers with tongs so that they blacken on all sides, approximately 10 to 15 minutes total. Remove from the broiler, and once cool enough to handle, remove and discard as much of the blackened skin as possible as well as the peppers' stems and some or all of the seeds (which are the source of the peppers' heat). Coarsely chop the peppers and set aside.

Repeat this procedure with the hatch chili peppers, if you have been lucky enough to procure fresh ones; the frozen or canned ones have invariably already been roasted, peeled, and seeded, in which case you can just chop them.

In a large mixing bowl, whisk together the flour and about 1 tablespoon each of the salt and pepper and toss the beef in the mixture to coat. Heat 2 tablespoons oil in a Dutch oven until just smoking, then add the beef, working in batches, and let sear until dark brown on all sides. Using tongs, remove the cooked beef to a plate and continue to cook remaining beef.

Add the onion and garlic to the hot pot and season with salt and pepper. Cook over medium-high heat, scraping the bottom of the pot with a wooden spoon to dislodge browned bits, and adding another tablespoon of oil if necessary to keep the fond or the onion from scorching. After the onion has begun to soften and brown, about 3 minutes, add the cumin, coriander, and oregano and cook for another 2 minutes, then stir in the tomato paste and beer. Bring to a boil, and cook until the liquid is reduced by about two-thirds. Stir in the stock and return the beef to the pot. Add the reserved poblano and hatch chili peppers, bring to a boil, reduce the heat to a simmer, and cook, covered, for about 90 minutes, until the beef is fork tender.

Remove from the heat and serve in bowls, with the jalapeños, cilantro, tortillas, and sour cream alongside, as well as lots of cold beer, preferably from New Mexico.

Serves 6 to 8

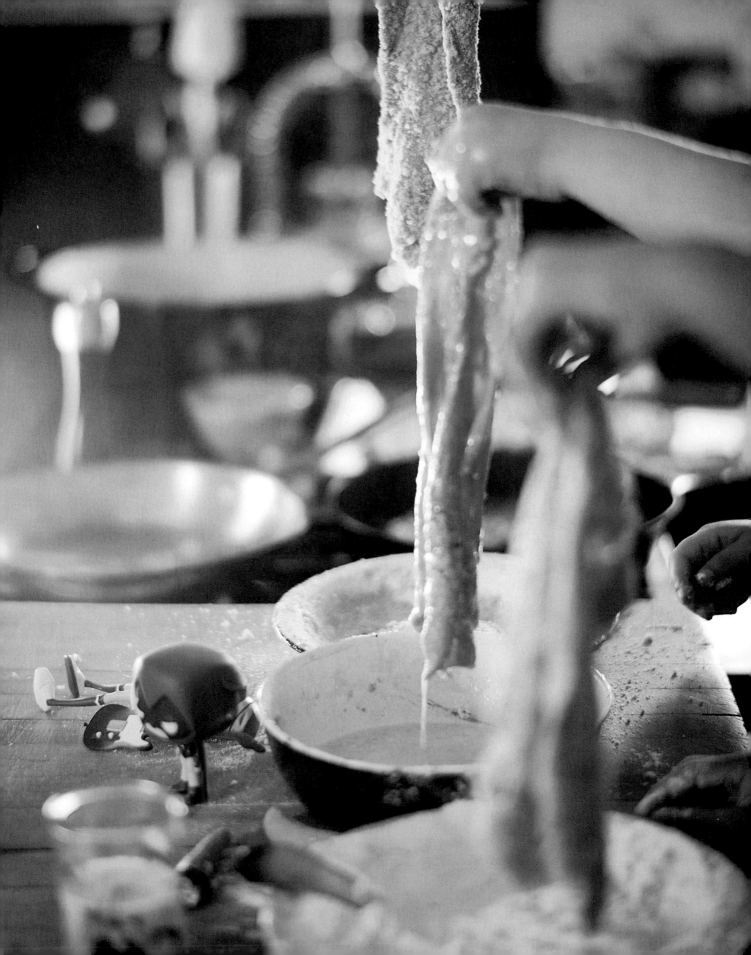

VEAL MILANESE

This is a father-daughter favorite around my house. Actually, it's a dish that I usually prepare for Ariane *and* her best friend, Jacques. My wife doesn't eat carbs, of course—she's too busy honing her body into a lethal weapon to consider simple pleasures like a pounded veal chop, breaded and fried.

We share the work. The kids set up a breading station, and between them, they handle flouring, egging, and coating the veal with bread crumbs before being allowed to gingerly lay the cutlets into hot oil in the pan. No injuries yet!

1 cup all-purpose flour

Salt and freshly ground black pepper to taste

2 cups panko bread crumbs

1 cup finely grated Parmesan cheese

2 large eggs, beaten

8 veal leg cutlets (5 to 6 ounces each), pounded to ¼-inch thickness

2 cups peanut oil

SPECIAL EQUIPMENT

Deep-fry or candy thermometer

Preheat the oven to 200°F. Place the flour in a rimmed plate or shallow bowl and season with salt and pepper. Combine the bread crumbs and cheese in another rimmed plate and mix well. Place the eggs in a third rimmed plate and season with salt and pepper.

Season each piece of veal with salt and pepper on both sides. Dredge each piece in the flour, patting off the excess. Next dredge each piece in egg, letting the excess drip off, then dredge each piece in the bread crumb mixture, pressing so that they adhere well. Place each piece of prepared veal on a sheet pan.

Place a wire rack on another sheet pan and place it in the center of the warmed oven.

Add the oil to a large, tall-sided skillet and bring it to 375°F, monitoring the temperature with the deep-fry thermometer. Carefully slip the veal into the oil, working in batches of two or three pieces at a time to avoid bringing down the temperature of the oil, which you should continue to monitor as the veal cooks. Cook until the cutlets are browned on both sides, about 6 minutes, then carefully remove the cutlets with tongs, and transfer to the warmed oven. Continue with the remaining pieces, season them with additional salt as desired, and serve.

Serves 4 to 8

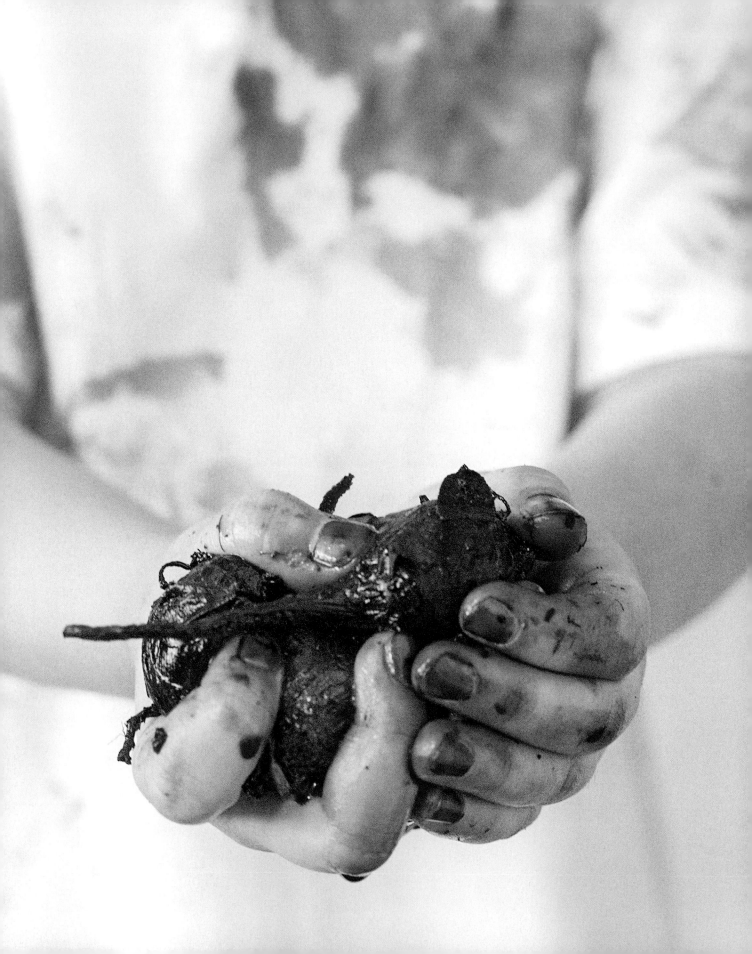

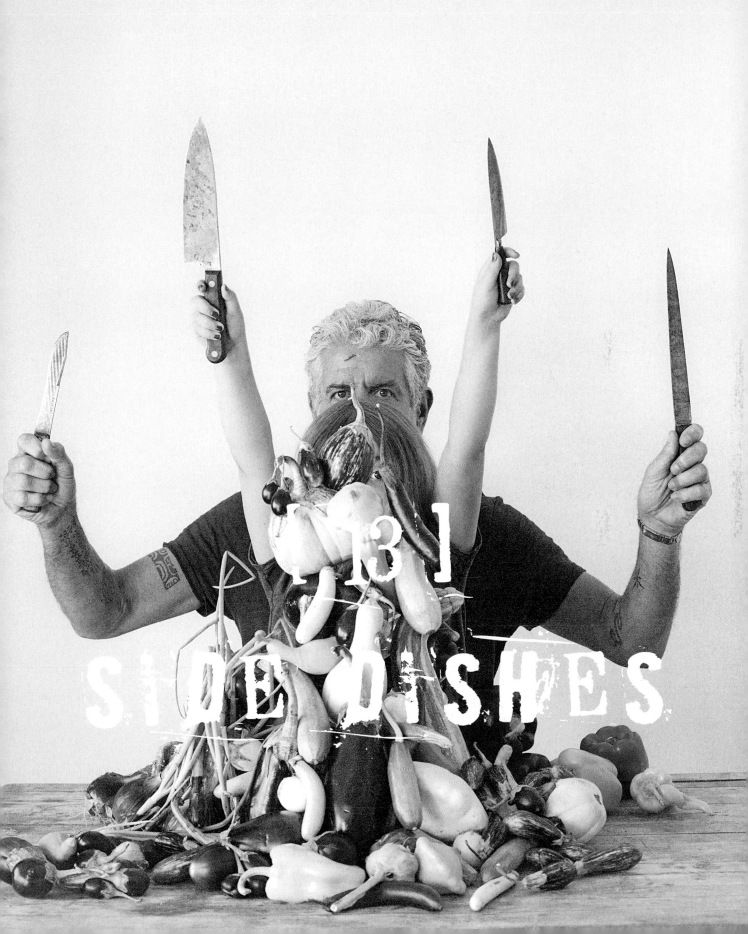

[13]

SIDE DISHES

RATATOUILLE

Don't prepare this recipe, as I did, for a table full of Provençales. They will likely compliment you on your "nice vegetable dish" but will *not* call it "ratatouille." They have a point. Ratatouille is traditionally sort of sludgy. All the components are cooked together, encouraged to "marry."

I just can't.

In a break with the "right way" to do things, I cook all the vegetables separately, highlighting their differences, while (ideally) honoring the original flavor profiles. This version is fresher and crisper—and undeniably prettier.

1 to 1¼ cups extra-virgin olive oil

1 medium red onion, peeled and diced

4 garlic cloves, peeled and finely chopped

½ cup tomato paste

6 sprigs fresh thyme, leaves only, chopped

2 medium zucchini, trimmed and diced

Salt and freshly ground black pepper to taste

1 medium yellow squash, trimmed and diced

1 large red bell pepper, cored, seeded, and diced

1 medium eggplant, diced (but save the internal pieces without skin for baba ganoush or another dish—it's crucial that each piece in this dish have some skin attached)

1 to 2 teaspoons high-quality aged balsamic vinegar

2 sprigs fresh basil, leaves only, coarsely chopped

In a large, heavy-bottom sauté pan, heat ¼ cup of the oil over high heat. Add the onion and garlic; when the onion is translucent and just beginning to brown, reduce the heat and stir in the tomato paste and thyme. Remove from the heat and transfer the mixture to a sheet pan to cool.

Wipe out the sauté pan (or use a clean one) and heat 2 tablespoons of the oil in it over high heat. Add the zucchini and sauté over high heat until tender and beginning to become golden brown at the edges. Season with salt and pepper, remove from the heat, and transfer to the sheet pan with the onion mixture, keeping it segregated.

Repeat this procedure with another 1 or 2 tablespoons of the oil as needed, and the squash, pepper, and eggplant, cooking each vegetable separately, seasoning with salt and pepper, and allowing it to cool on the sheet pan. Wipe out the pan between vegetables.

Once the vegetables have cooled to room temperature, combine them in a large mixing bowl and toss gently. Add the balsamic and remaining oil to taste. Adjust the seasoning with salt and pepper, add the basil, and let the mixture sit at room temperature for 3 to 4 hours to let the flavors marry. Serve at room temperature.

Serves 6 to 8 as a side dish

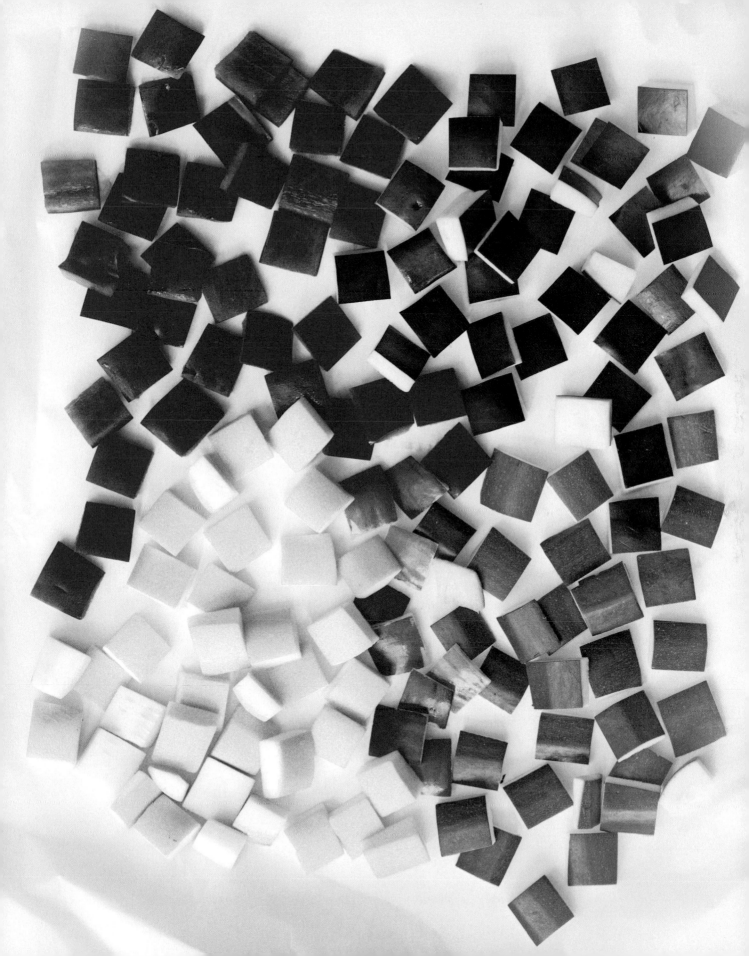

SAFFRON RISOTTO

Years ago, in response to a short piece about risotto in the food pages of a New York newspaper, a well-known Italian restaurateur wrote an angry and impassioned editorial, denouncing the piece, in particular its assertion that you could half-cook risotto before spreading it out to cool, then finish the cooking when your guests arrive. *No* respectable Italian would *ever* do such a thing, wailed the restaurateur.

Which struck me as amusing. Because I'd worked for the prick—and I never saw risotto cooked any other way while in his employ. At any given moment, there'd be two full sheet pans of half-cooked risotto sitting on a station, and another two in the walk-in refrigerator.

Does this cheat impact the quality of the risotto? Yes. Most assuredly. But how much? So much that it's worth abandoning your guests for twenty-five minutes while you stand there in the kitchen, stirring fucking rice? So much that any of your friends can even tell the difference? No disrespect to your friends, but I sincerely doubt it.

Just be careful to not overcook it during the initial "blanch"—and finish it correctly. You want a fairly soupy, porridgy consistency. Your risotto should not stand up in a heap.

And please, please, please: If you're making risotto as an entrée, or as a course all its own, do not overload it with ingredients. Wild mushrooms, truffles, asparagus—whatever. Pick one.

And don't even think about truffle oil.

Pour half the stock into a small, heavy-bottom pot and add the saffron threads. Bring to a low simmer over medium-low heat to begin to infuse the stock with the saffron.

In a medium, heavy-bottom pot, heat the oil over medium-low heat and add the onion. Stir well with a wooden spoon to coat with the oil and cook, stirring frequently, until the onion is soft and translucent but not browned, about 5 minutes. Stir in the rice, increase the heat to medium-high, and cook for 3 to 4 minutes, until the rice smells slightly toasty. Decrease the heat to medium-low and add the wine. Stir regularly until the wine has been absorbed by the rice and the sharp alcohol smell has cooked off.

Add the saffron-infused stock, a ladleful or two at a time, stirring regularly and adding more as each batch becomes absorbed. Once all of the saffron stock has been added, heat up the remaining stock using the same pot; continue to add that stock to the rice, stirring with each addition. Check the rice for doneness: It should be tender and cooked through, but not mushy. The mixture as a whole should be runny enough to cover the bottom of a bowl; add more stock as necessary so that the risotto doesn't sit up in a stiff lump.

Beat the butter and cheese into the hot rice mixture with the wooden spoon. Your goal is to incorporate some air into the mixture, to lighten the texture. Taste and season with salt. Serve immediately.

1½ quarts chicken stock

Generous pinch of saffron threads

¼ cup extra-virgin olive oil

1 small yellow onion, peeled and finely chopped

1½ cups carnaroli rice

½ cup dry white wine

4 tablespoons (½ stick) cold unsalted butter, cut into small chunks

½ cup finely grated Parmigiano-Reggiano cheese

Salt to taste

Serves 6 as a side dish

CREAMED SPINACH

There's no need to obscure the taste and color of fresh spinach with a béchamel sauce; some heavy cream and butter are all you need. The hardest and most important part here is making sure your spinach is completely grit-free.

Fill a large bowl with cold water and plunge the spinach into it, agitating a bit to get as much of the sand and dirt as possible to fall off the leaves and into the water below. Lift the spinach up and out of the water and into a colander; if there is a significant quantity of dirt and grit in the washing water, dump it out, rinse the bowl, fill it with cold water, and repeat the washing process. Let the excess water drain from the spinach, but don't dry it; the water that clings to the leaves is what you need to gently steam it.

Heat a large sauté or braising pan over medium heat and add the spinach, working in batches, turning it gently with tongs and letting it cook until it is just wilted and bright green, no more than 5 minutes. Transfer each batch of steamed spinach to a colander (a second one may prove useful here) and, when it's all been steamed and is cool enough to handle, wrap it in one or more clean dish towels or layers of paper towels and wring from it as much water as possible. Coarsely chop the spinach, then arrange it on a sheet pan to further cool and air dry for about 15 to 20 minutes.

In a medium, heavy-bottom saucepan, combine the heavy cream and garlic and bring to a simmer. Let simmer over low heat for 15 to 20 minutes, then strain out the mixture through the sieve into a bowl, discard the garlic, and return the cream to the saucepan over medium heat.

Stir the spinach into the warm cream, then add the butter and continue to stir until it is melted. Puree the mixture with the immersion blender or pulse it in the food processor. Taste and season with salt and pepper, and, if desired, nutmeg. Transfer to a serving dish and serve immediately.

3 pounds fresh spinach, roots and tough stems removed

1½ cups heavy cream

2 garlic cloves, peeled, crushed, and coarsely chopped

3 tablespoons unsalted butter, cut into cubes

Salt and freshly ground black pepper to taste

Freshly grated nutmeg (optional)

SPECIAL EQUIPMENT

Immersion blender or food processor

Serves 8 to 12 as a side dish

ROASTED CAULIFLOWER with SESAME

This shit is compulsively delicious. One adult could easily eat the entire head of cauliflower for dinner and feel good about it.

Preheat the oven to 450°F.

In a large mixing bowl, combine the cauliflower, oil, salt, coriander, oregano, and pepper and toss well to evenly coat the cauliflower with the oil and spices. Transfer to a sheet pan and arrange in an even layer, making spaces between the pieces as much as possible. Roast the cauliflower in the oven for 20 minutes, turning the tray and lightly tossing the pieces halfway through.

While the cauliflower roasts, combine the tahini, miso, vinegar, and 1½ tablespoons water in a small mixing bowl, and whisk until smooth.

Once the cauliflower is done, remove it from the oven, transfer to a mixing bowl, and toss with the sauce and sesame seeds to coat evenly.

1 head of cauliflower, broken by hand into florets

¼ cup extra-virgin olive oil

2 teaspoons salt

1 teaspoon ground coriander

1 teaspoon dried oregano

Freshly ground black pepper to taste

2 tablespoons tahini

1 tablespoon white miso

2 teaspoons red wine vinegar

1½ tablespoons water

3 tablespoons toasted white sesame seeds

Serves 4 to 6 as a side dish

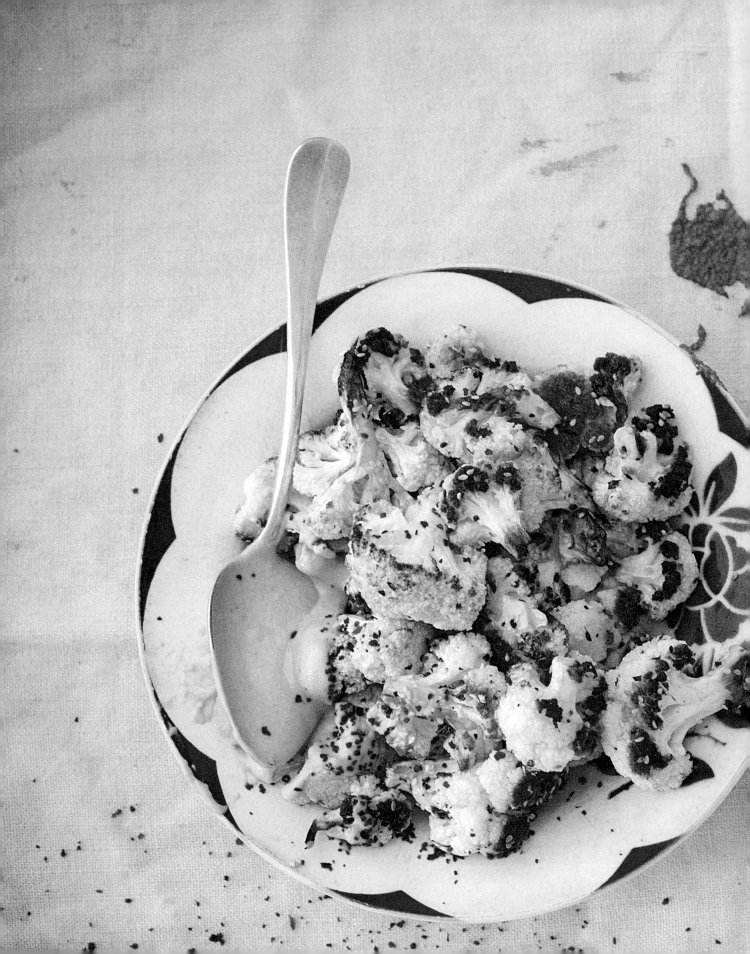

BRAISED BELGIAN ENDIVE

Straight out of Escoffier, by way of a dinner party in the Greenwich, Connecticut, of the early 1980s.

½ cup all-purpose flour

1 teaspoon salt

½ teaspoon freshly ground black pepper

2 to 3 tablespoons unsalted butter

4 heads of Belgian endive, washed, trimmed, and cut in half lengthwise

½ cup dry white wine

1 cup veal stock or Dark Universal Stock (page 260)

2 tablespoons finely chopped fresh parsley

In a shallow bowl or plate, whisk together the flour, salt, and pepper.

In a large, heavy-bottom sauté pan, heat 1 tablespoon of the butter over medium-high heat until it foams and subsides. Dredge the endive halves in the flour, patting off the excess, and place them, cut side down, in the pan. Let cook for about 3 minutes, then turn with tongs to sear on the opposite side for another 3 minutes. This may need to be done in two batches, with an additional tablespoon of butter; put the cooked endive aside on the holding plate while you cook the rest. Return all of the cooked endives to the pan, pour in the wine, agitate the pan slightly, and let it reduce to nearly dry, then add the stock, agitate the pan, and reduce the heat to a simmer. Cover the pan and let the endives braise until tender, about 10 minutes. Add the remaining 1 tablespoon butter, and, once it has been incorporated into the braising liquid, taste and season with salt and pepper as needed. Remove the endives and sauce to a serving platter, garnish with parsley, and serve.

Serves 4 as a side dish

MUSHROOM SAUTÉED WITH SHALLOTS

Because they are so full of moisture, screaming high heat is essential here for getting your mushrooms to brown, and not steam, in the pan, so really preheat the pan before adding them. Use only the small amount of oil called for here, and do not overload the pan. You are sautéing, not poaching. Do not screw this up with any of these common—but entirely avoidable—mistakes.

In a large, heavy-bottom sauté pan, heat the oil over high heat until it shimmers and just begins to smoke. Add the mushrooms and cook over high heat, tossing and stirring frequently with a wooden spoon or spatula, until the mushrooms become browned at the edges, and fragrant, about 4 minutes. The mushrooms should make a squeaking noise as they move across the pan.

Add the shallots and season with salt and pepper. Adding salt will cause the mushrooms to release their juices. Continue to cook over high heat until the juices have been sizzled away. Once the mushrooms are well browned and tender, add the butter, toss well to coat, then add the parsley. Remove from the heat and serve at once.

1 tablespoon canola or grapeseed oil

1 pound mushrooms, any variety, thinly sliced

4 shallots, peeled and finely chopped

Salt and freshly ground black pepper to taste

1 tablespoon unsalted butter

¼ cup finely chopped fresh parsley

Serves 4 to 6 as a side dish

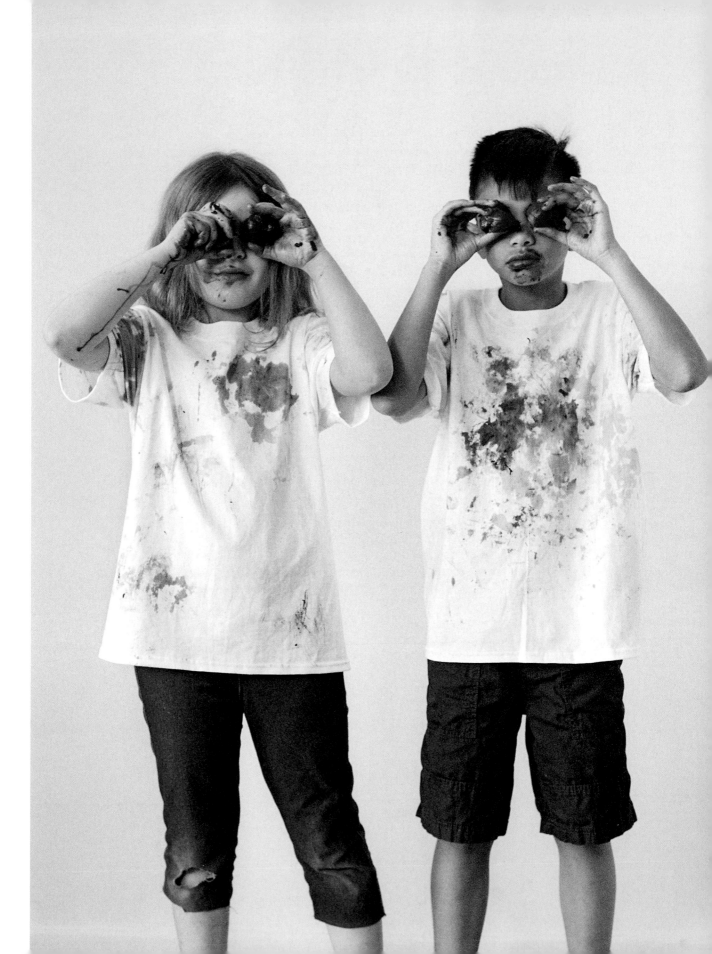

ROASTED BABY BEETS WITH RED ONION AND ORANGES

This is a staple dish in my home, where my daughter devours it. You need not use high-quality extra-virgin olive oil; opt for a neutral oil and let the beet, onion, and citrus juices do the work.

Preheat the oven to 450°F.

Toss the beets in a roasting pan with 1 tablespoon of the oil, and roast in the oven for 45 to 50 minutes, until a paring knife slips easily into the center. Once the beets are cool enough to handle, slip off and discard the skins.

Let the beets cool to room temperature, then cut into ¼-inch-thick slices. Toss in a mixing bowl with the onion, orange, vinegar, the remaining 1 tablespoon oil, and, if using, mint. Season with salt and pepper and serve.

1 pound baby beets (6 to 8 beets), scrubbed and trimmed

2 tablespoons canola or grapeseed oil

½ medium red onion, peeled and thinly sliced

1 navel orange, peeled and cut crosswise into ¼-inch-thick wheels

2 teaspoons cider vinegar

12 fresh mint leaves, torn (optional)

Salt and freshly ground black pepper to taste

Serves 4 as a side dish

FRIED POLENTA CRESCENTS

Sure, you can make pedestrian polenta triangles, but it's not so difficult to make the more visually interesting crescents.

Combine the polenta and stock in a large bowl, stir a bit, cover, and refrigerate at least 4 hours and up to 12. (Skip this step, and accept a longer cooking time—60 rather than 30 minutes. Your call.)

Transfer the polenta and stock to a large, heavy-bottom saucepot. Stir it and bring it to a boil, then reduce to a simmer and cook, stirring regularly but not necessarily constantly, for about 30 minutes. Once the polenta is tender and has absorbed all of the liquid, stir in 2 tablespoons of the butter and the cheese, whip well with a wooden spoon, season with salt and pepper, then remove from the heat.

1 cup medium-coarse polenta (also known as "corn grits")

5 cups water or chicken stock

4 tablespoons (½ stick) unsalted butter

1 cup finely grated Parmigiano-Reggiano cheese

Salt and freshly ground black pepper to taste

4 to 6 tablespoons extra-virgin olive oil

Grease a half sheet pan with 1 tablespoon oil and turn the hot polenta onto it. Wet or oil a spatula and use it to get the polenta as evenly distributed as possible across the tray; bang it decisively against the countertop to knock out any air bubbles. Let cool to room temperature, then wrap in plastic wrap and refrigerate for several hours, until completely chilled.

Transfer the polenta from the refrigerator to a cutting board, lifting it in one or two sections, using the spatula and an abundance of caution. With a 2- or 3-inch-diameter round cookie cutter, cut as many large circles from the polenta as you can. Cut each in half to form crescents. (If you want to get fancy, use a smaller cutter to cut away a section from each large circle to form a true crescent shape. This process can also be done freehand.)

In a large, heavy-bottom sauté pan, heat 1 tablespoon oil and 1 tablespoon butter together until the butter foams and subsides. Working in batches, fry the crescents in the pan for 3 to 4 minutes per side, until golden brown on the edges, turning them carefully with a spatula and draining them on a cooling rack when done. As they cook and absorb fat, you may need to add the remaining butter and oil, a tablespoon or less at a time. Season with salt and pepper as needed and serve with Fegato alla Veneziana (page 217).

Serves 6 to 8 as a side dish, with probable leftovers

Pommes Anna

If using a cast-iron skillet here, make sure it's well seasoned to avoid the heartbreak of incomplete detachment when flipping the potatoes out of the pan to serve. For entertaining, I suggest making this several hours before guests arrive, and gently reheating it in a 300°F oven.

Preheat the oven to 400°F.

Peel the potatoes, and working quickly to avoid their discoloring, slice them very thinly in the food processor. Place the slices in a single layer on paper towels or clean kitchen towels and pat them dry.

Use a pastry brush to generously coat a 10- to 12-inch cast-iron or nonstick ovenproof skillet with some of the melted butter. Arrange a layer of potato slices in an overlapping circle in the bottom of the skillet. Brush these with the melted butter, season with salt and pepper, then top with another layer of potatoes in an overlapping circle. Brush with butter, season, and repeat until all of the potatoes have been added to the pan, seasoned, and buttered.

Brush the parchment paper lid with butter, press down gently on the potatoes, and cover with the lid. Cook in the oven for 30 minutes, then rotate the pan and cook for another 15 to 30 minutes, until the potatoes are golden brown and easily pierced with a paring knife. Remove from the oven, let rest 5 minutes, remove the parchment lid, then run a spatula around the edges of the cake to loosen any stuck edges. Invert a large plate over the pan, and working quickly and decisively, invert the potato cake onto the plate.

4 pounds Yukon Gold potatoes (about 10 to 12 large potatoes)

½ pound (2 sticks) unsalted butter, melted

Sea salt to taste

Crushed black peppercorns to taste

Special Equipment

Food processor fitted with thin slicing blade

Parchment paper, cut into a circle the same diameter as the pan

Serves 4 to 8 as a side dish

GARBANZOS WITH CHERRY TOMATOES

Here, good olive oil is essential.

2 cups cooked garbanzo beans, drained

⅓ cup plus 1 tablespoon best-quality extra-virgin olive oil

4 garlic cloves, peeled and thinly sliced

Juice of 1 lemon (about 2 tablespoons)

½ teaspoon salt, plus more to taste

1 pint ripe cherry tomatoes

2 tablespoons coarsely chopped fresh Italian parsley

In a medium-sized, nonreactive bowl, combine the beans, ⅓ cup oil, garlic, lemon juice, and salt and mix well. Cover and let sit at room temperature for 3 to 4 hours. (If letting marinate any longer, up to 24 hours, cover and refrigerate.)

Heat the oven to 400°F. (Ideally you're roasting some chicken thighs or a piece of fish on the bottom rack of the oven, and have room on the top for the tomatoes.) On a sheet pan, toss the tomatoes with 1 tablespoon oil. Place in the oven and cook for 15 to 20 minutes, until the tomatoes are warm and softening but not yet bursting. Remove from the heat and stir into the garbanzo bean mixture, along with the parsley. Taste and adjust seasoning as desired.

Serves 4 to 8 as a side dish or atop toast

KOREAN-STYLE RADISH PICKLES

Do not let the pungent intensity put you off; these pickles are delicious and essential to the Korean Fried Chicken (page 165) experience.

In a medium mixing bowl, whisk together the water, vinegar, sugar, and salt. Add the radish and stir gently, then transfer everything to a glass or ceramic casserole dish. Cover and let sit at room temperature for 8 to 12 hours, or overnight. Transfer to the refrigerator and let sit for at least another 24 hours, and up to 3 days, before serving.

¼ cup water

¼ cup white vinegar

¼ cup sugar

2 teaspoons salt

1 large daikon radish (about 1 pound), peeled and cut into ½-inch cubes

---

Serves 10 to 12 as a side dish for fried chicken

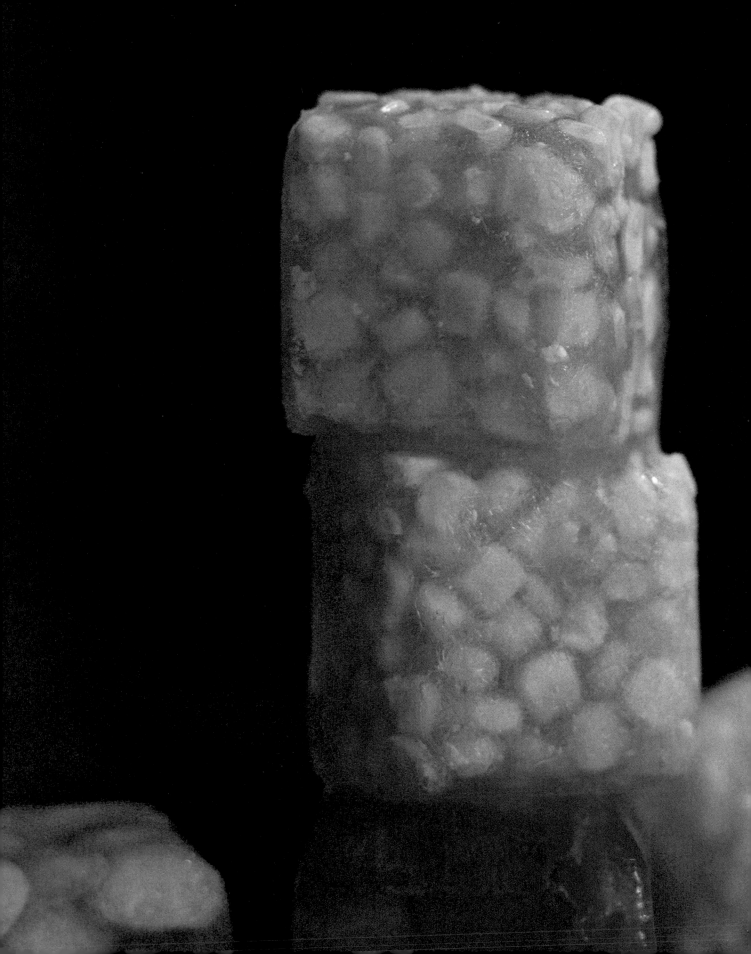

SUCCOTASH

A completely acceptable vehicle for frozen lima beans, and perhaps the only reason they ought to exist and endure.

In a large, heavy-bottom sauté pan, heat the butter over medium heat until it foams and subsides. Add the onion and bell pepper; cook and stir until the onion is translucent but not yet browning. Add the garlic and cook for another minute, then add the tomato and season with salt and pepper. Once the tomato begins to break down and release its juices, after about 2 minutes, stir in the lima beans, water, and herbs. Cook and stir occasionally over medium-low heat for about 15 minutes, then stir in the corn and cook for an additional 5 minutes. Taste and adjust the seasoning if desired, then serve.

Serves 8 to 10 as a side dish

2 tablespoons (¼ stick) unsalted butter

1 small yellow onion, peeled and finely diced

1 medium to large red bell pepper, cored, seeded, and diced

3 garlic cloves, peeled and finely chopped

1 large ripe red tomato, peeled, cored, seeded, and finely chopped

Salt and freshly ground black pepper to taste

2 cups frozen lima beans, thawed

1 cup water or Dark Universal Stock (page 260)

1 tablespoon finely chopped fresh oregano

1 tablespoon finely chopped fresh thyme

2 tablespoons finely chopped fresh parsley

2 cups corn kernels

BUTTERMILK BISCUITS

Don't be afraid: Biscuits are easy as long as you do a few crucial things right, as per below. I've tried making these with lard, duck fat, and Crisco, but the best, fluffiest results come from ice-cold butter.

Preheat the oven to 450°F.

Let the frozen butter sit at room temperature for 5 minutes, then cut it into ½-inch cubes. Transfer the cubes to a small mixing bowl and place it in the refrigerator.

In a large mixing bowl, whisk together the flour, sugar, salt, baking powder, and baking soda. Get the butter from the fridge and add it to the flour mixture, taking care to distribute it evenly. Working with a quick but light hand, use a pastry cutter to incorporate the butter and flour until it looks like coarse crumbs with some pea-size lumps. Add the cold buttermilk all at once and stir the mixture with a wooden spoon, using as few strokes as possible until the dough just comes together. Flour your hands and gently knead the dough five to ten times, just enough to bring it together a bit more and flatten some of the butter lumps.

Lightly flour a clean cutting board or other work surface and transfer the mixture to it. Use gentle pressure to press out the dough to a more or less even ¾-inch thickness. Cut as many biscuits as possible, using a simple grid pattern. Transfer the biscuits to the prepared sheet pan, leaving about 1 inch between each one.

Use a pastry brush to brush the top of each biscuit with the melted butter. Transfer to the oven and cook for 10 to 12 minutes, until they are golden brown and fragrant. Serve hot.

Makes about nine 3-inch biscuits or fifteen 2-inch biscuits

8 tablespoons (1 stick) frozen unsalted butter, plus 1 tablespoon unsalted butter, melted

2 cups all-purpose flour, plus about ¼ cup more for kneading and rolling

2 teaspoons sugar

1 teaspoon salt

2 teaspoons baking powder

½ teaspoon baking soda

¾ cup cold buttermilk

SPECIAL EQUIPMENT

Sheet pan lined with parchment paper

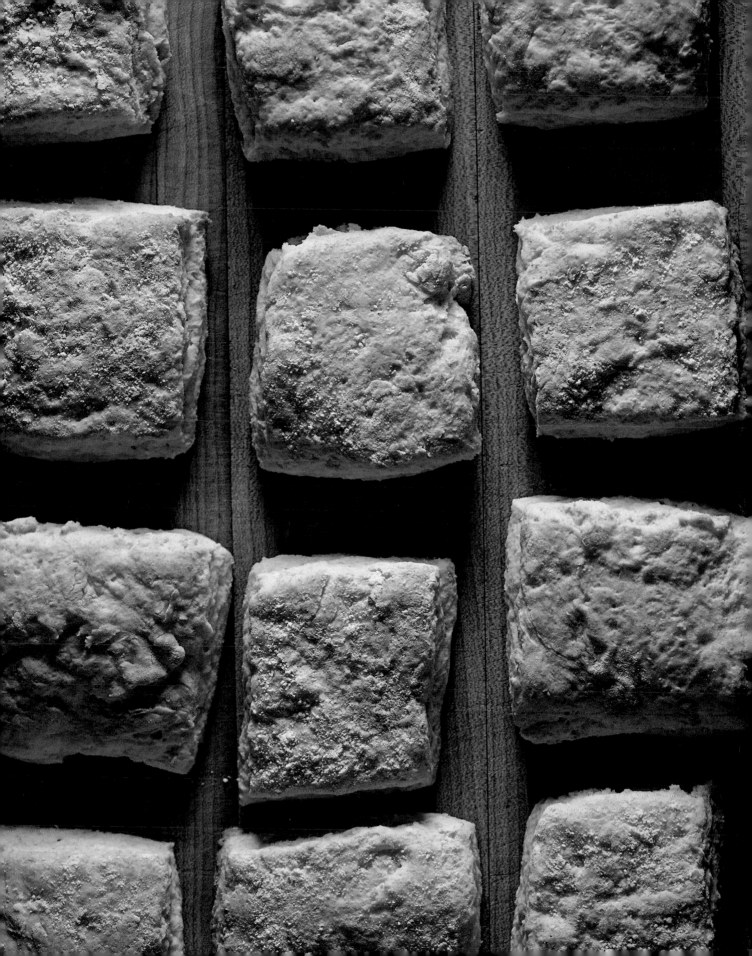

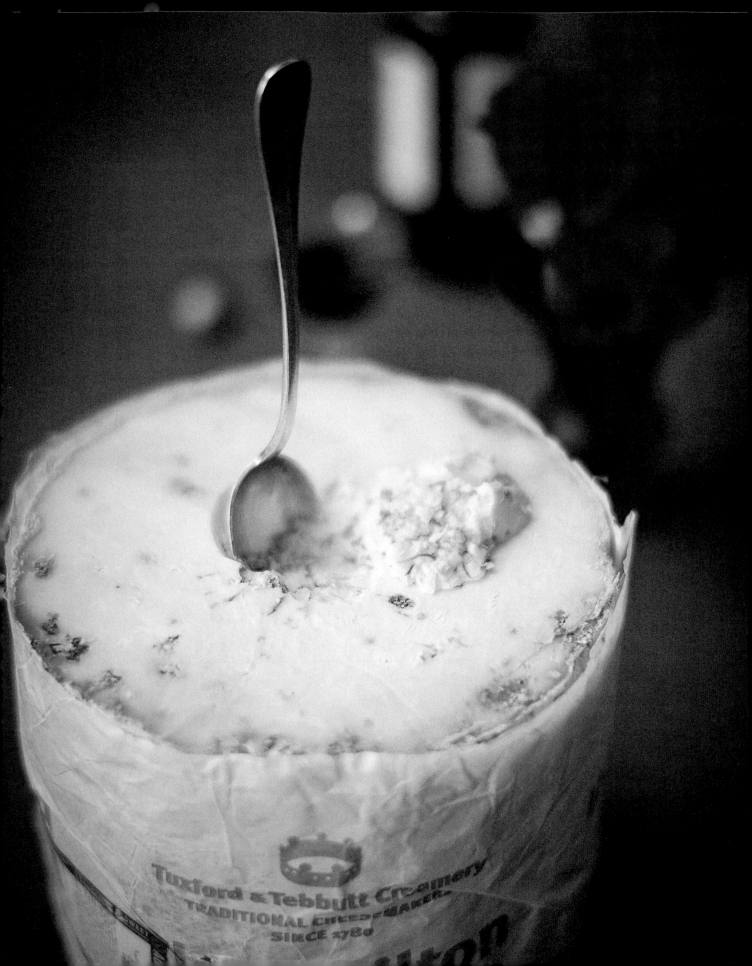

Tuxford & Tebbutt Creamery
TRADITIONAL CHEESE MAKERS
SINCE 1780

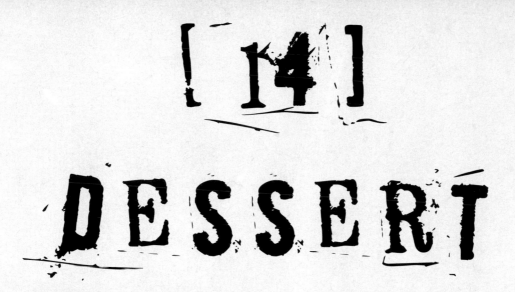

[14]

DESSERT

Fuck dessert.

Okay. I don't mean that. I like dessert just fine. But if I had to live without one course for the rest of my life, dessert would be the one to go. I certainly don't know how to make pastries. Perhaps this explains my career-long suspicion of pastry chefs: They can do something that I absolutely cannot.

I may just not be a sweets guy. Sure, they tell you refined sugar is poison—and they're probably right. But they said that about heroin, too—and that turned out okay, didn't it?

Alright, maybe not.

I do, in fact, on occasion, enjoy a little bite of chocolate or something sugary at the end of a good meal. But *then* . . . I want cheese.

Cheese is magic. The cheese course, irreplaceable. All the knowledge accumulated by mankind and all the mysterious forces of the natural world reside in cheese.

Not just any cheese will do. What I want after a good meal is that king of cheeses: Stilton. And I would like some good port with that.

Sure, there may be "better" cheeses out there.

Maybe.

But I doubt it.

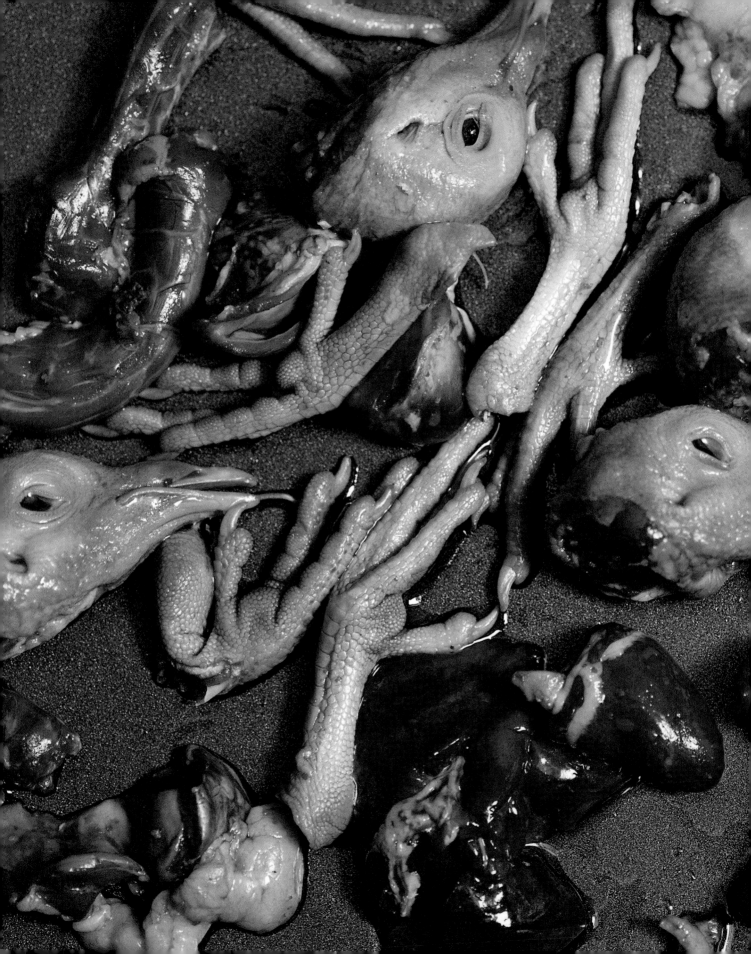

[15]

STOCKS, SAUCES, AND DRESSINGS

If you cook, you need stock. It's that simple.

Real (as opposed to commercially made) stock is the most important factor in making soups, sauces, and stews that taste like they've been made by a highly trained professional versus a mere professional.

Make stock. Freeze it in small batches. Use it all the time.

DARK UNIVERSAL STOCK

Veal bones are nice. Stock and demi-glace made from roasted veal bones are even better—but many of my former colleagues have abandoned the old school in favor of lighter stocks: veal stock made from unroasted bones (which they claim is less bitter), or "demi-glace" made from roasted chicken bones. I am somewhat sentimental about doing things the traditional veal way, but as I've been out of professional kitchens for a long time, I say whatever floats your boat. Chicken bones are certainly easier to come by.

What follows is a perfectly serviceable recipe for universal stock. I encourage you to load your freezer with small containers of it.

It's as versatile as a blank canvas—a perfect background waiting for you to fill.

As a rule of thumb, you will be reducing this stock with red wine, straining it through a fine-mesh sieve, and infusing or garnishing with appropriate elements depending on the main ingredient.

If, for instance, you're making a sauce later for lamb, you can jack it with lamb flavor by reducing it with roasted lamb scraps, perhaps some rosemary and garlic, and some red wine. For a duck sauce, throw in some duck bones, heads, and/or feet if you have them, plus some bay leaves and maybe an orange rind. Nicely browned turkey bones and a sprig each of sage, rosemary, and thyme will customize it for turkey gravy, and pork bones, pig ears, and red wine or beer will do the job for a porky sauce.

Preheat the oven to 400°F. Oil 2 large roasting pans.

In one of the pans, toss together the chicken bones with the tomato paste and flour to more or less evenly coat. Arrange them in an even layer and roast in the oven, turning and stirring the contents occasionally to keep bones from scorching, until the bones are browned, about 60 minutes.

While the bones roast, in the second pan, combine the onions, carrots, and celery and roast them as well, stirring regularly, until they are browned, about 30 minutes.

Transfer the bones and vegetables, but not any grease or other pan residue, to a large, heavy-bottom stockpot and fill the pot with cold water. Add the thyme, parsley, bay leaves, and peppercorns and bring the mixture to a high simmer, keeping vigilant in the last few minutes and reducing the heat to a low simmer before the mixture boils. Let simmer for at least 6 hours—better to let it go for 8 or 10—and use a ladle to skim off and discard the foam and oil as it rises to the top. There is no need to stir the stock as it simmers.

Remove the pot from the heat. Remove as many bones as you can with tongs, and discard them. Set up a sieve over a bowl or second stockpot—you may need to recruit a helper for this part, as you do not want to slip and lose everything you have just worked for—and carefully strain the stock, either by pouring it or ladling it through the sieve. Repeat the straining process a few times, until you are satisfied with the clarity of your stock. Transfer the stock carefully to storage containers, and chill in the refrigerator. Store in the refrigerator for up to 4 days, and up to 3 months in the freezer.

2 tablespoons canola oil

4 pounds chicken bones or as many as will fit into a large heavy-bottom stockpot

2 tablespoons tomato paste

2 tablespoons all-purpose flour

2 large white onions, peeled and coarsely chopped

3 medium carrots, peeled and coarsely chopped

2 ribs celery, coarsely chopped

4 sprigs fresh thyme

4 sprigs fresh parsley

3 bay leaves

1 teaspoon whole black peppercorns

Makes about 6 quarts

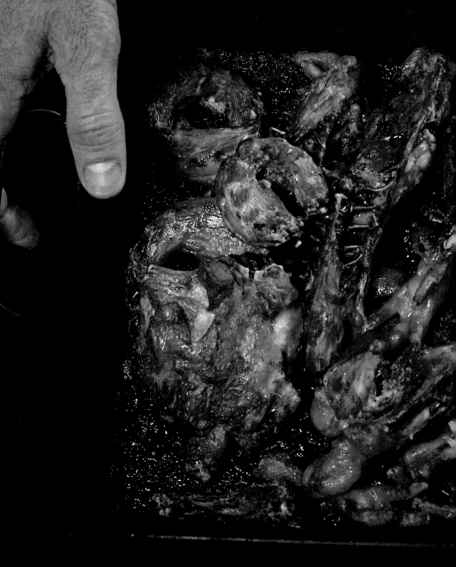

DARK UNIVE

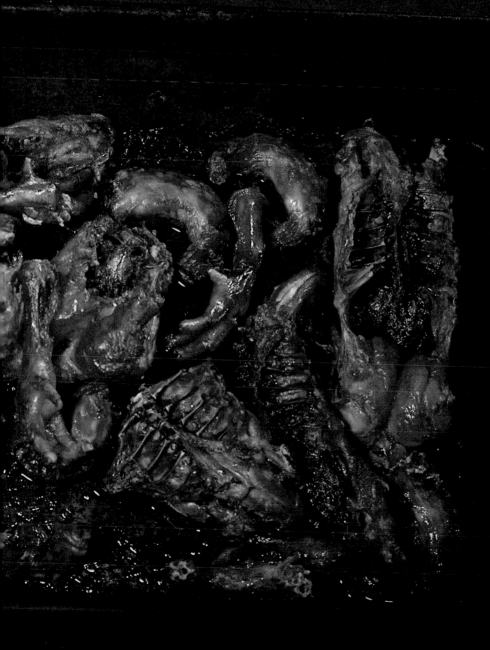

SHELLFISH STOCK

Got shrimp shells? Lobster heads? Crab carapaces? Smash them up a bit, load them into plastic bags, and freeze them. When you have the inclination, roast them in the oven and make a thick, dark, rich shellfish stock that can be, frankly, transformative. Freeze it in old-school ice cube trays or small containers; use it within three months.

1 tablespoon canola oil

Approximately 2 quarts lobster, shrimp, and/or crab shells

3 ounces tomato paste

1 large white or yellow onion, peeled and coarsely chopped

2 carrots, peeled and coarsely chopped

2 ribs celery, peeled and coarsely chopped

4 sprigs fresh thyme

4 sprigs fresh parsley

3 bay leaves

1 teaspoon whole black peppercorns

Preheat the oven to 425°F. Oil a roasting or sheet pan and add the shells. Toss the shells with the tomato paste to coat them as evenly as possible. Roast in the oven for about 15 minutes, taking care to not let them brown or scorch, which will turn your stock into bitter garbage.

Transfer the roasted shells to a large, heavy-bottom stockpot, along with the vegetables and aromatics, and cover by 2 inches with cold water. Bring to a simmer and calibrate the heat so that the pot bubbles lightly but does not boil. Use a ladle to skim off and discard the foam and scum that rises to the surface; you may find yourself doing several rounds of this in the first 30 to 45 minutes. Once the foam and scum slows, let the stock simmer for at least 6 hours. Do not stir the stock as it simmers; this will only muddy the proverbial waters.

Remove the pot from the heat. Remove as many large shell pieces as you can, using tongs, and discard them. Set up a sieve over a large bowl—you may need to recruit a helper for this part, as you do not want to slip and lose everything you have just worked for—and carefully strain the stock, either by pouring it or ladling it through the sieve. Repeat the straining process a few times, until you are satisfied with the clarity of your stock. Transfer the stock carefully to storage containers, and chill in the refrigerator. Store for up to 4 days in the refrigerator, and up to 3 months in the freezer.

Makes 2 to 4 quarts

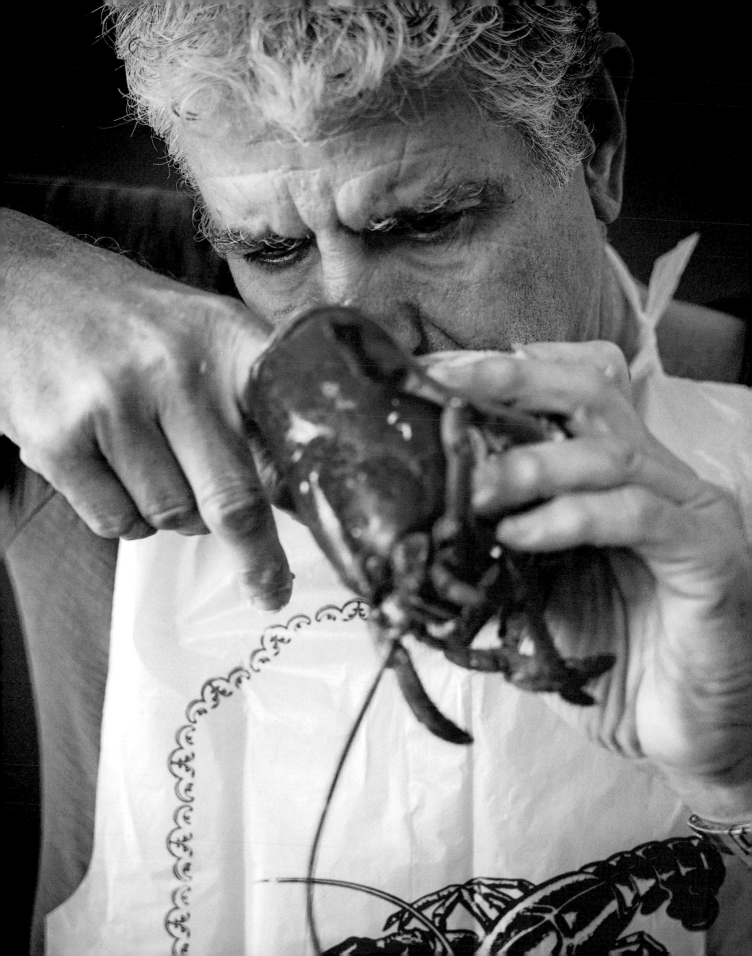

Octopus Stock

½ tablespoon canola oil

10 octopus tentacles, beak removed and discarded and tentacles cut into bite-size pieces

1 teaspoon whole black peppercorns

1 medium white or yellow onion, peeled and coarsely chopped

4 whole garlic cloves, peeled

1 carrot, peeled and coarsely chopped

1 rib celery, coarsely chopped

This is an enchanted liquid that makes seafood stews richer, deeper, and better.

In a large, heavy-bottom pot, heat the oil over medium-high heat until it shimmers. Working in batches, lightly sear the octopus pieces until they release their natural juices, 1 to 2 minutes. Use tongs to remove the octopus pieces to a plate or bowl and drain and discard the liquid. Return the octopus to the pot and add the peppercorns, onion, garlic, carrot, and celery. Fill the pot about three-quarters full with cold water, bring to a boil, then reduce to a simmer. Gently simmer for 1 to 1½ hours. Strain the stock, discarding the solids, and refrigerate or freeze.

Makes 2 to 4 quarts, depending on the volume of the pot

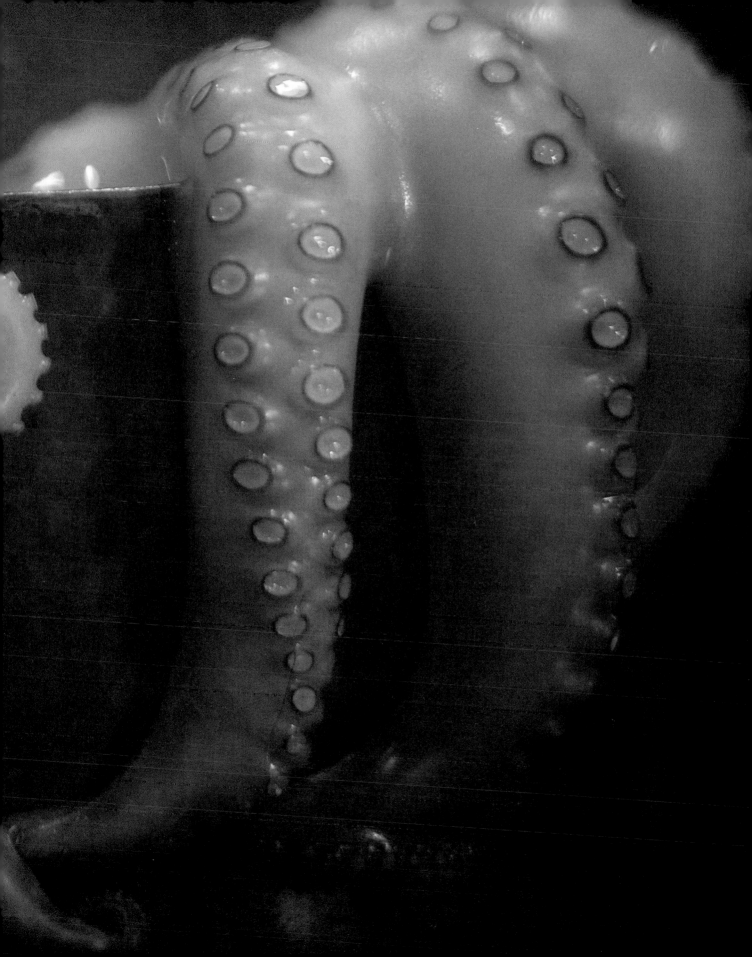

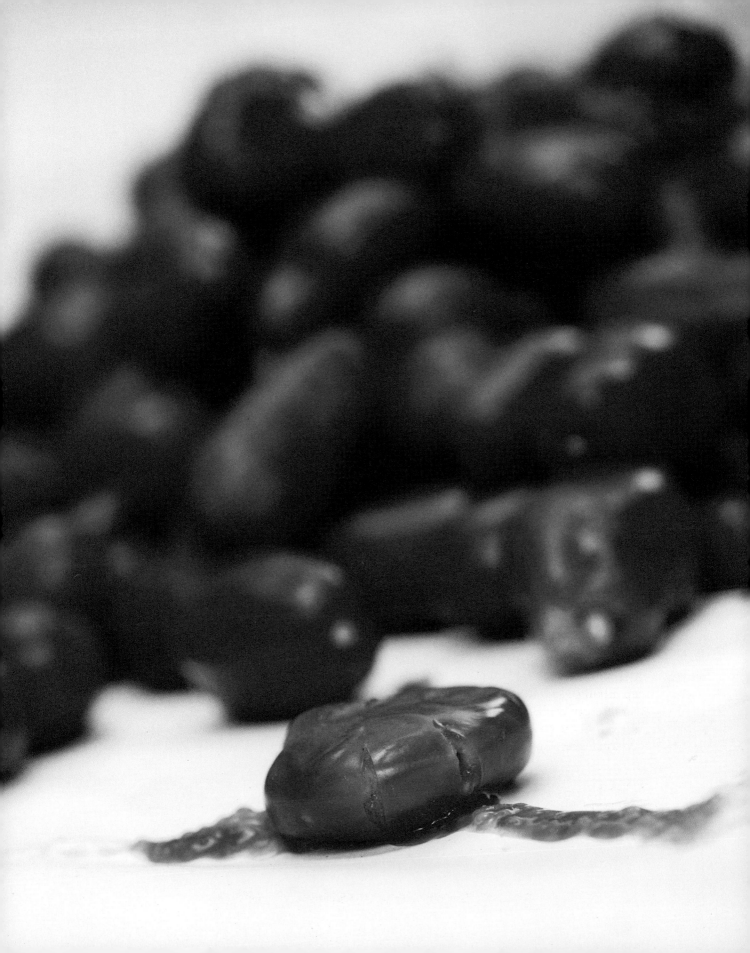

POMODORO

Tomato sauce doesn't need a lot of ingredients. In fact, it *shouldn't* have a lot of ingredients. It should be quick and easy, and it should taste fresh—like tomatoes in season. It's *tomato* sauce after all. *Not* oregano sauce. Or garlic sauce. Let me stress this again, so you know I'm serious: *It's about the tomatoes.* And it should take no more than 45 minutes—preferably far less—of actual cooking time.

Fill a large, heavy-bottom pot with water and bring it to a boil. Use a paring or serrated knife to cut an X into both ends of each fresh plum tomato. Once the water boils, add the tomatoes to the pot, working in two batches if necessary to avoid overcrowding the pot or reducing the temperature too drastically. Allow the tomatoes to simmer in the water for about 30 seconds, until the skin begins to loosen and peel away from the flesh. Using tongs, remove the tomatoes to the ice-water bath. Once the tomatoes are cool enough to handle, peel off and discard the skin, squeeze out and discard the seeds, and coarsely chop the flesh.

In a large, heavy-bottom sauté pan, heat the oil over medium-low heat and add the onion, garlic, and pepper flakes. Let cook 1 to 2 minutes, stirring to keep the aromatics from browning, then add the chopped plum tomatoes and the canned tomatoes and their juices, squeezing the canned tomatoes by hand to crush them up a bit before they go into the pan. Stir well, season lightly with salt and pepper, and let cook for 20 to 25 minutes, stirring occasionally, until the tomatoes have completely broken down.

Remove the sauce from the heat and use the immersion blender to puree the sauce. (You may wish to carefully transfer the sauce to a large, deep mixing bowl, which will make it easier to manipulate the blender.) Return the sauce to gentle heat, add the butter, and cook and stir until the butter has been incorporated into the sauce. Stir in the basil leaves. Taste and adjust seasoning as necessary.

Makes about 5 cups

10 ripe red plum tomatoes

¼ cup extra-virgin olive oil

1 medium yellow onion, peeled and finely chopped

4 garlic cloves, peeled and crushed

¼ teaspoon red pepper flakes

1 (28-ounce) can peeled plum tomatoes and their juices

Salt and freshly ground black pepper to taste

2 tablespoons (¼ stick) unsalted butter

6 fresh basil leaves, gently torn into a few pieces

SPECIAL EQUIPMENT

Ice-water bath (large bowl filled with ice and cold water)

Immersion blender

HOLLANDAISE SAUCE

Yes, I still loathe the concept of brunch. And when *Kitchen Confidential* came out over fifteen years ago, I apparently scared innumerable readers off the pleasure of hollandaise. I'd like to gently recant here and say that a sauce made well, with fresh ingredients, served just after it comes together, can still be a beautiful thing.

But still—fuck brunch.

1¼ pounds (5 sticks) unsalted butter

⅛ teaspoon crushed black peppercorns

⅛ teaspoon salt, plus more to taste

3 tablespoons white wine vinegar

1 tablespoon cold water

6 egg yolks

1 to 2 tablespoons freshly squeezed lemon juice

In a small, heavy-bottom saucepan, melt the butter over medium heat, using a slotted spoon to skim the white foam off the surface. Remove from the heat and pour the clear yellow liquid butter into a second small, heavy-bottom saucepan, taking care not to include any of the milky-looking liquid that remains at the bottom of the pan. Keep the clarified butter warm, but not hot.

In a third small, heavy-bottom saucepan, use a wooden spoon to combine the peppercorns, ⅛ teaspoon salt, and vinegar and cook over medium heat until the vinegar boils and almost completely evaporates (a state of near-dryness known as *au sec*). Remove the pan from the heat and stir in the cold water with the wooden spoon.

Transfer the mixture to a medium stainless-steel bowl, making sure to scrape it well with a spatula so as to not lose any of the reduction, which gives the sauce its essential flavor. Add the yolks to the bowl and whisk well.

In a medium, heavy-bottom saucepan, bring a few inches of water to a low simmer and place the bowl with the yolks over the simmering water. Whisk constantly, making sure you hit all the surfaces of the bowl, until the yolks are pale yellow, thick, and creamy. The more air in the eggs, the less likely they will be to curdle over the heat.

Remove the bowl from atop the simmering water and begin to whisk in the clarified butter, starting with a few drops at first and adding another ladleful after each one is incorporated. If the mixture becomes too thick to beat, add a small amount of the lemon juice.

Once all the butter has been incorporated, whisk in the lemon juice and season with salt to taste. Strain the mixture through a fine-mesh sieve into a clean bowl or pot and serve immediately, or within 90 minutes, keeping the sauce warm but not hot.

Makes about 2 cups

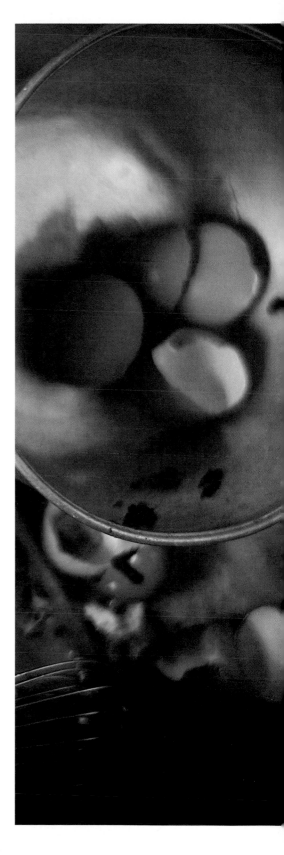

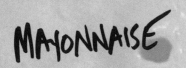
MAYONNAISE

Some recipes call for the prepared stuff, but some, like chicken salad, demand a homemade mayonnaise. It's one of a category of emulsified dressings in which two unmixable liquids are held in suspension by a third—in this case oil and vinegar, brought together by egg yolks. The notion of an emulsion gets some cooks panicky, but there's no reason to sweat it. As long as you use the freshest possible eggs, beat the yolks well, and go slow and steady when incorporating the oil, you shouldn't have any trouble. And if you do, if the emulsion breaks because you've added more oil than it can hold? Whisk in another beaten egg yolk and watch the thing come back to life.

2 egg yolks

1½ tablespoons white wine vinegar

½ teaspoon salt, plus more to taste

½ teaspoon dry mustard

1¾ cup vegetable, canola, or grapeseed oil

1 tablespoon freshly squeezed lemon juice, or to taste

In a large mixing bowl, beat the egg yolks well with a whisk. Whisk in ½ tablespoon of the vinegar, then add the salt and mustard and whisk well.

Begin to add the oil, in a very slow and steady stream, whisking constantly. You may wish to enlist the help of a friend—one of you whisks while the other pours. Once you see the emulsion begin to form, you can add the oil a little faster, but do not dump it in. The emulsion breaks when the matrix is overloaded with oil.

If the mixture starts to become too thick to beat, you can thin it with some of the remaining vinegar. Continue to add the oil, then whisk in any remaining vinegar. Taste the mixture and adjust with the lemon juice and additional salt if desired.

Makes about 2 cups

Béchamel Sauce

Make sure that you have both a whisk and a wooden spoon or spatula close at hand, as you'll be switching back and forth between the two tools as you build the roux, which is the base for the béchamel.

In a medium, heavy-bottom saucepan, heat the butter over medium heat until it foams and subsides. Whisk in the flour and stir it well with a wooden spoon, incorporating it into the butter until a dry paste forms. Reduce the heat and continue to cook and stir, taking care not to let the mixture get browned.

Meanwhile, in another saucepan, heat the milk to a simmer, then gradually whisk it into the pan with the flour-butter mixture (the roux), continuing to whisk until the mixture is smooth. Season with salt and pepper and, if using, a judicious amount of nutmeg. Continue to cook over medium-low heat, stirring regularly, until the sauce is thick enough to coat the back of a wooden spoon.

6 tablespoons (¾ stick) unsalted butter

6 tablespoons all-purpose flour

4 cups whole milk

Salt and pepper to taste

Pinch of freshly ground nutmeg (optional)

Makes about 4 cups

Blue Cheese Vinaigrette

In a mixing bowl, combine the cheese, mayonnaise, oil, vinegar, and lemon juice and whisk together to make a homogenous mixture. Thin with a tablespoon of water if necessary. Taste and season with salt and pepper.

8 ounces best-quality blue cheese, crumbled

½ cup Mayonnaise (opposite) or store-bought mayonnaise

¼ cup canola oil

¼ cup red wine vinegar

2 tablespoons freshly squeezed lemon juice

Salt and freshly ground black pepper to taste

Makes about 2 cups

MIXED FRUIT CHUTNEY

6 dried figs, quartered

8 dried apricots, quartered

¼ cup raisins

1 Granny Smith apple, peeled, cored, and grated

1 cup finely grated fresh pineapple

2 tablespoons freshly squeezed lemon juice

1 tablespoon finely grated lemon or lime zest

1 teaspoon salt

1 teaspoon ground cayenne pepper

1 teaspoon freshly ground black pepper

A dab of this stuff will relieve the crushing boredom of skinless grilled chicken breasts, steamed vegetables, and other such punishing foods.

Place the figs, apricots, and raisins in a small bowl and cover with hot water. Let soak until softened, about 1 hour. Drain the fruit and add to a medium, heavy-bottom saucepan, along with all the remaining ingredients. Mix well, bring to a boil, and reduce to a simmer. Add a splash of water if it looks too dry. Cook, stirring frequently, until the mixture has thickened and become somewhat sticky, about 15 minutes. Remove from the heat, transfer to a clean container, and refrigerate, uncovered, until well chilled. Will keep in refrigerator for up to 2 weeks.

Makes about 2 cups

Red Wine Vinaigrette

In a medium mixing bowl, combine the vinegar and garlic and season with salt and pepper. Let sit 30 minutes, then remove and discard the garlic. Add the mustard and slowly whisk in the oil, continuing to whisk until the mixture is emulsified. Fold in one or more of the optional additions, as suits your taste.

Makes about 1½ cups

½ cup red wine vinegar or sherry vinegar

1 garlic clove, peeled and crushed

Salt and freshly ground black pepper to taste

1 teaspoon Dijon mustard

1 cup best-quality extra-virgin olive oil

Optional additions: 1 tablespoon rinsed and chopped capers; 1 tablespoon chopped cornichons; chopped fresh dill, parsley, or basil to taste; ½ teaspoon red pepper flakes or hot sauce; 1 teaspoon finely grated citrus zest

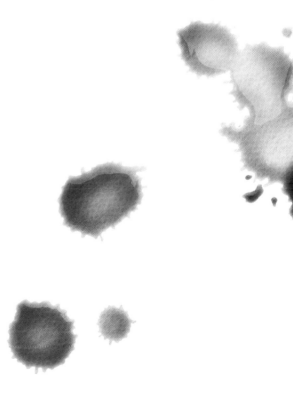

Pico de Gallo

10 ripe Roma tomatoes

1 large or 2 small red onions, peeled and diced

2 jalapeño peppers, minced

¼ cup freshly squeezed lime juice (from 3 to 4 limes)

2 tablespoons canola oil

Salt and pepper to taste

Place the tomatoes on a cutting board and cut approximately ½-inch slices from all four sides of each tomato using a serrated knife or very good and sharp chef's knife. (The idea is that you want intact pieces of tomato with the structure that the skin provides.) Cut each of these slices into a small dice and transfer to the mixing bowl. Add the diced onions, peppers, lime juice, and oil and toss together with a wooden spoon to combine. Taste and season with salt and pepper. Serve alongside quesadillas.

Makes about 7 cups

NUOC MAM CHAM (VIETNAMESE DIPPING SAUCE)

In a small mixing bowl, whisk together the lime juice, sugar, and ¾ cup water. Add the fish sauce in increments, tasting as you go and adjusting with lime juice and fish sauce to get the best balance of flavors. Add the pepper and garlic and let sit for at least 30 minutes before serving. Cover and refrigerate for up to 1 week.

Makes about 1 cup

¼ cup freshly squeezed lime juice (from 3 to 4 limes), plus more to taste as needed

3 tablespoons sugar

2 to 3 tablespoons best-quality Vietnamese fish sauce, or to taste

1 fresh red Thai chili pepper, finely sliced

1 garlic clove, peeled and finely chopped

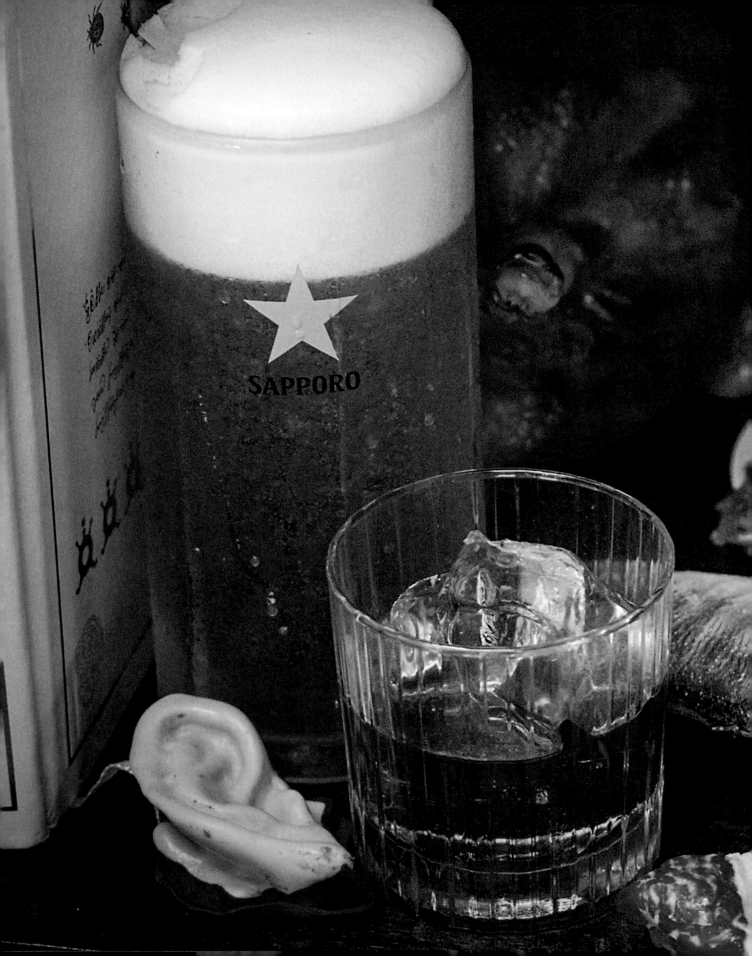

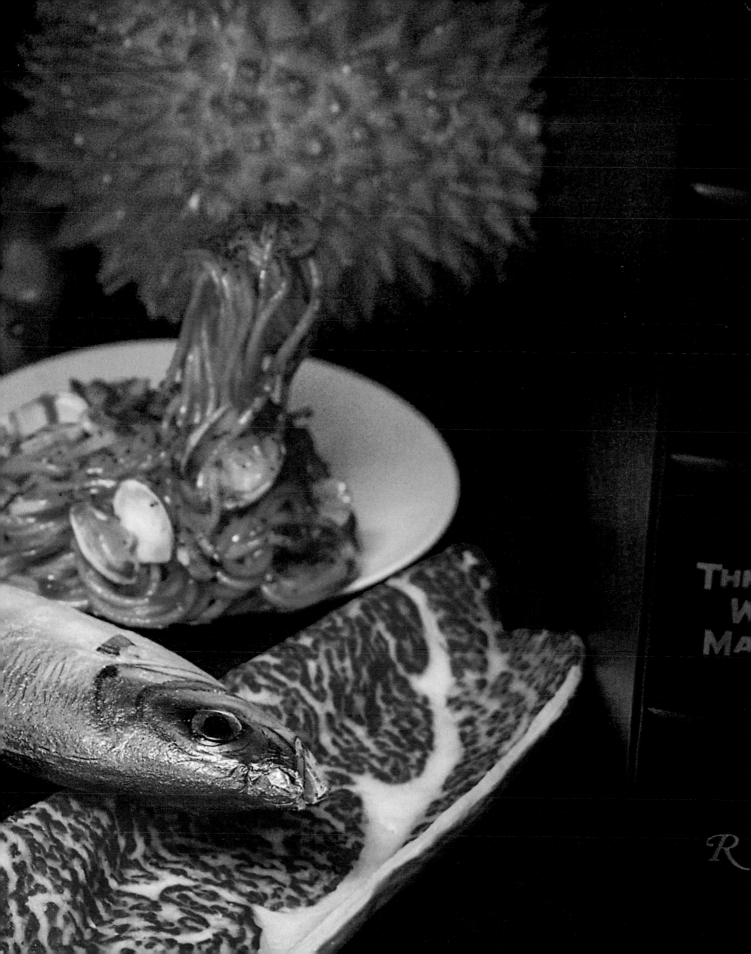

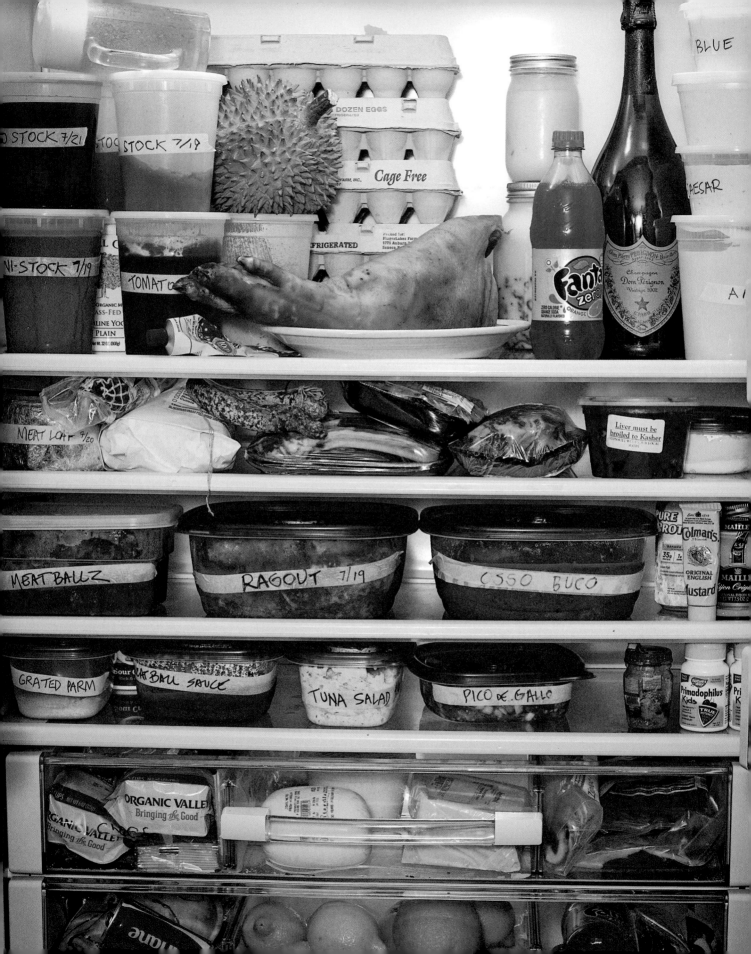

INDEX

Note: Page references in *italics* indicate recipe photographs.

ANTHONY BOURDAIN is the author of the *New York Times* bestsellers *Kitchen Confidential* and *Medium Raw; A Cook's Tour;* the collection *The Nasty Bits;* the novels *Bone in the Throat* and *Gone Bamboo;* and the biography *Typhoid Mary: An Urban Historical*. He has written for the *New York Times* and *The New Yorker,* among many other publications. He is the host of the Emmy and Peabody Award–winning docuseries *Anthony Bourdain: Parts Unknown* on CNN, and before that hosted *No Reservations* and *The Layover* on Travel Channel, and *The Taste* on ABC. He lives in New York City.

LAURIE WOOLEVER is a writer, editor, and longtime lieutenant to Anthony Bourdain. Her work has appeared in the *New York Times, GQ, Food & Wine, Lucky Peach, Saveur, Dissent,* among other publications. Woolever is a graduate of Cornell University and the French Culinary Institute, and is a former editor at *Art Culinaire* and *Wine Spectator*. She lives in New York with her husband and son.

BOBBY FISHER is a photographer based in New York City, not a dead chess champion buried in Iceland. He prefers Nikon to Canon and women to men, but will do anything for money and adventure. He loves hotel rooms with obstructed views and eating fish for breakfast. Fisher's work has been featured in *Rolling Stone, GQ, Food & Wine,* the *New York Times,* as well as the books *L.A. SON* by Roy Choi and *The Red Rooster Cookbook* by Marcus Samuelsson.

THANK YOU

R YOUR BUSINESS

REUSE OR RECYCLE
FROM AND CHILDREN. DO NO
ANY OVER NOSE AND MOUTH AND CIPATING STORE
BEDS, CARRIAGES OR PLAYPENS.

RPI

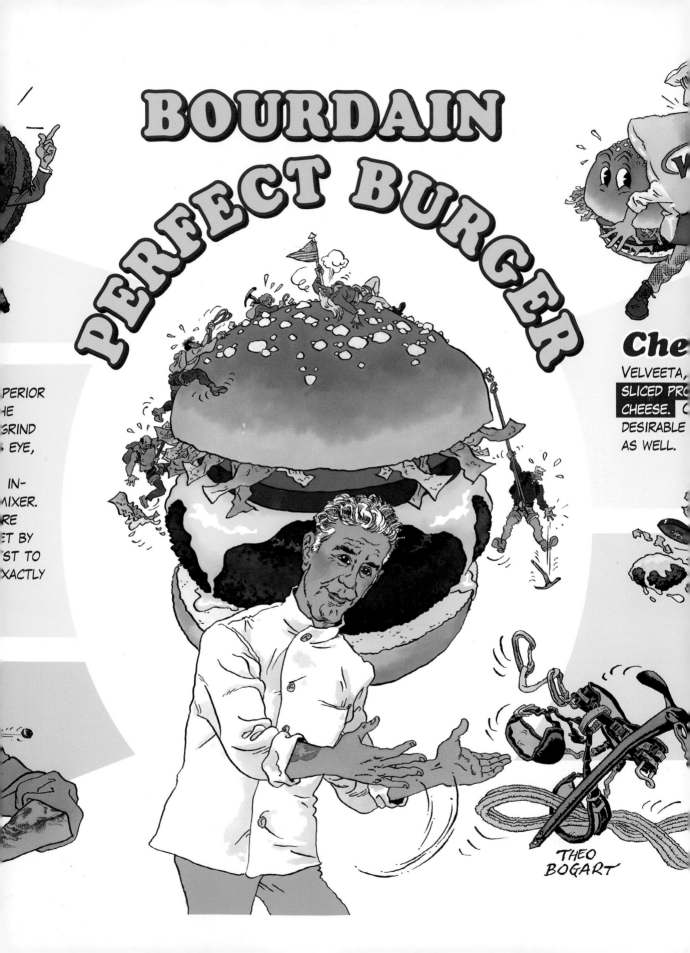

BOURDAIN
PERFECT BURGER

...PERIOR
...HE
...GRIND
... EYE,

...IN-
...MIXER.
...RE
...ET BY
...ST TO
...XACTLY

Che

VELVEETA,
SLICED PRO...
CHEESE. C...
DESIRABLE
AS WELL.

THEO BOGART

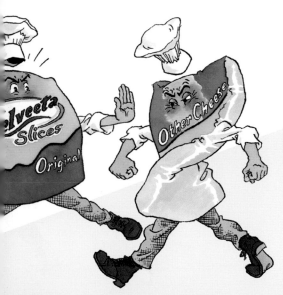

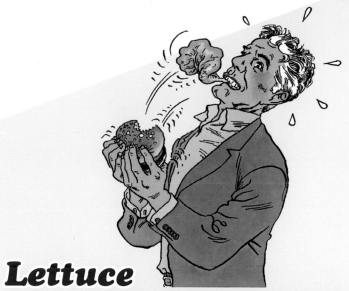

Lettuce

HAS THE POTENTIAL TO BE A SLIPPERY TOPPING. SOME PEOPLE ALLEVIATE THIS BY CUTTING THE LETTUCE INTO A WIDE JULIENNE SO THAT IT WON'T PULL OUT WHEN YOU BITE THE BURGER. IF YOU HAVE A SINGLE BIG LETTUCE LEAF, IT MIGHT PULL OUT OF THE SANDWICH WHEN YOU EAT IT. IT ALSO CAN INTERFERE WITH GRIPPING THE BURGER IN A SINGLE HAND.

ese

AMERICAN CHEESE, OR A SIMILAR ...CESSED CHEESE, IS THE BEST MELTING ...THER CHEESES MIGHT HAVE MORE ...FLAVORS, BUT THEY DON'T MELT

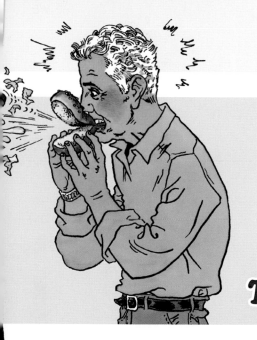

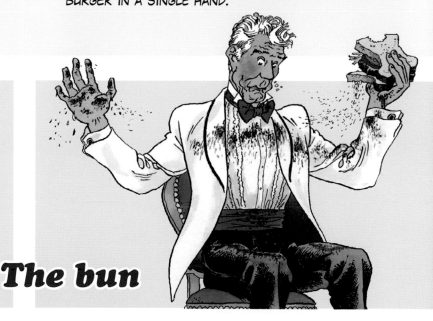

The bun

THE STORE-BOUGHT BUN NEEDS TO BE SOFT, MOIST, AND DENSE; SEEDS CAN ADD EXTRA CRUNCH AND FLAVOR. WHEN YOU BITE THROUGH IT, IT HAS TO COMPRESS OR THE FILLING WILL FLY OUT THE OTHER SIDE. THIS CAN BE ACHIEVED IN A NUMBER OF WAYS, BUT A SLICE OF BREAD IS NOT AS GOOD AS A BUN BECAUSE IT IS POROUS. YOU ALSO WANT TO STAY AWAY FROM BREAD THAT HAS TOO MUCH CRUST OR A HARD CRUST.

The burger patty

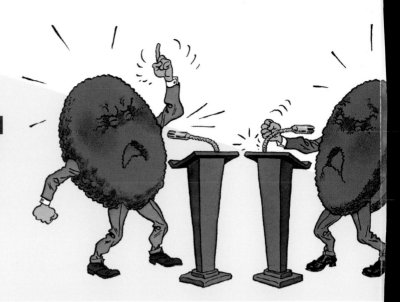

As for the patty (the heart of any hamburger) **the debate over one patty vs. two patties is a matter of taste.** It all depends on the ratio of the surface area to the interior of the patty. If you prefer the flavor of the browned Maillard reaction, then you could make two thin patties. If you like the flavor of rare meat, then you should cook one thicker patty.

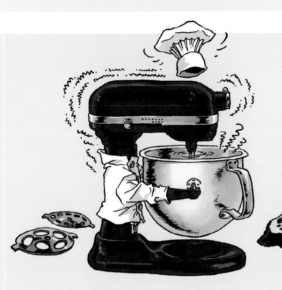

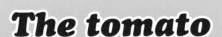

The extra effort to grind your own meat pays off in s[...] textures and flavors—and it allows you to customize [...] leanness and the tenderness. Use top-quality meat and [...] it well: our favorite is a blend of short rib and aged r[...] mixed with a bit of hanger steak.

Grinding your own meat is easy with a[...] expensive attachment for your stand [...] Use a medium plate to produce a text[...] that is somewhat finer than you can g[...] hand-chopping. We've found that it's b[...] add a little salt to the ground meat e[...] one hour before cooking it.

The tomato

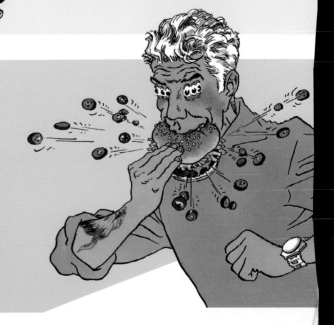

Should be a single slice of a larger tomato, like a beefsteak tomato. The interior of the tomato is not as slippery as the skin, so a larger interior surface area will have more friction and help the tomato stay in place. The last thing that you want is to use several slices of a smaller tomato, like a plum tomato. **They'll slip out when you eat them.**